Is It REVIVAL? Or APOSTASY?

A Biblical Evaluation of Today's Evangelical Christianity

PHILIP SMITH

First Edition

NEWMAN SPRINGS PUBLISHING
320 Broad Street
Red Bank, NJ 07701

First originally published by Newman Springs Publishing 2023

Unless noted, all scriptural references in this book are from the King James Version of the Bible. Other translations are sometimes used for easier reading if they do not deviate from the original translation of the Hebrew and Greek manuscripts.

ISBN 979-8-88763-724-2 (Paperback)
ISBN 979-8-88763-725-9 (Digital)

Printed in the United States of America

For their love and guidance in directing my
steps in the solid foundation of faith,
this book is dedicated to my parents,
Wesley and MaryEllen Smith

Contents

Preface

I understood long ago that the reason for various denominations within Christianity was that they originated from specific doctrinal prioritization. Though most mainstream orthodox denominations still claim the Gospel of the Bible to be vital, some have been influenced to compromise these doctrines of the faith they were founded upon. There is also the nondenominational Charismatic movement and many other independent churches not associated with any denomination. Not too long ago, Christianity seemed to be a melting pot of believers of all kinds who held to the basics of the faith. Today, however, the beliefs of many who call themselves Christians are rapidly shifting. By the late 1990s, I had realized the significant schism within Christianity. Seeing the growing criticism against the teachings of many nationally known Evangelical pastors, I began searching for answers to such discord within the body of Christ. I found scriptural evidence that many believers had been hoodwinked in one area or another and was inspired to be a witness for biblical discernment and truth. In 2013, I began writing this book, which was intended to be a short booklet highlighting the importance of identifying today's satanic assault against the Gospel of the New Testament. As a result of the necessary material to cover, it evolved and expanded into a larger body of work examining specific false teachings and doctrinal mistakes many have made.

Introduction

To the follower of Jesus, the Bible should be a continuing classroom of knowledge, wisdom, and truth to be embraced. When convinced that the Bible is written in truth and that it is God's divinely inspired manuscript preserved through the centuries for such a time as this, we should know that it behooves us to diligently study it. In Martin Luther's time, five hundred years ago, there would have been no Protestant Reformation of freedom from Catholicism's religious bondage without his and others' divinely inspired determination to proclaim the truth of Holy Scripture. In the same manner, today's willing ambassadors for biblical truth now attempt to inform the Protestant Church of its mistakes in preaching a watered-down Gospel and the acceptance of liberal or heretical doctrines.

The widening gap between the discerning Christian and the deceived Christian is becoming very evident. According to the words of Jesus in several passages, the discerning believer will one day be separated from the deceived believer—one to eternal life, the other to eternal punishment. Therefore, a trumpet of warning must sound to all Christians. The overall message of this book is simple—it exposes the false teachings within the Evangelical Church that have led us away from the doctrinal truth of the cross of Christ.

The body of Christ is split mainly into two camps—the orthodox camp and the growing "New Revelation" camp. Though both groups may appear on the surface to be fundamental (Evangelical) in their beliefs and teaching, they are, in reality, traveling different paths. Though there are believers in both camps who are genuinely "born again," many do not appear to grasp that Satan, our enemy, is ruthlessly sneaky and has already distracted millions through false doctrines and perversion of Scripture, thus risking the crown of eternal reward they believe is due them. The New Testament tells us that digressing from or adding to the simple Gospel of salvation puts us in a jeopardized position on the day when Jesus Himself will judge us (John 5:22–27 and 2 Corinthians 5:10). Hence, I have written this book not for the ridicule and criticism of God's people, but out of compassion for them.

I have not attended a theological seminary nor have I ever been in church leadership. Yet by carefully studying my Bible, I find that it gives easy answers, to which many pastors appear to be blind to, perhaps because the try to look at Scripture through thick theological glasses, thus having overanalyzed and over rationalized certain Bible passages. Yet they have bypassed the obvious stated within the full context or by not comparing Scripture against itself. The misinterpretation of Scripture is then passed on to the congregation, leading to deception within the body of Christ today. In addition, the conformity of the organized church is largely based on tradition and man's preconceived ideas of what pleases God, thus distorting the simple Gospel to accommodate these incongruous ideas and traditions. Therefore, the followers of Jesus within every denomination and nondenominational church can easily travel a road of deception or religious bondage.

I found that the Bible actually reveals there will be no end-time worldwide spiritual revival, but neither will there be a grand exit from the church. Rather, the New Testament tells of a great apostasy of ignorance and doctrinal neglect within the end-time church. This expository book—*Is It Revival? Or Apostasy?*—explains the gradual increase of apostasy and heretical teachings within the body of Christ and why God has allowed it to happen.

We must carefully listen to the words of Jesus in Luke 12:51: **Suppose ye that I am come to give peace on the earth? I tell you, Nay; but rather division.**

It is noteworthy that Jesus said this to His disciples only—His initial chosen group. The division Jesus spoke of was not the conflict between believers and unbelievers over the meaning of life or the existence of God, but of division within the religious world over a coming change. When reading the full context of Luke 12:49–53, we find that because of Jesus's "baptism" which He was about to endure in His death, burial, and resurrection, He thereby informed the disciples of a coming division and separation between the old religious law and the truth of new divine doctrine. Jesus had offended the religious scribes and Pharisees with His nonreligious Gospel; He therefore had to explain to His followers the kind of upheaval that His Gospel would bring to the world of religion.

Jesus was familiar with rejection and controversy: in John 7:5, we read how even His own brothers didn't believe He could be the promised Messiah. In Mark 6:4 (NIV), Jesus said: **Only in his hometown, among his relatives and in his own house is a prophet without honor.** Similarly, I have also encountered Christians close to me who scoff at my warning and critical judgment call against false teaching within the church. Since I am familiar to them personally, they see my biblical discernment as only my opinion of the Scriptures or of my overly critical rant. However, Jesus told us to **judge not according to appearances, but judge with a righteous judgment** (John 7:24 NKJV). Those who know the truth are therefore mandated to make a judgment call against any within the church who oppose the doctrine of the new covenant Gospel.

The apostle Paul encouraged the church at Philippi: **And this I pray, that your love may abound yet more and more in knowledge and in all judgment** (Philippians 1:9). This verse contains powerful words. Followers of Jesus must have the **love** and the **knowledge** of Scripture to boldly profess all judgment in **truth**.

Biblically speaking, unity in the body of Christ is in the agreement over precise interpretation of the fundamental doctrines of the faith. When the foundation of the saving Gospel is compromised, God raises up discerning informers, similar to the **watchmen upon the walls** in Isaiah 62:6. Though in today's religious hierarchy environment, the watchmen and ambassadors for truth who attempt to warn of doctrinal error are usually squelched and ignored. They are perceived as nitpicky and against everything progressive; they are assumed to be the cause of discord within the body of Christ. But the Scripture quotations in this book will prove this false notion. As a result of ignoring these "apostasy watchmen," a large portion of the worldwide Evangelical Church continues to veer off course into false doctrine, religious bondage, and wrong focus. These deviations are defined as "apostasy"—a straying from the truth. The definition of "heresy" is somewhat similar—the deliberate denial of truth. A cult religion teaches heresy. But a teacher of God's Word or whole denominations can become apostate if the Gospel is neglected or changed. Both apostasy and heresy positions are destructive and condemning—personifying an ignorance or abandonment of scriptural truth.

The apostle Peter tells us to read Scripture with the context in mind: He said **that no prophecy of the scripture is of any private interpretation** (2 Peter 1:20). Though a segment of Scripture or even a single verse may have many applications, it, however, has only one meaning. Context is key. We cannot read into Scripture what only makes sense for us today. We must first know who wrote the passage…to whom was it written…and what did they mean by it. Just as we would comprehend any other book, correct interpretation of the Bible is found by the practice of exegesis—conclusions made by following the text. Eisegesis is the opposite—to isolate a passage, or single verse—reading into it an interpretation of our choosing. However, Bible truth is not a concept of the past: the factuality of God's Word must be our conviction. We cannot keep the Bible in our back pocket, then pull it out to search for passages that fit the teaching of our favorite pastor or any preconceived notions we might have. When encouraged to extract a personal "what does this passage mean to you?" way of studying Scripture, the Bible then becomes a situational ethics book—a sort of "as one sees it" evaluation. This eventually causes doubt that there is any such thing as literal Bible truth, and that it's okay to interpret a personal rendition of what Jesus the Savior came for. In addition, when kindhearted pastors add a little of their own leaven of interpretation to biblical truth, their preaching, over time, becomes perverted.

As I am personally guilty of, we as Christians have also channel surfed Christian television, seeking after the teaching of our favorite nationally known celebrity pastors. We've attended Christian conferences and seminars—chasing after the latest inspiration or divine anointing and learning how we can receive our promised blessing. We hear of a "new direction" the Holy Spirit is supposedly taking the body of Christ. These are all misnomers according to Hebrews 1:1–2. Read this passage carefully: There are no hidden "new revelations" we must search for, aside what is already stated in Scripture. The preaching of any pastor or the teaching within Christian seminars and conferences is beneficial only if it is derived from sound Bible doctrine and of the simple words of Jesus concerning the Gospel of salvation. Following after the teachings of a single person with an assumed "great anointing" proves the immaturity of many Christians, which is partly to blame for the doctrinal disunion within the worldwide church today.

Because of all this and other distractions, we are living in an era of great deception, which aligns perfectly with New Testament prophecy of the end times we live in. Many in the faith shall "fall away," as Paul warns in 2 Thessalonians 2:3. Though there are nominal Christians who become disillusioned and drop out of church attendance altogether, many other of the faithful still within the church are falling away from the truth of God's Word. This is not my opinion but is scriptural discernment; as it says: **knowledge shall be increased** (Daniel 12:4), and at the same time, there shall come **a falling away** prior to **the day of Christ** (2 Thessalonians 2:2–3).

King Solomon wrote: **A wise man will hear, and will increase learning** (Proverbs 1:5). Solomon's words apply very much to believers today. In order to "increase learning," we must "hear" with understanding according to the Scriptures. Peter also warned us to be on guard in all spiritual matters; he said: **Be sober, be vigilant; because your adversary the devil, as a roaring lion, walketh about, seeking whom he may devour: whom resist steadfast in the faith** (1

Peter 5:8–9). Much of the content and warning of this book you've begun to read pivots on this passage. If we neglect to personally search out the primary Gospel message of Scripture and rely only on our pastor's interpretation of it to secure our eternal destiny, we will have no excuse on the Day of Judgment if finding we had been deceived into believing false doctrine. In addition, if we trust only in our answered prayers as proof of our salvation, we have missed the mark by a long shot. Or if we believe that we're on the right spiritual track because we continue in financial prosperity, we also risk losing eternal life. Those within the religious cults, such as Mormonism, Jehovah's Witnesses, Hinduism, and Islam, also claim to have their prayers answered and are prosperous as well. How then is answered prayer or financial success any evidence of spiritual discernment? It is no evidence whatsoever!

A brief evaluation of other religions

Among the major world religions, we find that

- Buddhism teaches that there is no Supreme God;
- Hinduism teaches that sin is nonexistent, and salvation of the soul is unnecessary;
- Islam teaches that Jesus was not the Son of God;
- Jehovah's Witnesses teach Arianism—that Jesus was created by God and was not eternal;
- Mormonism teaches that Jesus was a created being and that man can become as God is;
- Catholicism teaches that man can become as God, that pagan practices are compatible with the Gospel of Jesus, that a priest has divine authority to forgive sins, and that repetitious Rosary prayers to Mary brings cleansing of soul and closeness to God.

Rampant within Protestant Evangelical Christianity are very similar heretical doctrines and teachings, of which many Christians ignorantly embrace.

Sounds impossible? Think again. Liberal, compromising, and perverted doctrines and theologies of today have far digressed from the biblical truth that was preached in most Protestant congregations just sixty years ago.

Though some current-day false teachers are named within these pages—just as the apostle Paul did in his writings—it is not my intent to hatefully slander them but only to compare the Word of God against their wrong interpretations of it.

How can the reader of this book be assured that the following pages contain correct interpretation of the Scriptures? It is simple: within this book, there are no isolated Bible verses that derive a single theological position. Scripture must be compared against itself. And Strong's Exhaustive Concordance of the Bible aids in deciphering the truth and the real meaning of many misunderstood words and passages.

My prayer is that these pages will be seen as knowledge from the Bible and **speaking the truth in love** as Ephesians 4:15 tells us to do.

Chapter 1

A Lifelong Need for the Gospel

This first chapter is crucial to the topics discussed in this book. We must understand and agree on the basic beliefs of the Christian faith and of conversion to Christ before any false doctrines relevant to the Gospel can be determined.

Unregenerate man doesn't know he's a sinner until finding that the Bible tells him so. **For all have sinned, and come short of the glory of God** (Romans 3:23). Unless we were raised in the church, the awareness of certain activities that God considers "sin" or "abomination" were likely not apparent to our natural mind. Though we may have had bad feelings when acting against our moral conscience, it likely wasn't thought of as an offense to God. But after hearing the Gospel message and discovering our ignorance and guilt of sin and having a heartfelt response to it, we should naturally begin to loath our unrighteousness and repent of it. This is the beginning of a changed heart toward God.

After turning from the world's way of carnality to God's way of peace, righteousness, and spiritual insight, a spark of inspiration ignites our desire to share what we've learned and experienced. The Savior Himself tells us what to do next. In the King James Version of Matthew 28:19, Jesus tells His disciples: **Go ye therefore, and teach**

all nations. Other translations say: **Go and make more disciples.** Either translation is correct: It is the Great Commission from Jesus the Savior—to teach and spread the good news as you go your way. Today, this commission to spread the Gospel continues; yet to successfully convey it to others requires a scriptural study of the core of the Gospel message itself, which is the deity of Jesus the Savior.

The Gospel of Jesus is directly connected to the term "*born again.*" In John 3:3, Jesus told Nicodemus the Pharisee that man cannot comprehend the spiritual kingdom of God unless he is "*born again*"—a position of inner spiritual understanding and connection to holiness. It is the transformation of a changed heart, which completely restructures our perspective of life. According to some, the proper response to this Gospel requires a verbal "sinner's prayer" of acceptance and repentance. In truth, there is no Bible passage telling that our name has been recorded in heaven's Book of Life for having only verbalized a confession of sin. Instead, a changed heart is what brings inward renewal and God consciousness. The thief on the cross next to Jesus had a *born-again* experience, though he probably didn't realize it. According to the text (Luke 23:39–43), the thief admitted his wrongdoing only to the other thief, then asked Jesus to remember him in His eternal kingdom. This indicated his remorse for the sin he'd committed and at least some awareness of coming judgment. Jesus then told the thief he would soon be with him in paradise. The Savior knew his heart had changed, and this reversed his eternal destiny.

God forgives our sin when we grieve over it and determine to forsake it. **If we confess our sins, he is faithful and just to forgive us our sins, and to cleanse us from all unrighteousness** (1 John 1:9). The word "confess" in this verse means "acknowledge": God accepts acknowledgment and sorrow for our sin whether or not we verbalize a "sinner's prayer." Our heart and conscience must confirm a conviction that our sin opposes His Righteousness. When reading in our Bible of God's holiness and in comprehending our severe lack of it, forsaking our sin should be a natural desire. Arriving at this stage of self-abhorrence, we then begin the renewing process of inner change toward spiritual and eternal matters. However, at the point of conversion to Christ, though our heart is changed, it is impossible to instantly obtain awareness and total understanding in all God's ways of holiness. It will take time in learning and studying the Scriptures to discern it.

Romans 8:7 states: **Because the carnal mind is enmity against God: for it is not subject to the law of God, neither indeed can be**. Here, Paul uses the term "carnal mind." Strong's Exhaustive Concordance of the Bible explains this as "*a thought process inclined toward human nature*." We all have a human nature, which is "against God," as Paul says. After accepting Christ as our personal Savior, though we may do our best to walk with God, we can still be carnally minded simply by default or for not taking more time to read and study our Bible—which keeps us better attuned to God's ways. Ephesians 4:23 says: **And be renewed in the spirit of your mind**. The Concordance describes this word "renewed" as: "regenerate," "renovate," "reform," and "repetition." After turning from sin, we should be inspired to the repetitious reading, meditating, and study of God's Word. It's a lifetime process leading us away from human carnality. It is our lifelong need for the Gospel of salvation.

Identifying with the inner transformation of the heart and mind, Jesus also said we must **enter through the narrow gate** (Matthew 7:13 NIV). The salvation Gospel is not about inviting Jesus to walk beside us for better success in life. In doing this, we have entered through the wrong gate—a very wide gate. Rather, the "narrow gate" is described that way for a specifically defined belief in a Savior who is God and coming to the conviction of our own sinfulness and alienation from His righteousness. It's a very uncomplicated Gospel. Entering through this narrow gate of belief naturally leads to comprehension of the narrow way of a lifetime journey, as Jesus said in Matthew 7:14.

Distinguishing the spirit from the soul

Unregenerate man has at best only a vague awareness of his invisible soul and spirit, since the physical body is so conspicuous. In addition, there is usually no distinction between our soul and our spirit: It's a hard concept to grasp unless we study our Bible to find the explanation. First Thessalonians 5:23 distinguishes the body, soul, and spirit as separate entities. Our soul is our own mind and personality. Our spirit enables us to contact, receive, and worship God through the study of His Word; we then **worship God in spirit and in truth** as John 4:24 says. If we seek a spirit realm foreign to Bible truth, the enemy takes control, kindling our interest in *spirit enlightenment*, and we become ensnared with evil deception. When a person dies without responding to the salvation Gospel, their unsaved soul continues to exist void of a righteous "spirit connection" with God the Father. But when we seek God's forgiveness for sin through Jesus the Savior, we are then "saved" or "*born again,*" and the Spirit of Christ, the Holy Spirit, comes to live within our spirit, giving His thoughts, feelings, and intentions. When listening to the Holy Spirit, we know it is different from our mind, will, and emotions we constantly live with.

> ***Until we personally accept Jesus as our Lord, we are not yet "born of the Spirit of God," and we cannot be aware of the "righteous spiritual realm."***

The commandments of God

The narrow lifelong journey Jesus spoke of is in no way connected with religious dos and don'ts. Neither can we gain eternal life by only obeying the Ten Commandments. These commandments are in the Bible to show us how God must be worshipped and to inform us what sin is. Keeping these commandments is coupled with faith in Jesus throughout the New Testament. In Matthew 5:17–18, Jesus says: **Think not that I am come to destroy the law, or the prophets: I am not come to destroy, but to fulfill. For verily I say unto you, Till heaven and earth pass, one jot or one tittle shall in no wise pass from the law, till all be fulfilled.**

In John 15:10, Jesus said: **If ye keep my commandments, ye shall abide in my love**.

The apostle John wrote: **For this is the love of God that we keep his commandments: and his commandments are not grievous** (1 John 5:3).

In 2 John, verse 6, he says again: **And this is love, that we walk after his commandments.**

This is a major component of how we abide in Jesus: we love and forgive one another, and we keep the commandments—which are not the works of obedience—but are written in our hearts (Hebrews 8:10) as the laws of the kingdom of God, which becomes natural to the regenerate mind.

When reading the Ten Commandments in Exodus 20 and meditating on the ramifications of each one, we find they are the divinely given statutes of holiness and ethics. They are not pinpointed laws for specific conditions only, but rather, they apply to all areas of life. Hebrews 8:14 says: **How much more shall the blood of Christ, who through the eternal Spirit offered himself without spot to God, purge your conscience from dead works to serve the living God?** When we trust in the blood of Christ for the remission of sin, our **conscience** is then cleansed from **dead works**, and God's Ten Commandments become not a rule book we must live by but are the standard and confirmation of our intent toward righteousness.

In John 14:15, Jesus said: **If you love me, keep my commandments**. And He says in John 14:21 (NKJV): **He that has my commandments and keeps them is he that loves me: and he that loves me shall be loved of my Father, and I will love him and will manifest myself in him**.

Even though Jesus admonishes us in other passages to forgive, love, and show mercy to others, these are not the commandments He is talking about here. The proof is in Matthew 19:16–19 where Jesus not only told the rich man to keep the commandments, but also recited the fifth through ninth commandments to him.

Speaking of the sixth commandment in Matthew 5:21–22, Jesus said: **You have heard it said…"Thou shalt not kill"; and whosoever shall kill shall be in danger of the judgment: But I say unto you that whosoever is angry with his brother without a cause shall be in danger of the judgment**.

This is a far-reaching commandment. For instance, any who think they belong to a superior race by skin color or by origin are murderers. Racial discrimination is hatred against our fellow man: it is **anger...without a cause** and will not escape the judgment. First John 3:15 says: **Whosoever hateth his brother is a murderer: and ye know that no murderer hath eternal life abiding in him**.

There are sixty-nine passages in our Bible about keeping the commandments of God. King David relied on God's guidance in His spoken Word—the Ten Commandments. In Psalm 119:105, he writes: **Thy word is a lamp unto my feet and a light unto my path**.

In the New Testament, 1 John 2:4–5 states: **He that saith I know him, and keepeth not his commandments is a liar, and the truth is not in him. But whoso keepeth his word, in him verily is the love of God perfected: hereby know we that we are in him**.

The apostle John also wrote in Revelation 22:14: **Blessed are they that do his commandments that they may have right to the tree of life and may enter in through the gates into the city**.

The Ten Commandments are therefore an integral part of the Gospel message. It is impossible to know God and at the same time be unaware of them.

Defining the Gospel

Our lifelong need for the Gospel is explained in Matthew 24:13: Jesus said, **But he that shall endure unto the end, the same shall be saved**. Enduring till the end—in conviction of a particular belief—is what Jesus meant. It is a steadfast belief in the literal Son of God who went to the cross and died for our sin. Being *born again* of the Spirit causes a lifetime of humbleness and repentance before God the Father. Jesus didn't tell us to repent of our sin, then move on with life as usual. The Gospel of salvation is not a matter of only accepting it—but also requires the heart's understanding of the Savior's sacrifice. After arriving at the point of humbleness and hopelessness before God, the Gospel is very simple to understand.

In Mark 1:15, Jesus said: **The time is fulfilled. The kingdom of God is at hand. Repent ye, and believe the gospel**.

Here, Jesus states nothing of vocalizing repentance of sin as a means by which we enter the kingdom of God. Instead, it is a heart issue—a change of mind that steers us in a new direction, which then propels us to verbally declare the Gospel message. Paul encourages us saying: **That if you confess with your mouth the Lord Jesus, and believe in your heart that God has raised Him from the dead, you will be saved** (Romans 10:9 NKJV). Paul didn't mean that only speaking out your belief in Jesus would bring salvation. Rather, it is necessary to first **believe in your heart that God has raised Him from the dead**, as the verse also says. It must be a conviction and determination of the heart toward the eternal Lord Jesus—your personal Lord and Savior.

In 1 Corinthians 15:3–4, Paul tells of the simplicity of this Gospel and of its sound doctrine: he says, **Christ died for our sins according to the scriptures; and that he was buried, and that he rose again the third day**.

This is the Gospel. The importance of believing in it is also revealed by Paul in Romans 3:23–24, giving us the simple explanation of our alienation from God and then the solution for it: **For all have sinned, and come short of the glory of God; being justified freely by his grace through the redemption that is in Christ Jesus**.

Acts 10:43 reveals how simple the forgiveness of sins can be: **that through his name whosoever believeth in him shall receive remission of sins**.

In Luke 9:23, Jesus said: **If any man will come after me, let him deny himself, and take up his cross daily, and follow me**.

This means we should give our lives to Him—daily submitting and surrendering to God's will—not our own selfish will. It is to esteem the Gospel of the death, burial, and resurrection of the Lord Jesus Christ as priority.

In John 6:29, Jesus said: **This is the work of God, that ye believe on him whom he hath sent**.

When we believe "on" Jesus the Savior—not just "in" Him—we become conscious of the spirit realm, and we realize our human wretchedness, resulting in sorrow for sin.

In John 6:47, Jesus then says: **He that believeth on me hath everlasting life**. The verse immediately preceding shows the exact interpretation: **Not that any man hath seen the Father, save he which is of God, he hath seen the Father** (John 6:46). Jesus was with the Father before He came to earth, which defines Him as eternal as the Father is eternal. Therefore, in John 6:47, Jesus was saying, "He that believes on *my deity* has everlasting life."

And of course, the primary Gospel verse we all know, John 3:16, says: **For God so loved the world that he gave his only begotten Son, that whosoever believeth in him should not perish, but have everlasting life**.

By itself, however, John 3:16 should not be the only passage we lean on to claim eternal salvation, simply because we must also **come to the light** as Jesus says a few moments later in John 3:21. We must embrace this Light of Righteousness by turning from our unrighteous ways. The simple words of John 3:16 explain how and why we are saved: it is by a belief that Jesus was and is the only begotten Son of God. He was not symbolically God; neither was He God's sacrificial representative for the purpose of our earthly pleasure. Jesus was God come in the flesh, and His flesh was sacrificed for our eternal life. It's amazingly simple! Yet many Christians have now theologically neglected "the light" of John 3:21 in a willful distancing from the righteousness God offers—ignorantly justifying a progressively deceptive and different gospel. If they desire eternal life, they must turn back and embrace the Gospel of the Bible once again. Second Peter 2:20–21 tells us that the believer who diverts from the Gospel will be worse off than the one who hears the Gospel and does not accept it. Both are on a path leading to hell. But Jesus was on a mission to redeem as many souls as possible. He was a hellfire preacher—speaking of and warning of the torments of hell far more than the glory of heaven. In essence, the good news message of our Bible is the "Rescuing Gospel"—the rescue from hell.

Though God is merciful and will not condemn those who don't have the mental capacity to understand, the rest of humanity is very accountable. When our life is over, we will be judged and rewarded as per our response to the Gospel of Jesus and how we utilized our time, talent, and excess. We won't be rewarded for our perfect church attendance record...or the success rate of our prayers...or that we had memorized Scripture. We won't be rewarded for any earthly achievement or the financial success we attained. All of it becomes meaningless in comparison to the invisible and spiritual kingdom of God and the Gospel of His righteousness in truth.

Jesus said: **I am the door: by me if any man enter in, he shall be saved, and shall go in and out, and find pasture. I am come that they might have life more abundantly** (John 10:9–10).

Did Jesus mean we could have an abundantly fulfilled life in a materialistic sense? Or that we would gain more satisfaction in our earthly accomplishments when we seek His Righteousness? No! We cannot add Jesus and His Gospel to our life. The Gospel of Jesus must be our inward conviction—separate from the physical realm. In the revealed fullness of New Testament doctrine, we find that earthly satisfaction and success or physical health and comfort are not rendered as benefits of the Gospel. When Jesus said: **And shall go in and out, and find pasture**, it means that if we first enter through Jesus, the Door of Righteousness, we can find pasture when returning from our daily earthly responsibilities. The **life more abundantly** which Jesus spoke of in John 10:10 is of spiritual contentment and communion with Him—completely separate from our physical environment.

First Timothy 6:17–19 says:

> **Charge them that are rich in this world, that they be not high-minded, nor trust in uncertain riches, but in the living God, who giveth us richly all things to enjoy; that they do good, that they be rich in good works, ready to distribute, willing to communicate; laying up in store for themselves a good foundation against the time to come, that they may lay hold on eternal life.**

This passage does not link the spiritual realm with the physical realm: it distinctly separates the two. Though our heavenly Father gives us material blessings to enjoy, inner peace must be prioritized through the Gospel of righteousness, having nothing in common with earthly blessings and physical comforts. In Luke 11:5–12, Jesus explains that if we ask God for physical necessities, He will supply them; then in verse 13, He said if we ask for the Holy Spirit, God will give it. Yet within the text, there is no indication that the material realm and the spiritual realm are somehow connected: one cannot benefit the other.

The sixth chapter of Romans is also basic to the knowledge of the Gospel; yet some of us cringe when reading Romans 6:3: **Know ye not, that so many of us as were baptized into Jesus Christ were baptized into his death?**

This is hard for some to swallow. We don't want to die to ourselves: we don't want to submit to a religion of death. Instead, we want to experience all the earthly blessings of the Christian life, which many pastors tell us we can have. Yet this is contrariety to the sound doctrine of the Gospel. The follower of the biblical Jesus is indeed following a doctrine of death unto carnality. Though our heavenly Father may give us good material things to enjoy in life, these should not be seen as well deserved for having placed our faith in Christ.

Romans 6:5 then reveals the ultimate promise of everlasting life: **For if we have been planted together in the likeness of his death, we shall be also in the likeness of his resurrection.**

Though this is a powerful verse of spiritual understanding, it may seem a bit gloomy to be likened to Christ at His death, and we may begin a misguided effort to coerce God into preserving our lives in earthly comfort. In a very real sense, our kindhearted philanthropic pursuits and our generous church giving could easily counter or replace our spiritual maturity when we don't prioritize the real Gospel.

Romans 6:11 further encourages spiritual maturity of believers: **Likewise reckon ye also yourselves to be dead indeed unto sin, but alive unto God through Jesus Christ our Lord.** Here the apostle Paul desires the reader to reject sin and to be spiritually discerning and mature. But when we as Christians pursue earthly contentment and prosperity above the kingdom of God—or as conducive to it—we deviate greatly in a spiritual sense. Paul states in 1 Corinthians 15:50: **Now this I say, brethren, that flesh and blood cannot inherit the kingdom of God; neither doth corruption inherit incorruption**. Christians not giving priority to spiritual things tend to slip into unperceived idolatry. But when we discern the spiritual Gospel of the Bible, we easily become disassociated with earthly things. We should also mourn for the unsaved around us who seek temporal earthly satisfaction, rather than eternal life.

The new man

Ephesians 4:23–24 says: **And be renewed in the spirit of your mind; and that ye put on the new man, which after God is created in righteousness and true holiness**.

This passage does not tell us to put on a new attitude in order to gain righteousness. But rather, **put on the new man**, which is supernaturally offered to us by God. In other words, we cannot change our lifestyle or put on a positive attitude to be made holy. Instead, we are renewed in our mind from a faith in Jesus, which results in **the new man** from within. When we turn from our sinful nature, we are given **the new man** to reside in if we choose. We still have the potential to revert to the "old man"—the old carnal nature. But when daily choosing spiritual righteousness over fleshly things, we then walk in the Spirit, thus gaining peace of mind. Being "saved" but yet remaining in the "old man" nature also gives tendency to continue striving in the old method of "works" for salvation.

Other portions of Scripture further explain what **the new man** is all about. The book of 1 Corinthians is insightful for comprehending how Jesus becomes one's Lord, instead of only one's Savior. First Corinthians 2:11 speaks to carnal believers, informing them that **the things of man** are wisdom only to himself, but **the things of God** no man knows except through the **Spirit of God**. First Corinthians 3 then continues to address the unfruitfulness of carnal believers. The apostle Paul states that they are saved because they have chosen Jesus as their Savior; but they have not given heed to the **new man** made available to them. The fruit they produce is only **wood,**

hay, and stubble because they live in carnality, having **envy, strife, and divisions**. But those who determine to move on to maturity in Christ will find love, peace, and contentment, which produces **gold, silver, and precious stones** as Paul says in 1 Corinthians 3:12. First Corinthians 3:15 (ESV) then says: **If anyone's work is burned up, he will suffer loss, though he himself will be saved, but only as through fire**.

When studying 1 Corinthians, chapters 2 and 3, in conjunction with the concept of "the new man" in Ephesians 4, we find that those who mature in the ways of God will be greatly rewarded. But those who choose to live carnally in Christ will have little heavenly reward.

Chapter 2

The Flock Ravaged

In the same manner as Jesus ascended to heaven, he shall return to earth one day. We as Christians anticipate this event. Though according to Matthew, chapters 13 and 24, and Mark 13 (which we will later discuss), many end-of-the-age believers will fall asleep spiritually from the lullaby of unperceived deception, making them unprepared for the Savior's return. False doctrines passionately taught by current-day false teachers leaves the Gospel message obscured in religious preoccupation, contrived works, and distortion of Bible truth. Therefore, Christianity, as a whole, is in a state of disunion over primary issues of the faith. The flock of God's redeemed have been ravaged, swindled, and deceived by false teachers and false prophets for many years now. But we shouldn't be surprised: Jesus told us there would be end-time false prophets. How do they have such successful influence over us? It is for our own laziness to find biblical knowledge. Though when a follower of Jesus studies God's Word more in depth, any false teaching we may read or hear is easily exposed as contrary to sound doctrine.

Carefully read 1 John 2:24–27: it gives great insight to the body of Christ. Notice in verse 24 the apostle John uses the phrase **from the beginning**, and then in verse 26, **them that seduce you**, and in verse 27, **But the anointing which ye have received of him abideth**

in you, and ye need not that any man teach you: but as the same anointing teacheth you of all things, and is truth, and is no lie, and even as it hath taught you, ye shall abide in him.

Notice how the text doesn't say that we don't need pastors and shepherds of the flock to guide and teach us. But it says **the anointing**—the Holy Spirit—has been our teacher **from the beginning** of our conversion, and that we can and should be a student of God's Word for ourselves.

Then the ultimate reason for what the apostle John has just stated: **And now, little children, abide in Him; that, when He shall appear, we may have confidence, and not be ashamed before Him at His coming. If ye know that he is righteous, ye know that every one that doeth righteousness is born of him** (1 John 2:28–29).

This plainly says it all. When discerning the fullness of 1 John 2:24–29, we know that we will abide in the righteousness of the Lord Jesus Christ when we take sound doctrine to heart and live by it.

Shepherds over the flock—the body of Christ—have a divine command to preach the truth from the heart of God, and to exegetically expound upon the Scriptures. Though if we blindly follow our pastors' teaching only because of his loving and compassionate ways, we may easily believe everything he says. How can we know for certain that his interpretation of the Gospel aligns with sound Bible doctrine if we don't make a personal separate study? When studying God's Word and asking the Holy Spirit to show us the truth, we then comprehend it and are assured of the "anointing of truth" to abide in Christ Jesus.

The New Testament indicates that all believers should have discernment of what constitutes sound doctrine and how it differs from false doctrine. Those who lead the flock are chiefly responsible to speak out with further exhortation as Paul instructed Timothy to do in 2 Timothy 4:2: he said, **Preach the word; be instant in season, out of season; reprove, rebuke, exhort with all longsuffering and doctrine**.

This passage, among others, reveals that precise and accurate teaching of the "doctrine" is foremost. This is why it is so important to search for and become a part of a doctrinally sound Bible-based church. Finding what we think is a good church full of good-hearted people and led by a dynamic pastor and his team is no guarantee that Bible truth is being taught there.

Unfortunately, I have already found it to be true—that the knowledge and warning I share with Christians largely falls on doubting and unreceptive ears. Many believers seem to be skeptical of new or different views than their own. It seems that many are not willing to even research beyond their own sphere of limited knowledge. This falls in line with Romans 11:5–6: **Even so at this present time also there is a remnant according to the election of grace. And if by grace, then is it no more of works: otherwise grace is no more grace**. What follows in Romans 11:7–8 is even more amazing: **But the election hath obtained it, and the rest were blinded (according as it is written, God hath given them the spirit of slumber, eyes that they should not see, and ears that they should not hear)**.

This passage cannot possibly apply to the unbelieving masses. Read the full context beginning at Romans 11:1. Even today, a spirit of slumber shrouds many believers—having blind eyes and deaf ears to the true Gospel. They are blinded by complacency and unperceived deception. God allows it to happen for the purpose of separating righteousness from unrighteousness. The carnal must be distinguished from the spiritual—a necessary reveal of the hearts of believers who have reverted to religious works or false doctrine. Dependence on religion or belief in a false gospel becomes a sad cycle that even many in church leadership ignorantly hold to because they either don't or can't accept God's grace in the Savior as totally sufficient as Romans 11 shows us.

Erring brethren within the church are spoken of in 1 Corinthians 5: in verses 12–13 (NIV), Paul says, **What business is it of mine to judge those outside the church? Are you not to judge those inside? God will judge those outside. Expel the wicked men from among you**.

Aligning with this passage, I find I am scripturally justified to make a judgment call against those within the body of Christ who err in their interpretation of the Gospel. We cannot judge the motives of the human heart, but we can test the spirit of truth and the spirit of erring false doctrine through the Word of God. In 1 John 4:1, we are told: **Beloved, believe not every spirit, but try the spirits whether they are of God: because many false prophets are gone out into the world**. In other words, John tells us we should test according to Scripture everything we hear or read. In the Epistles of the New Testament, we are told to cling to sound doctrine. Yet how can we be knowledgeable of truthful doctrine if we neglect an understanding of it?

In Titus 1:9, referring to a bishop or pastor, it says: **Hold fast the faithful word as he has been taught, that he may be able by sound doctrine both to exhort and to convince the gainsayers**. This **faithful word** (sound doctrine) is not only a cutting edge by which we can convince against wrong theology—but also that even a slight deviation from it steers us off course from the narrow way of salvation Jesus spoke of.

Proverbs 30:6 warns: **Add thou not unto his words, lest he reprove thee, and thou be found a liar**. Carrying this Old Testament warning into the new covenant era we live in, we find that any addition to the Gospel of salvation is actually false teaching that directs people down a religious or self-benefiting path with no eternal value. As such, even though a pastor is loved and respected, his teaching and preaching is still subject to scrutiny and rebuke if necessary.

In Paul's Second Letter to Timothy, he exhorts: **Study to show thyself approved unto God...rightly dividing the word of truth** (2 Timothy 2:15).

This is primarily a very instructive verse: we are required to study God's Word by making careful comparison between passages. In doing so, we will find correct interpretation of the Bible and also discover whether or not our lives are pleasing to our Father in heaven.

Correct interpretation of the Bible comes by reading within the context and balancing Scripture against itself.

Paul gives an exhortation and warning to immature believers in 1 Corinthians 2:5: he says, **That your faith should not stand in the wisdom of men, but in the power of God**. In surrounding context, we see Paul was emphasizing "Christ crucified" as the only saving power of God. All other **enticing words of man's wisdom** (verse 4) were, in effect, useless.

Because Paul is writing here to a specific body of believers, the implication is that they should not be swayed by any eloquent or convincing talk of things unrelated to the Gospel. This admonition to the Christians at Corinth showed them the narrow path of following the true Gospel of Jesus. When we also take this admonishment to heart, it should result in the understanding of precisely why the followers of Jesus are in the world: it is to proclaim the Gospel of God's grace and righteousness. Christians are not required to convince unbelievers that angels exist or that miracles are possible. Rather, they are to confidently and humbly **make more disciples** as Jesus instructed in Matthew 28:19.

Immaturity of believers is also spoken of in Ephesians 4:13–14:

> **Till we all come in the unity of the faith, and of the knowledge of the Son of God, unto a perfect man, unto the measure of the stature of the fullness of Christ: that we be no more children, tossed to and fro, and carried about with every wind of doctrine, by the sleight of men, and cunning craftiness, whereby they lie in wait to deceive.**

Notice how Paul warns of fraudulent and corrupt communication being taught even among Christians. This **cunning craftiness**, as Paul calls it, is ongoing even today: it causes not only spiritual immaturity but also deception from and ignorance of the real Gospel message. Sermons and seminars on how to improve your life, realize your goals and potential, or how to better influence others—all filtering through supportive Bible verses and stories of how God used common people to be transformed into victorious overcomers, is grossly misapplied. Though we can learn lessons from those in the Bible who failed or be inspired by the stories of men and women who triumphed, the ultimate soul-saving message of our Bible is that sinful humankind needs Jesus the Savior. When we correctly interpret and apply the fullness of God's Word, we then become victorious overcomers in a spiritual sense only. Though God directs our steps and gives us confidence to succeed in life's goals and dreams—perhaps inspired by examples in His Word—there is, at the same time, a higher calling for Christians to proclaim the simple life-changing spiritual message from the Bible.

But because many of us wanted scriptural endorsement of an earthly benefit for believing in Jesus, God lets us find it **by the sleight of men, and cunning craftiness** (Ephesians 4:14). Through dynamic yet falsified *New Revelation* teaching from pastors we admire, we were enticed to a broad and beautiful floral-laced avenue. Awestruck with enthusiasm to pursue a more rewarding journey in Jesus, we failed to notice the warning sign at the turn reading "Deception Road," and we began traveling a path of unperceived friendship of the world and **enmity with God** as James 4:4 warned of.

Cult religion

Do you remember Bhagwan Shree Rajneesh? He was the mystic East-Indian guru who moved his commune to a Central Oregon ranch in the 1980s. Bhagwan's followers wore only red clothing and had a rather free but devout lifestyle. Many of them gave up all that they had in exchange for a life of peace and safety within the Rajneesh community. The teachings of Bhagwan Shree Rajneesh were obviously not Bible based, and we as Christians knew them to be a cult, led by a false teacher.

After a few years of controversy with Oregon authorities and Bhagwan's deportation for criminal activities, the Rajneesh commune disbanded, and in 1990, Bhagwan Shree Rajneesh died from heart failure at age fifty-eight.

Non-Christian cult groups, like the Rajneeshees, that spring up, then fade away, are not what Jesus was talking about in Matthew 24:4

where he warned his disciples to **take heed that no man deceive you**. Jesus was not addressing unbelievers who have potential to join a cult religion in their quest for the meaning of life. Rather, he is speaking to his own followers who had already believed the truth.

In Scripture, a false prophet (false teacher) is described primarily as one who arises among God's own people. It is not referring to a non-Christian cult leader who teaches wacky ideas about God and life—but is one who distorts and mangles Scripture—ignorantly spreading false prophecy and doctrinal lies within the body of Christ.

Acts 20, Galatians 1, and 2 Peter 2 are among the many Bible chapters warning us specifically to beware of a changed gospel—a cult-type religion developing within the church.

In Acts 20, we read that Paul is about to depart from Greece and go to Jerusalem where he is uncertain of what will befall him. He encourages and warns the people in verses 30–31, saying: **Also of your own selves shall men arise, speaking perverse things, to draw away disciples after them. Therefore watch, and remember, that by the space of three years I ceased not to warn every one night and day with tears**.

When carefully discerning Paul's emotional plea and his reference in verses 26–28, echoing Moses's warning to the people (Deuteronomy 13:1–3) to not follow after false prophets who draw the listener away from the truth, we know that we also must be on alert for unsound doctrine in our day. Applying the message of Deuteronomy 13 to the church today, we find that the enemy's purpose of a false prophet (false teacher) is to turn people away from the New Testament doctrine of salvation. When a false prophet within the church reveals a sign or miracle that comes to pass by way of unsound doctrinal teaching, we are thus deceived just as the Israelites many times were. And yet the Israelites were specifically warned beforehand about the "signs and wonders" of false prophets! The New Testament gives many similar warnings for our time as well. In 2 Peter 2:1–2 (NIV), the apostle Peter states:

> **But there were also false prophets among the people, just as there will be false teach-**

> **ers among you. They will secretly introduce destructive heresies, even denying the sovereign Lord who bought them...bringing swift destruction on themselves. Many will follow their shameful ways and will bring the way of truth into disrepute.**

This is happening in many congregations large and small. The false teachers of our day proclaim doctrines that reject the Incarnation of Jesus the Savior. One example:

> *Nationally known, celebrity and motivational pastor, Bishop T. D. Jakes of The Potter's House mega-church in Dallas, Texas, believes and teaches "modalism"—that there are merely three aspects (modes) of the divine revelation. Jakes teaches that the Trinity Godhead is actually One God who manifests Himself in "three expressions," and at different times. Theologically, this is a denial of the Apostles' Creed of "three co-existing persons" within the Trinity Godhead. This doctrine, believed by Oneness Pentecostalism, renders many false assumptions—that Jesus the Son first came into being when he was born in Bethlehem; that through skillful ventriloquism, spoke to himself at his baptism in Luke 3:22; and at his ascension was transformed into spirit mode. This subtle yet dangerous falsehood of the nature of Christ opposes over a dozen Bible passages stating that Jesus "the Son" eternally and literally exists in the form of deity. The doctrine of "modalism" thus desecrates the core of the Gospel of Salvation.* ("TD Jakes and Steven Furtick Affirm Modalism," YouTube)

Counterfeit Christianity

Does your pastor quote and interpret Scripture? Of course he does! Is this evidence that he's been appointed and anointed by God? No! In Luke 4:10–11, Satan quoted and interpreted Scripture to Jesus in hopes that he would believe a counterfeit version of it. Satan knows Scripture very well and will twist its divinely intended meaning to deceive the shepherds of the flock and laity alike. Our natural carnal-minded tendencies will also lead us into disassociation with the fundamental Gospel of the Bible. The enemy of our soul keeps guard over our negligence of God's Word—focusing our attention on worldly distractions and distortion of Bible truth—strategizing how to reverse our eternal destiny.

Today, a huge counterfeit segment of Christianity is growing alongside the true disciples of Jesus. Because of the popularity of *New Revelation* teaching, and its being flaunted by the Christian media, this group seems to be larger in number—giving impression of an end-time spiritual awakening. Yet in Jesus's Sermon on the Mount addressing the crowd, He said: **Because strait is the gate, and narrow is the way, which leadeth unto life, and few there be that find it** (Matthew 7:14). The minimal number of those finding the truth is what Jesus referred to—it is a belief in Himself as the eternal God and a humbleness of the heart which leads to life eternal. Notice that Jesus did not say, "*Because many are the lifelong duties of the obedient, therefore few can endure, and few shall find eternal life.*" To the contrary, this is not the Gospel's "narrow way." Here in Matthew 7:14, Jesus not only refers to the saved versus the unsaved, He is also speaking of those who see and believe the truth versus those who do not—even among His own followers. We read in John 6:63–66 that many who had followed Jesus turned back after learning that the words He spoke were only spiritual and profited the flesh nothing.

The "strait gate" we must enter through is seeing and believing a precise doctrine and interpretation of Jesus the Savior, and the "narrow way" is a lifelong continuation in that belief. It has nothing whatsoever to do with one's own church attendance record or religious duties and good works—which the natural mind attempts to apply to salvation. But by studying God's Word, building line upon line and precept upon precept in our faith, we are transformed into a lifestyle of righteousness and holiness—living by the Spirit and not the flesh. It is a continual contrition of the heart and forgiving those who offend us. This was meant to be an easy lifelong accomplishment after the heart has been genuinely converted through the realization of God's love for us by sending His Son for our redemption.

But Satan loves organized religion: it feeds right into his plan of deception. Though a congregation may grow in number, this isn't a sign they've been taught by those who maintain biblical truth. Today, the enemy has blinded religious pastors and false teachers of the flock, who cleverly justify their unfocused and undiscerning imaginations—presenting inspiring messages to their congregations. If the listener does not personally study his or her Bible, their exposure to the salvific Gospel is limited for being piggybacked from their pastors' interpretation of it. Does he have heedful exegetical skills? Or is his interpretation and theology inclined toward a cunningly tainted doctrine that profits the flesh? We must listen with discerning ears because every pastor believes that he teaches and preaches the truth. That's why we are encouraged and even scripturally mandated to find gospel truth and to be personally convinced of our own faith, which brings a decisive hope *in* our faith.

Isaiah 55:8 says: **For my thoughts are not your thoughts, neither are your ways my ways, saith the Lord**.

This verse is not addressing the heathen or unbelievers but God's own people. Read what follows in Isaiah 55:11–12. It states that God's Word shall produce a harvest, and **it shall accomplish that which I please, and it shall prosper whereto I sent it. For ye shall go out with joy, and be led forth with peace**.

Did you notice the word "prosper" in the passage? It says: **God's Word shall prosper**, meaning "come mightily" as the Concordance reveals—having nothing in common with tangible prosperity, as some incorrectly apply to the verse. Verse 13 continues: **Instead of the thorn shall come up the fir tree, and instead of the brier shall come up the myrtle tree: and it shall be to the Lord for a name, for an everlasting sign that shall not be cut off**. Today we see just the reverse in many cases: thorns and briers have sprung up, dividing the church over controversial issues such as prosperity. This has happened because the very next verse has been neglected: **Thus saith the Lord, Keep ye judgment, and do justice: for my salvation is near to come, and my righteousness to be revealed** (Isaiah 56:1). Salvation and righteousness must therefore be in a completely different category from earthly prosperity and wealth.

Today, whole denominations and independent churches are not in total doctrinal unity with one another mainly because Christian pastors and shepherds of the flock have not kept judgment in the **righteousness to be revealed**—the new covenant Gospel of Jesus the Savior. Because our ways are not God's ways, as Isaiah 55:8 says, even the shepherds of God's flock can be tripped up when trying to decipher and apply biblical instruction in their own wisdom, thus corrupting the understanding of the listener.

The apostle Paul tells Timothy, his son in the faith, how to pass on the spiritual wisdom he was taught: **And the things that thou hast heard of me among many witnesses, the same commit thou to faithful men, who shall be able to teach others also** (2 Timothy 2:2).

Paul was insistent that the particular Gospel of Jesus be accurately conveyed to future generations of the faithful. However, the Gospel's misinterpretation of our previous generation continues to be a threat to the spiritual well-being of today's believers. Many Christians are not only focused on financial achievement but also focused on feelings and experience rather than scriptural fact. The clarity and simplicity of the Gospel has become twisted, muddled, or not prioritized; in fact, it isn't even understood by many. In addition, our survival-mode mentality takes over, and we turn to our spiritual teachers for easy Bible answers. This is how last-day Christians are deceived and then become apostate: they do not discern the real Gospel because of their passionate desire to experience God's manifestations, supernatural supply, and blessings of abundance.

In many church congregations, there has been a gradual shift from biblical truth to human sentiment and the desire for wealth. It has resulted from a deluge of ear-tickling and rational-sounding "imaginations" taught by undiscerning pastors. This unsound teaching has nothing whatsoever to do with the basics of New Testament doctrine and the reason for it. Because they are so loved and admired, many pastors and bishops have acquired inflated egos. The enemy has deceived them to believe that their teaching aligns with Scripture, rather than Scripture being searched to find the base for sound teaching. This, in turn, does not advance the kingdom of God in the slightest but sends them and the listener down the road of spiritual unfruitfulness and destruction. Our spiritual passion is eternally beneficial only if our beliefs have been exegetically derived through the Word of God.

Chapter 9 of this book reveals a particular current-day well-known pastor who is so profoundly passionate to see revival happen that he cannot see of his own deception. This pastor absolutely loves God but has not discerned the difference between a spiritual revival and a revival of manifestations. He has not discerned the sound doctrine of the Gospel of salvation for his error of searching out passages that only appear to support his desire and agenda for revival.

The truth of sound doctrine

Today, many people doubt and don't believe there is any such thing as literal truth—especially biblical, spiritual, or doctrinal truth. Could the Muslim's Quran be the truth? Could the Book of Mormon be the truth? Where is spiritual truth proclaimed? The Bible tells us and even warns us to not be deceived by any subsequent teaching. In John 18:37–38, Jesus explained to Pontius Pilate that He bore witness unto the truth of life, and that those who heard His voice will know of spiritual truth. Jesus had explained perfectly the truth of salvation to Pilate, but he was uninterested and couldn't comprehend what Jesus said, replying: **What is truth?** Pilate then turned and walked away—maybe because he perceived Jesus's words as only metaphoric and couldn't imagine how things unseen could be truthful. Yet the Christ—the Man of Truth Himself—had stood right in front of Pilate, explaining the simple spiritual basics to him!

Old Testament prophets, Jesus, and New Testament apostles were contenders for and interpreters of spiritual truth and of sound doctrine. We as Christians should know that the salvation Gospel of the Bible is reality, yet in much of the church today, this Gospel is under attack by the false prophets. We've also been subtly encouraged to act upon an interpretation of the Gospel that resonates with us personally, which easily leads to beliefs based more on cultlike feelings, emotions, and a works-based performance kind of faith. Rather than obeying God, we have become focused on experiencing God and His presumed promise of miracles and increase. All too many Christians prioritize works for Christ, rather than examining the doctrine of Christ Himself. Ultimately, it is to our spiritual detriment if we are seduced to believe in a different Jesus or another gospel than the Bible tells of.

Our application of Scripture should align itself with the message of the life, the death, and the resurrection of Jesus Christ. I observe, however, that many Christians seek an experience from God or a blessing from God, rather than sharing His Gospel with the unsaved. This is the result of unsound doctrine being taught by false prophets and prophetesses who, as Jesus said, will **teach and seduce my servants, and commit fornication** (Revelation 2:20). Revelation 2:24 then tells that the listener had not discerned the truth of the Gospel because they were seduced by the false prophets who had deceived them—**But unto you I say…as many as have not this doctrine, and which have not known the depths of Satan as they speak**.

Millions of Christians have already been swept into the delusion of Satan's "depths" through seductive false teaching. Rational and logical-sounding false doctrines are undetectable to the Christian ear not attuned to sound doctrine. Twisted passages, astutely and scrupulously presented, convince the listener of *New Revelation* truth. Yet these apostate "revelations" of Gospel perversion profit the believer nothing in the end.

The false teachers among us are not aware that they themselves are false teachers because the enemy has blinded them in deception. Though when reading of Jesus's warnings about deception, we might automatically think we are immune—*Jesus couldn't possibly be warn-*

ing me personally—I'm focused and sincere, and my prayers are being answered! This kind of naivety leaves you wide open to deception of the sneakiest kind.

Revelation 2:26 then gives insight to the spiritual victory of those who do not listen to the false prophets: **And he that overcometh, and keepeth my works unto the end, to him I will give power over the nations.**

Think of it! This is Jesus our Savior speaking! What are the "works" Jesus wants us to keep? Is Christ telling us that we shall overcome because of our close intimacy with Him on a daily basis? Or shall we overcome by our obedience to the Ten Commandments? No! We overcome through a persevering belief in the sound doctrine of the Gospel of salvation—the death, burial, and resurrection of the Lord Jesus. This is the only "works" required of us. In Revelation 2:20–21, Jesus warns of the false prophets and the deceived who listen to them:

> **Notwithstanding I have a few things against thee, because thou sufferest that woman Jezebel, which calleth herself a prophetess, to teach and to seduce my servants to commit fornication, and to eat things sacrificed to idols. And I gave her space to repent of her fornication; and she repented not.**

This is probably the most important passage in the book of Revelation for end-time Christians to contemplate and understand. Sanctification unto holiness and separation from the world's system must be our criterion. Though God is merciful and gives most of us a space of time to repent of our mistaken beliefs and apostasy, there is also no promise of time enough to return to the truth of salvation. Those who remain seduced by an altered apostate gospel will experience **great tribulation, except they repent of their deeds** (Revelation 2:22). This is a future-tense warning, applying to the current reader of the text. The next verse proves it: Revelation 2:23 says, **And all the churches shall know that I am he which sear-**

cheth the reins and hearts: and I will give unto everyone of you according to your works.

This speaks of our eternal future—after our earthly mortal life ends. What we believe in and prioritize in this life will one day be judged and personally recompensed for eternity.

Jesus told His disciples: **Behold, I send you forth as sheep in the midst of wolves: be ye therefore wise as serpents, and harmless as doves** (Matthew 10:16).

Today, the followers of Jesus need to be wise as serpents through the understanding of Holy Scripture simply because we are **in the midst of wolves** who teach unsound doctrine. We must be knowledgeable of the new covenant Gospel and of Satan's devises against it.

Jesus also said: **If any man have ears to hear, let him hear** (Mark 4:23). The Savior desires that we understand the truth of God's Word and that we act upon it and not be turned aside by any other doctrine. When we **have ears to hear** and take it to heart personally in conviction and truth, we cannot be swayed by the lies of the enemy.

In John 10:27–28, Jesus said**: My sheep hear my voice, and I know them, and they follow me: and I give unto them eternal life; and they shall never perish, neither shall any pluck them out of my hand**. Know therefore that we cannot be plucked out of fellowship with Jesus the Savior if we remain in the truth and perseverance of His Gospel.

Chapter 3

The Origin of Apostasy

Where did false teaching about Jesus and His Gospel originate? More importantly, why can't many devout Christians recognize their own apostasy from the simple and sound doctrine of the Gospel? How have we become so blind or lazy to discern it? The answer is in 1 Peter 5:8–9: **Because your adversary the devil, as a roaring lion, walketh about, seeking whom he may devour: whom resist steadfast in the faith**.

When reading this passage carefully within its surrounding context, we see that the devil's main attempt is to derail us from sound doctrine. It is not to devour us in physical infirmity or to tempt us into gross moral sin. Owing to the fact of our original fallen nature, we usually sin many times of our own volition. Don't blame every sin on Satan's leverage and temptation; he knows right well of the Scriptures—that **if any man sin, we have an advocate with the Father, Jesus Christ the righteous** (1 John 2:1). When we are convicted by the Holy Spirit and by repenting of our sin, move on even stronger in the faith! We must therefore be steadfast not only through our afflictions and temptations of the flesh but primarily steadfast and secure in sound Gospel doctrine belief. As mentioned above, the apostle Peter reveals that the devil is **as a roaring lion**—a skilled and loud mouthpiece of convincing false doctrine in the ears of the faithful—**seeking whom he may devour** in a spiritual sense unsuspectingly. The enemy's successful strategy of recent years has removed many from a faith in Jesus, the sacrificed Son of God, to a faith in Jesus, the giver of all blessings. Christians know they should not willfully sin against God by breaking His Ten Commandments, but many have unwittingly sinned by succumbing to doctrinal apostasy—a digression from scriptural truth—which is actually a violation of the first commandment: **Thou shalt have no other gods before me** (Exodus 20:3).

Primary deterrents to the Gospel have progressed undetected even among more mature believers. But as sincere disciples of Jesus, we must be on guard: we are required to recognize unsound doctrine relating to the Gospel of salvation and resist the devil's convincing and conciliating derailment in a seductive and perverted gospel. We must be steadfast in our simple faith in the Savior who is God. It is bedrock for traveling the "narrow path" Jesus spoke of in Matthew 7:14.

Perhaps to the new or naive believer, New Testament admonishments referring to "the doctrine" may not seem relevant to salvation, and thus, a propensity to neglect the meaning of it easily develops through the schemes of the enemy. Maybe you don't see anything theologically wrong with the teaching in your own church or denomination. And hopefully your pastor has not deviated doctrinally from Scripture. But how do you know for sure? Deception upon deception is gradual. It hasn't taken a year or even a decade. In fact, you may not have noticed any change in the preaching of the Gospel within your own lifetime. Apostate ideas that move us away from the saving Gospel have taken roughly 160 years to creep their way into the Protestant Church. It began in secular society with the gullible Bible-ignorant masses being deceived through heretical theologies of non-Christian men and women. The God of the Bible and man's relationship to Him were either maligned or totally ignored in these teachings. Gradually, over many decades, these deceptive unbiblical doctrines have penetrated the church unnoticed, causing an unperceived apostasy from the Gospel. This happened because faithful believers did not keep guard against unsound doctrine. Though many Protestant pastors and Bible scholars still declare doctrinal truth, diverse **doctrines of devils** (1 Timothy 4:1) became mingled with the Gospel, propelling much of the church into a theological downward spiral. And we aren't likely at the bottom just yet.

Over the last century, many quirky teachings and ideas have been introduced within Christianity. For the most part, these teachings surrounded the Gospel and did not attack its primary core. Today, however, the enemy is in major onslaught mode to remove the core of the Gospel message, which spiritually destroys many lives and the effectiveness of the church in society.

If you're not familiar with a perverted gospel being preached today within mainstream Christianity, you must be made aware of the *Human-Only Jesus gospel* being taught. The listener must be alert and informed because this unsound anti-Gospel doctrine is obviously not stated as *the Human-Only Jesus gospel.* If it were, devout followers of Jesus wouldn't dare give it any credence. Though because of Satan's deceptive seduction, many believers now believe in a gospel of a loving savior who was not God. How? Because this false doctrine is hidden deep within logical sounding yet fabricated theological gobbledygook. It is called "*The Born-Again Jesus*" doctrine. This dangerous teaching is largely undetected as the catalyst for other disparaging, heretical, and apostate indoctrinations, which are explained in the following chapters of this book.

This chapter is very important. It is packed with tidbits of information and insight you'll find fascinating. What follows is a sequence of past non-Christian teachers of philosophical false notions that have now perverted the preaching of many of today's Evangelical Christian pastors.

Sounds impossible? Think again!

Idolatrous philosophy mingled with Bible doctrine

In the 1800s an awakening in the occult and spiritism led to the *New Thought* movement. *New Thought* is a broad term encompassing diverse beliefs emphasizing experiencing God's presence for practical purposes such as healing and success. All teachings of *New Thought* philosophy revolved around the idea that "*God is a Universal Mind—an impersonal force that manifests itself within all people.*"

Phineas P. Quimby (1802–1866) was the father of *New Thought* theology. He was a philosopher, mesmerist, and spiritual teacher. Quimby wrote many books on what we as Christians would know to be erroneous interpretations of life, death, and the Bible.

In Quimby's writings, he states: "*The spiritual realm transcends the physical realm, and 'thought power' and positive thinking are true. Sickness comes from the mind, but 'right thinking' heals it*" (Quotations of Phineas Parkhurst Quimby, Google search).

Though Quimby's statement has a component of faith, it is not a biblical kind of faith nor does sickness originate in the mind; neither was Quimby's method of healing scriptural.

Quimby's *New Thought* theory about Jesus is that He was not God Incarnate but showed the way to become divine in nature, and that God, the *Universal Creative Intelligence*, is within all humans equally. Some within this movement believed in reincarnation and that with each lifetime, a closer perfection to divinity was achieved and that the term *salvation* actually means "*oneness with the impersonal life force*"—thus unlocking one's potential for success and healing.

The prevailing belief about life after death is that regardless of outward actions, most people will ultimately obtain salvation—theorized as "equal status with God."

Mary Baker Eddy (1821–1910) claimed to have been healed from a sickness by Phineas Quimby and was thus inspired by his writings. Mrs. Eddy became influential in her New England community and beyond, writing books on science and health. She was also a practicing hypnotist and conducted seances—incorporating some biblical teaching with spiritism (witchcraft).

Mary Baker Eddy was the founder of the *Christian Science* movement, which is still active today, but is neither Christian or scientific in nature and belief. From her many writings, she states:

"Spiritual reality is true and everything else is an illusion" (Mary Baker Eddy Quotes, Google search).

This statement by Eddy may sound somewhat reasonable in a figurative sense; however, this would also presume that when Jesus physically healed someone, it was just an illusion. Though to the person who was healed by Jesus, it certainly was no such thing.

Mrs. Eddy also stated: *"The Christian view of the atonement of Jesus is erroneous"* (Mary Baker Eddy Quotes, Google search).

Here, in a willing denial of multiple New Testament passages referring to the blood of Jesus, it is easily assessed that Mary Baker Eddy's teaching was biblically flawed and heretical.

Charles Wesley Emerson (1837–1908) was a proponent of the teachings of Mary Baker Eddy and the cultic doctrines of her *Christian Science* movement. Charles Emerson was a minister in the Unitarian Church—a liberal non-Judeo-Christian denomination that taught "freedom of conscience," that truth is determined by human reason and experience, and that man is the final authority. Unitarianism denies the Trinity Godhead and the deity of Jesus.

In 1877, during his Unitarian ministerial position, Charles Emerson enrolled at Boston University Conservatory of Oratory. When the School of Oratory closed at Boston University in 1880, Emerson left his ministry in the Unitarian Church and reopened the school he had attended and became its president. It was later named Emerson College.

During Emerson's leadership at this institution, he published a number of books including four volumes of *The Evolution of Expression*, which became the core text in the school's curriculum. Charles Emerson believed that the ability to communicate was the key to achieving one's full potential, and that when a student completed his academic program, they would have success in any area of life they pursued.

In the 1890s, the faculty and student body of Emerson College were heavily involved in the "metaphysical cults" (beyond the physical realm)—teaching Phineas Quimby's *New Thought* philosophies of word and thought power and Mary Baker Eddy's doctrines of spiritism.

In 1892, a young man named Essek W. Kenyon (1867–1948) enrolled at Emerson College, originally to study acting. In 1893, while attending the school, Essek Kenyon had a *born-again* experience and later developed his own philosophies from additional study of Scripture, initially proving to himself that the doctrines of Phineas Quimby's *New Thought* "positive confession" and "prosperity theology" were true.

Essek W. Kenyon went on to become founder and president of Bethel Bible Institute in Spencer, Massachusetts, and later became pastor of New Covenant Baptist Church.

In the early years of Kenyon's Christian walk, though his heart may have been sincere, he made the huge mistake of neglecting exegetical Bible truth and favored searching for passages that would seemingly support the teachings of men. Though in his later ministry and by observation of those who analyzed Essek Kenyon's sermons, he appeared to have removed himself from this method.

In his lifetime, E. W. Kenyon wrote eighteen books, including *The Wonderful Name of Jesus*, published in 1916. Sounds wonderful enough, and yes, there is inspiration and some truth in this book in that we, as believers, have the authority to use the name of Jesus to claim victory over Satan's devises and attacks. But *The Wonderful Name of Jesus* also contains heresy and false teaching. The great error in this particular book by Kenyon is the supposed revelation that the blood of Jesus was insufficient on its own, and that after His death on the cross, Jesus spent time in hell to finish His payment for the sins of humanity. This doctrine makes a blasphemous statement against the Gospel of salvation. It is the twisting of Scripture for the purpose of claiming equality with Christ. Let's discover how and why.

On page 47 of *The Wonderful Name of Jesus*, twenty-fourth edition, 1964, Essek Kenyon states of Jesus's death on the cross: "*If his physical death paid it, then every man could die for himself.*"

Kenyon's theory was obvious: since man couldn't die for his own sins to become saved, and since Jesus, also being a man, became the only righteous Chosen One, it was pointless for Him to die only a physical death. He needed also to die spiritually for the sins of the world.

Kenyon reasoned that Jesus's actual shedding of blood and physical death wasn't enough, and that God the Father rejected Him further by letting Him descend into Gehenna, thus causing His spiritual death and suffering further torment.

This, however, is a confused theology. How could Jesus be the Son of God as the Bible states (which definitively means that He is an eternal member of the Trinity Godhead), but yet He also died spiritually? Though Kenyon reasoned this was factual, we find in the four Gospel books of the New Testament that Jesus spoke of Himself as "Lord" during His earthly ministry. Therefore, Jesus could not lose His Lordship status at the cross. The Bible clearly states that Jesus was both human and God: He held a unique position of deity called *Hypostatic Union.* Jesus was and is the eternal God who was sent to occupy human form and for a specific purpose.

Interestingly enough, Essek Kenyon wrote: "*The Deity of the Man of Galilee is the crux of Christianity. If this can be successfully challenged, then Christianity has lost its heart and will cease to function; it will become a dead religion*" (*The Wonderful Name of Jesus*, p. 13).

Kenyon's statement here was true; although his theory that Jesus was tormented for three days in hell renders an opposing theology—that the Savior possessed no deity whatsoever before His death on the cross. Our Bible emphatically states, however, that Jesus was divine during His life on earth. Since an eternal divine Creator cannot be overpowered by His own creation, Kenyon's theory is impossible, though it seems he hadn't considered this angle.

When biblically educated of the fundamental doctrine of the Gospel of faith, we are assured that the particular theory of Jesus's torment in Gehenna is unsound doctrine that thoroughly negates His deity. E. W. Kenyon's theory of the spiritual death of Jesus is a dangerous false doctrine we must vehemently reject if we desire eternal life. It is a different gospel—a theological lie that goes against Bible teaching and the work of the Holy Spirit.

Perhaps if we are unaware of certain passages, we may not think about what happened to Jesus when his physical body died. To a certain extent, it may seem unnecessary to ponder this. However, to theorize as factual truth that Jesus was also dead spiritually while his body was in the tomb is treading on dangerous and heretical doctrinal ground.

In the century that has passed since Essek Kenyon wrote *The Wonderful Name of Jesus*, his theory of the three-day spiritual death of Jesus has evolved into oppositional teaching of the cornerstone of the Gospel of salvation and "*the crux of Christianity*," as Kenyon rightly claimed. Yet because of Kenyon's book, many who have latched onto his false teaching about Jesus have now carried it even farther down the road of apostasy.

The scriptural evidence that Jesus did not descend into hell (Gehenna) for the purpose of suffering is in several New Testament passages and especially in the words of Jesus Himself while He was on the cross. Luke 23:46 records that Jesus stated: **Father, into thy hands I commend my spirit**—not into the hands of Satan.

In John 19:30, Jesus also said: **It is finished**, meaning His suffering for the sins of humanity had ended. In this passage, the word *finished* in the Greek language is *teleho*, which means "completed payment." We therefore know by the spoken words of Jesus Himself that the payment made for our sin was accomplished during that six-hour period on that day.

Jesus also said to the repentant thief next to him: **Verily I say unto thee, today shalt thou be with me in paradise** (Luke 23:43). Though some have argued that because the original Greek manuscript had no punctuation marks—and when the comma is taken out of this King James verse, it could be interpreted as not necessarily that particular day that the thief would be with Jesus in paradise. Does this decisively connote Jesus's immediate descent into a place of torment for more punishment? No! This is a desperate attempt by some to prove by any hint of elucidation that we as Christians are in some way equal with Jesus the Savior in His power and authority.

It really doesn't matter if Jesus was referring to that particular day or a later day that the thief would be with Him because the scriptural account of the crucifixion indicates that Jesus died before the thief died. So even if we leave the punctuation where it is, meaning thus that Jesus was indeed referring to that particular day on which the thief would be with Him, then was Jesus just waiting for this forgiven thief, welcoming him into paradise when he arrived a short time later? But then, excusing Himself for an important task, made an abrupt descent into Gehenna for additional agony? No! The Bible is noticeably lacking any explanation of such an occurrence—and for good reason! Jesus's descent into hell for more torment would deduce unequivocally that He was not God—but human only.

The mistaken theory is that since Jesus was the first ever to be raised from spiritual death, we can follow suit after Him by repenting from sin. This is blasphemous theology. Why? It's very simple: if Jesus died spiritually on the cross, then He wasn't God before the cross; and if He wasn't God before the cross, the salvation Gospel of the New Testament is completely lost—or, at best, is incorrect, and we could legitimately remove the many passages referring to Jesus's deity—which then leads us to trust only in our good works to gain salvation.

The apostle Peter states in 1 Peter 3:18–19: **For Christ also hath once suffered for sins, the just for the unjust, that he might bring us to God, being put to death in the flesh, but quickened by the Spirit: by which also he went and preached unto the spirits in prison**.

The key distinction here is that Jesus was **put to death in the flesh but quickened by the Spirit**. Though Jesus died physically, His Spirit was **quickened**, meaning "vitalized"—not suffering loss. Here we also find the Greek term **once suffered** (*hapax pascho*), meaning "a one-time sensation of pain." Jesus was put to death in the flesh and in that suffered a one-time sensation of pain; there was no additional payment required of him.

Ephesians 4:8–9 accounts that Jesus **also descended first into the lower parts of the earth...**in order to...**lead the captive and give gifts unto men**.

These passages are very specific: they show that Jesus died only in the flesh. Though it says He **descended first into the lower parts**

of the earth, it tells exactly why this happened: it was to lead the righteous dead out of their holding place and to give them reward. It says nothing about Jesus suffering in Gehenna for further payment for the sins of humanity—or that he "*wrestled with the devil,*" as some have claimed.

On page 47 of his book *The Wonderful Name of Jesus*, E. W. Kenyon states: "*When Jesus died, his spirit was taken by the adversary and carried to the place where the sinner's spirit goes when it dies.*"

The Bible states nothing of the sort. No demonic being could possibly carry the Spirit of Jesus away; this would decisively conclude a dissolving of His Lordship status. And many passages in the New Testament indicate that only the body and blood of the Lord Jesus was sufficient. Therefore, the payment for our sin ended at the cross and did not linger in limbo—or was to be determined by a spirit-wrestling match. The particular wording of the "three-day" prophecy in Matthew 27:63; Luke 18:33, 24:7, and 46; and John 2:19 proves this theory incorrect. Read these passages for yourself and discover the substantiating truth.

On page 64 of his book, Kenyon states: "*After Jesus' spiritual death and becoming united with Satan and nature, was born-again in hell after paying the price before he was raised from the dead.*"

Theologically speaking, this is blasphemy. There is no such passage in all of Scripture that would support Kenyon's statement. Obviously, Kenyon didn't realize his statement was a blasphemous teaching that discredits the blood atonement of the cross. To say that Jesus Christ was reborn, or *born again* (in the biblical definition), theologically renders His humanity only—that He was not God prior to the cross.

If Jesus was only a man, how could He have paid for the sins of humanity? He couldn't! If the Bible is truth, then Jesus was a member of the Triune Godhead before He came to earth and remained so during His life on earth. He therefore couldn't have possibly been "*united with Satan and nature*" at His death as Kenyon claims. Good and evil have no commonality. Therefore, the mistaken conclusion is that Jesus was not a member of the Godhead before He came to earth—or that He acquired a state of unrighteousness on the cross. Again, blasphemy!

Further proof that Jesus did not suffer in hell is found in the prophecy about the coming Savior in Isaiah 53:10: **Thou shalt make his soul an offering for sin**. Strong's Concordance identifies this Hebrew word "soul" as a "body," "person," and "breath." God required only the physical sacrifice of His Son: it was His "*breath of life*" that was sacrificed—not His Spirit. The Trinity Godhead was not broken at the cross: Jesus did not cease to be God for even a moment. But on page 65 of E. W. Kenyon's book, he states: "*His death on the cross was insufficient by itself and he needed to suffer in a spiritual sense in hell to complete the atonement.*"

This statement by itself proves Kenyon didn't biblically scrutinize his theory carefully enough. Had Jesus paid spiritually, then by definition, He was not conceived by virgin birth, and He would not be God Incarnate. Jesus did not acquire a sin-nature on the cross, resulting in a spiritual rebirth at His resurrection. Second Corinthians 5:21 says: **For he hath made him to be sin for us, who knew no sin; that we might be made the righteousness of God in him**. This passage doesn't mean that Jesus was "made sin," thus requiring a descent into hell. Here, the Greek word "made" is *poieo*, meaning "to bear." Jesus was made to bear our sins. He did not become sin.

E. W. Kenyon's theology demotes the Savior to a mere human level. Putting faith in a *human-only Jesus* is a false cult religion; it will not give you eternal life. That is why the Bible makes it clear in many passages that the Son of God existed before the world began—and then became God in the flesh. Putting faith in this eternal Lord Jesus is what saves the believer. If we have no Alpha and Omega eternal Savior, we have no eternal salvation.

Essek Kenyon was sincere, but his doctrine was wrong: it was "another gospel" for the theological conclusion that it renders the Bible's Gospel of salvation as meaningless.

In searching the New Testament to see how frequently the term "Lord Jesus" appears and just how it is used, we know this is of huge importance. In reading these many passages without the word "Lord" in them, we deduce exactly what E. W. Kenyon ignorantly and unwittingly taught: that Jesus was not Lord before the cross—but only after the cross.

Again, looking at Romans 10:9 (NKJV), Paul says: **That if you shall confess with your mouth the Lord Jesus, and shall believe in your heart that God has raised him from the dead, you shall be saved.**

Notice how Paul says it was "the Lord Jesus" who was raised from the dead. In other words, "the Lord" went to the cross, physically died, and was then raised. The eternal Lordship position of Jesus was unbroken!

Anyone can claim a belief in the man, Jesus—but this does not save them. This verse (Romans 10:9) states that to acknowledge the "Lord Jesus" does save, if you take Him to be your personal Lord and Savior. To believe that Jesus is your Lord and also *was* Lord at His birth is the confession unto salvation.

When a pastor upholds the truth of Romans 10:9...but also claims that we are equal with Jesus for being "*born again with Him,*" this theologically mistaken pastor is confusing the fundamentals of the faith and the crucial element of the Gospel of salvation. Christians are not deemed *born again* because Jesus was the first spiritually *born-again* man. They are *born again* for a renewed heart unto God and a belief in a Savior who is God. Christians cannot be *born again with Jesus* because Jesus was not spiritually *born again* at His resurrection.

Essek Kenyon's writings are in admiration of the cross, but he mixes this admiration with the idea that Jesus was also defeated there spiritually. If Jesus was spiritually defeated at the cross, then Colossians 2:15 makes little sense—**And having spoiled principalities and powers, he made a show of them openly, triumphing over them in it.**

How did Jesus triumph over principalities and powers? The previous verse (14) reveals it was through His cross! Therefore, Jesus maintained His deity status and was spiritually triumphant at the cross! He was defeated only physically. It's that simple.

First John 4:3 says: **And every spirit that confesses not that Jesus Christ is come in the flesh is not of God**. This is another very clear passage. Jesus "The Christ" came from the eternal realm to dwell on the earth in the confines of time and physical space as a human—then returned to eternity, remaining in physical form. Anyone who preaches that Jesus was not deity (God) when He came and lived on earth is preaching a false doctrine: they are not of God according to the apostle John.

Then there's the pivotal statement just a few verses later, which helps us determine further truth about the Savior. First John 4:6 (NKJV) says: **Hereby know we the spirit of truth and the spirit of error**. In context, we see that the spirit of truth states that Jesus came as God, and the spirit of error states he did not come as God—but was only a chosen man. In balancing Holy Scripture against itself, we find that the Bible tells us specifically that the physical death of the Lord Jesus was the price paid for our sin—simply because this deified Christ came in the flesh.

Essek Kenyon was obviously influenced and indoctrinated with the *New Thought* positive confession theology he was taught during his tenure at Emerson College. Though it seemed wonderfully advantageous, his first mistake was to meld this teaching with the Gospel of the Bible, which is why a major portion of his book *The Wonderful Name of Jesus* is focused on what we now discern as a misapplied and distorted interpretation of the presumed authority believers have over all things when verbally using the name of Jesus. But his second mistake was more severely apostate than the first: it was his theory of Jesus's spiritual death and rebirth, which deduced a *human-only Jesus gospel.*

We now realize how the unperceived human-only Jesus gospel was birthed through the "born-again Jesus" doctrine and why those promoting it are ignorant of its heresy. Offshoot destructive doctrines stemming from this false gospel prove that many of today's pastors continue to mangle the textual interpretation of many other Bible passages as well, which we now begin to explore...

Essek Kenyon was convinced that believers possessed power in their spoken words for their presumed equality with Jesus. He stated on page 98 of his book *The Wonderful Name of Jesus*: "*What I confess, I possess!*"

Even though by the time he wrote his book, Kenyon had likely rejected any *New Thought* and metaphysical cult-type teaching he'd been previously taught at Emerson College, he had nonetheless inadvertently coupled the *New Thought "power of positive words"* doctrine with the biblical doctrine of salvation.

Of course, stating positive words is soothing to the ear, but it is superstitious to believe that the words themselves cause reality. Taking this theory to an extreme, some Christians are now told that the name of Jesus has power to provide any physical thing we desire—or can deliver from every undesirable circumstance. This teaching is not in the Bible: it's a false notion leading to a misguided kind of faith. In Matthew 6:10, Jesus taught us how to pray, saying: **Thy kingdom come. Thy will be done in earth as it is in heaven**. Jesus never said, "*Declare anything you want, and you will have it.*" The apostle Paul says: **But in every thing by prayer and supplication with thanksgiving let your requests be made know unto God** (Philippians 4:6).

The New Testament does not tell us that God's will is to give us anything we proclaim simply because we have the authority to use the name of Jesus. And yet because of naivety, many Christians plow forward to the throne of God with prayer requests or prayer declarations which, to God in heaven, likely sound as if they come from a selfish five-year-old. Instead, what we discern from Scripture is that though prayer may change things outwardly, the real change is inward when we read, study, and comprehend the Word of God. We can then pray with proper understanding and mature boldness to see the right results—knowing that God's sovereignty supersedes our desires and specifically decimates any declarations of confessed acquisitions.

Word of Faith

Birthed out of Pentecostal and Charismatic Christianity, the Word of Faith movement likely adopted their name from Romans

10:8, which says: **The word is nigh thee even in thy mouth and in thy heart: that is, the word of faith which we preach**.

As previously referred to, Romans, chapter 10, is a key chapter for understanding that salvation is available to all people. Paul continues in verses 9–10, explaining exactly what the word of faith is all about: he says, **That if thou shalt confess with thy mouth the Lord Jesus and shalt believe in thine heart that God hath raised him from the dead thou shalt be saved. For with the heart man believeth unto righteousness; and with the mouth confession is made unto salvation**.

The **word of faith** stated in Romans 10:8 is therefore the **confession made unto salvation**, as verse 10 then says. It is not a spoken "word of claim" for something desired or a "word of declaration" for perfect health or financial prosperity as some might interpret.

Comparing the correct meaning of the term **word of faith** in Romans 10:8 with the words of Jesus in John 15:4—**Abide in me, and I in you**—we know this refers to a lifetime of confession of faith, which is unto salvation. Word of Faith Christianity has, however, concocted a doctrine theorizing that faith in Jesus encompasses earthly success, prosperity, and optimal health because of the believers' verbally professed "words of faith" for it. Indeed, we can apply our faith in God and the concept of "abiding in Jesus" to our earthly and physical lives. But we cannot biblically justify this faith by labeling perfect health and financial success as a result of abiding in Jesus. Though because Word of Faith pastors claim that the Bible speaks to this end, many of us have believed it is so.

Not only does the Bible not teach this doctrine, there is also a downfall to this theology: those who sit under Word of Faith teaching live in fear that they may fall short in their faith—that they don't measure up spiritually if and when they aren't healed from disease or do not prosper as they've been told they should. This is cruelty and confusion; the Bible nowhere declares such. But again, how can we know for sure? It is through careful research of the Scriptures! When we delve into this "word of faith" discrepancy with intent, we not only find the root error of a fabricated doctrine of men, but we also discover where it came from and why it is being preached within the church.

The Gospel of the Bible is simple and precise, yet when twisted slightly, it becomes perverted and useless. Though the majority of a pastor's preaching may be the truth, when teaching just one error that concerns the Gospel of salvation, he then becomes a false teacher. A little leaven leavens the whole lump (1 Corinthians 5:6 and Galatians 5:9). A small amount of false teaching connected to truth destroys the entire message. Many pastors may appear to have enlightened *New Revelation knowledge*, but there is no such thing outside of Bible exegete. Any presumed *New Revelation* that tampers with and slightly tweaks the simple Gospel of the Bible is nothing more than perversion and apostasy.

Again Jesus said: **This is the work of God, that ye believe on him whom he hath sent** (John 6:29). Then Jesus explains further in verse 40, saying: **That every one which seeth the Son, and believeth on him, may have everlasting life**.

Here, Jesus states that the **work of God** will begin when one **seeth the Son**—perceives Him as the Son of God—and when we **believeth on him**—meaning believing in His deity—we then **have everlasting life**. This is the true and intended scriptural definition of the stated **word of faith**, which many have deviated from for their false belief in a Jesus that was not the literal and deified Son of God.

Erring brethren

Kenneth Hagin (1917–2003) is considered by many to be the father of the Word of Faith movement within Christianity. At age fifteen, Kenneth Hagin experienced physical healing when the Lord delivered him from an incurable heart condition and blood disorder. He then gave his life to Christ and began preaching in Baptist churches at age nineteen. Since Baptists took issue with the subject of divine healing, he moved to the Assembly of God denomination. In the decades following, Kenneth Hagin became influential in the Charismatic Renewal, having great impact on the church in America and around the world. Hagin's beliefs and teachings were developed through his love of the Bible and his mentorship from Mom and Pop J. R. Goodwin of the Assembly of God denomination in Texas. Hagin's preaching and teaching ministry was also greatly influenced from books he'd read on the subject of healing by F. F. Bosworth, P. C. Nelson, and Smith Wigglesworth, to name a few. The theological teaching and testimonies in these writings further inspired Hagin to stay the course of the healing witness of Jesus.

According to Kenneth Hagin's personal testimony, when he was thirty years of age, the Holy Spirit began teaching him on the authority believers have through the name of Jesus as revealed in the first three chapters of Ephesians. It was during this time that Pastor Hagin changed his focus and began to preach with great enthusiasm. He began to teach that though Christians do not have a power within themselves to cause healing or to remove demons, they do have the authority by the name of Jesus to command victory and power over the enemy. Hagin declared that all believers have the very same authority as Jesus had—which is not exactly what the New Testament states, as we will discover.

When Kenneth Hagin was thirty-three, a Christian brother introduced him to a particular book that would also have great impact on him—*The Wonderful Name of Jesus* by Essek W. Kenyon. Still in the early stages of his ministry, Hagin also began experiencing "*personal visitations*" from Jesus, giving him encouragement and further "*New Revelation Knowledge*," as Hagin termed it. Between 1950 and 1959, Pastor Hagin had eight visitations from Jesus—some he claimed to have lasted over an hour. In one particular visitation, Hagin says Jesus explained the authority Christians have in His name over the enemy and then told him that E. W. Kenyon's doctrine of Himself was true.

When a full study of the New Testament is made concerning the authority of Jesus, we find it to be true—that Jesus the Savior does have all authority in the church, but Christians who use the name of Jesus in prayer cannot claim ultimate victory over all earthly and physical things. Rather, they must submit to God's sovereignty. However, being influenced by the *positive confession* doctrine of Essek Kenyon and others, Kenneth Hagin began to see it differently—that whatever the believer would declare, the believer would ultimately have.

As we have seen, many of Essek Kenyon's statements in his book are theologically incorrect concerning the deity of Jesus. Nonetheless, Kenneth Hagin was inspired by his visitations from Jesus and his personal endorsement of Kenyon's theology. Even though Assembly of God Pastor J. R. Goodwin had mentored and admired Hagin, he now disagreed with Hagin's embracement of E. W. Kenyon's theology, which Hagin began to teach as Bible truth.

Though Kenneth Hagin's personal visitations from Jesus are not disputed, some of the specific messages he received did not completely align with Scripture. Hagin therefore had to distort certain Bible passages and purposely ignore others that contradicted Jesus's personal statements to him.

All of this may sound as a doubtful and highly critical analysis of Kenneth Hagin's teaching and experience. But we are commanded in Scripture to **prove all things** (1 Thessalonians 5:21) and to investigate every doctrine—**Beloved, believe not every spirit, but try the spirits whether they are of God: because many false prophets are gone out into the world** (1 John 4:1). Paul also penned a warning to a young Gentile church at Galatia: **I marvel that you are so soon removed from him that called you into the grace of Christ unto another gospel** (Galatians 1:6). In the very next verse (Galatians 1:7), Paul explained why it is **another gospel**: it is because they that preach it **pervert the gospel of Christ**. This perverted (changed) gospel is therefore a gospel that does not save! Why else would Paul warn about **another gospel**?

The particular perverted gospel Paul referred to in Galatians 1 was a gospel of works, yet as we will now discuss, the gospel of which Kenneth Hagin taught inadvertently theorized a *human-only Jesus*—as E. W. Kenyon had also done unknowingly. The Kenyon/Hagin gospel is a far more dangerous and perverted gospel because it cuts away the nucleus of New Testament Christianity.

In Galatians 1:8, Paul says: **But though we or an angel from heaven preach any other gospel unto you than that which we have preached unto you, let him be accursed.**

If the real Jesus came to visit Kenneth Hagin, revealing to him a new or different revelation about Himself than what the Bible states, then according to the apostle Paul, either the real Jesus is accursed, or there must be an ever-changing gospel in heaven according to the whims of God the Father. Obviously, neither is true according to Scripture. Therefore, Kenneth Hagin's particular "visitation" wherein Jesus supported the teaching of E. W. Kenyon was indeed a deception. The Jesus impersonator who appeared unto Hagin on that occasion is "accursed" according to Galatians 1:8.

Seeing that there was very little material written on the subject of the name of Jesus (other than E. W. Kenyon's book), Kenneth Hagin began working on his own book, published in 1978, titled *The Name of Jesus*. Hagin's book is comprised mostly of his sermon commentaries, quotes from Kenyon's book, and stories from his past experiences. Unfortunately, when reading Hagin's book, it's hard to decipher his exact position: many statements are truth derived from Bible quotes, but others are preceded or followed by Hagin's commentary of contradictory scriptural error. Hagin quotes several passages taken out of their context to assume a different meaning: on page 6 of *The Name of Jesus,* Hagin pulls Matthew 28:18 completely away from the context. After His resurrection, Jesus is exhorting the disciples concerning the authority He has, saying: **All power is given unto me in heaven and in earth**. Hagin points out that because the word "power" in this verse is translated as "authority," it therefore means that Jesus's followers have the same authority to claim anything in prayer when His Name is used. Hagin then assumed that because Jesus's very next words in verse 19 are **Go ye therefore**, it was vital for Christians to realize the full power and authority they have to "go therefore in His Name" and to believe for anything they may ask, including healing and victory over every infirmity and sickness.

However, Hagin incorrectly interpreted the text. Read what Jesus actually said immediately afterward: **Go ye therefore, and teach all nations, baptizing them in the name of the Father, and of the Son, and of the Holy Ghost: Teaching them to observe all things whatsoever I have commanded you** (Matthew 28:19–20).

What "things" did Jesus command here? Go and heal the diseases and infirmities of all people? Or go and bring the dead back to life? Or go and search for demon-possessed people who needed to be delivered? No! The "things" Jesus commanded was to "teach" the salvation message and to "baptize them." The power of Jesus saves us from sin through the **name of the Father and of the Son and of the Holy Ghost**! Hence, this power and authority given to Jesus is primarily for the purpose of crushing the enemy's grip of sin!

Does this mean we shouldn't pray for healing or deliverance? Of course not! In Matthew 28:18, Jesus was simply not talking about healing at that particular moment, as Kenneth Hagin had assumed. In Mark 16:17–18, Jesus said: **And these signs shall follow them that believe; In my name they shall cast out devils... they shall lay hands on the sick, and they shall recover**. In this particular passage, we find Jesus has also given His followers the authority to pray "in His Name" for dominance over evil spirits and for relief and recovery from sickness. We do not have a divine power within ourselves to command or accomplish this, but we have the authority by Jesus's name to request it. We must understand that our prayers of authority and confidence are first rooted in the Savior's power of salvation through His cross. However, the atonement of Jesus did not remove every kind of adversity for those who would believe on Him. Paul told the Philippian church: **For unto you it is given in the behalf of Christ, not only to believe on him, but also to suffer for his sake; having the same conflict which ye saw in me, and now hear to be in me** (Philippians 1:29–30).

Here, Paul may be referring to physical sickness by using the word "suffer"; however, the main thought within the context is seen in the word "conflict" which Paul personally endured: it was the anxiety of his own persecution. Nowhere in his Epistles does Paul infer that the suffering of sickness and disease or the suffering of persecution will always be removed by prayers of faith.

On page 33 of Kenneth Hagin's book *The Name of Jesus*, he claimed to not have had a headache since he was seventeen. He states: "*When my head began hurting I would simply say, 'in Jesus's Name I do not have a headache!*" He then states that his headache always left! I have also found this kind of prayer to work in my own life. It doesn't seem likely that God wants us to have a splitting headache for no reason. Though what about a terminal health condition or cancer? Yes, we should pray against it in total faith and belief that God can remove the disease in us or in someone else. And what happens next reveals to us what God's will is at that moment. As Jesus said: **Not my will, but thine, be done** (Luke 22:42).

The authority of the believer is indeed Bible truth; however, there is better explanation relating to this authority contained within Hebrews 2:8, which Hagin didn't see or chose to ignore—**But now we see not yet all things put under him**. This sentence agrees with many other passages telling how and why we struggle against the enemy. If all adversity can be removed only by realizing and declaring the authority we have in the name of Jesus, then why do we still struggle with adversity? If **thou hast put all things in subjection under his feet**, as the first sentence of Hebrews 2:8 says, why must we ever experience sickness, disease, and oppression? Why even must our physical bodies die? Why wasn't all adversity, sickness, and death instantly removed after the resurrection of Jesus? The last sentence of Hebrews 2:8 explains why: because **not yet are all things are put under him**!

All things have been put under the authority of Jesus's resurrection power, but all things are not yet observed under His authority. Sickness, disease, and death have all been put under the feet of Jesus the Savior. Although we won't realize the fullness and totality of it until **in the twinkling of an eye, at the last trump...the dead shall be raised incorruptible, and we shall be changed** (1 Corinthians 15:52). This verse explains that physical corruption not only means the death of the body but also that the infirmities we now suffer will one day be removed and changed into **incorruptible** perfection at the Second Coming of Christ.

Therefore, our spiritual authority in Christ cannot encompass a declaration and confidence for total physical perfection and successful earthly living at all times. That's not the biblical interpretation of the authority in Jesus that we possess. Though this single verse, Hebrews 2:8, gives a great insight, the fullness of the text before and after reveals even more: though all things are put under the feet of Jesus, we must still suffer—**to make the captain of their salvation perfect through sufferings** (Hebrews 2:10).

The Son of the Trinity Godhead became human for the purpose of purchasing human souls and to make men and women witnesses to His saving power. Jesus did not come to earth, live his life, die, and then come back to life only to give His followers miraculous supernatural power through the Holy Ghost. Rather, the gift of the Holy Ghost upon a believer manifests and displays God's power in salvation. It is a power miraculous by nature but not dispersed in authoritative equality with the Father or the Son. It's an authority given for a witness to the Divine Power that saves from eternal death. In Acts 1:8, Jesus says: **But ye shall receive power, after that the Holy Ghost is come upon you: and ye shall be witnesses unto me**. Our heavenly Father bestows the Holy Ghost upon us not primarily as a conduit for healing but as a faithful witness unto salvation. Jesus Christ is described as **"the faithful witness"** in Revelation 1:5.

The "begotten at His resurrection" Jesus

On pages 16–18 of *The Name of Jesus (Legacy Edition)*, Kenneth Hagin theorizes that Jesus was not "begotten" by the Father until His resurrection from the dead. He states on page 17:

> *The Son of God was not born as He took on flesh. He preexisted with the Father. He just took upon Himself a body. When was it that Jesus was begotten? When He was raised upon that Resurrection morn! He died on the Cross and took our place in spiritual death. His spirit, His inner man, went to hell in our place. He tasted death for every man—spiritual death. Jesus is the first person ever to be "born again." Why did his spirit need to be "born again"? Because it was estranged from God the Father.*

This paragraph in Hagin's book covers several critical doctrinal mistakes intermingled with just one doctrinal truth—"*He preexisted with the Father.*"

Hagin states: "*The Son of God was not born as he took on flesh.*" This is untrue. The New Testament reveals just the opposite—that the Son of God was indeed "born in the flesh," meaning "begotten into the world" in a physical sense at that time.

There may be two opposing theological opinions over this issue—that is, until we read 1 John 4:9: **God sent his only begotten Son into the world, that we might live through him**. The Concordance translates: God sent (on a mission) His only begotten Son into the world. The apostle John is precise here: God did not send His Son "on a mission" when He was raised from the dead... but rather when He was begotten at His birth.

The problem in Hagin's above paragraph is that though he correctly and in a literal sense unites the spirit and body of Jesus at His birth, he then literally separates Jesus's physical birth from the term "begotten" in the sentences following. Since no Bible passage indicates that Jesus "*tasted spiritual death,*" He thus could not have possibly been "begotten" from a spiritual rebirth at His resurrection. Neither could the Spirit of Jesus be "*estranged from God the Father*" as Hagin claimed. It is blasphemous to state that the Savior was "not begotten of God in the flesh" or that the Eternally Righteous became unrighteous for three days, then returned again to righteousness. This makes no sense when reading that Jesus proclaimed He would raise Himself from the grave: **Destroy this temple, and in three days I will raise it up** (John 2:19). In John 2:21, we then find John's precise explanation of what Jesus meant: **He spake of the temple of his body**—which, after his death on the cross, was in the grave. This passage says nothing of Jesus's Spirit or His deity. Jesus didn't say that He would restore His Spirit from death or that He would make short a soon-coming severance of a spirit connection between the Father and Himself—but only that His body would rise! In addition, nowhere does the New Testament tell that Jesus was the first person to be *born again* in a spiritual sense.

On page 17 of *The Name of Jesus*, Hagin refers to Acts 13:33 as further evidence that Jesus was "begotten" specifically at His resurrection. It says: **God hath fulfilled the same unto us their children, in that he hath raised up Jesus again; as it is also written in the second psalm, Thou art my Son, this day have I begotten thee.**

Here, Paul refers to Psalm 2:7, which was the promise of a coming Messiah. Paul states that Jesus was **raised up again**—obviously referring to His resurrection from death. Since the events of Jesus's birth and resurrection occurred centuries after King David wrote this psalm, we know that from David's perspective, the Messiah must first be born on a particular day in the future, and then because the prophecy of His birth came true, the Messiah was indeed raised up again after His death on the cross. Paul's sermon in Acts, chapter 13, is a testimony of the sequence of historical and significant events leading up to the prophesied Messiah. Toward the end, Paul referenced Psalm 2:7: **Thou art my Son, this day I have begotten thee**. This was the pinnacle and crux of Paul's entire message, upheld by an Old Testament passage: it was Paul's interjected description of the prophesied begotten Messiah. But Hagin isolated Acts 13:33 as a significant event placed properly within the sequence of statements only...and thereby assumed Jesus couldn't have been begotten at his birth since Paul had already spoken of Jesus's death and resurrection in verses 28–30. Again Hagin wrongly interpreted the text.

The Gospel, according to E. W. Kenyon and Kenneth Hagin, theorizes that the cross of Christ was insufficient, and for a short period of time, the Savior of mankind was equal to Satan the deceiver of mankind. This is ludicrous if we take seriously the words of Jesus describing just how our redemption comes about: He said, **Verily, verily, I say unto you, He that believeth on me hath everlasting life** (John 6:47). Since Jesus spoke these words long before His journey to the cross, we know this was present-tense terminology. Jesus did not say, "*He that believes on me when I am raised up has everlasting life.*" Hence, our salvation is through a belief in the Jesus who was God Incarnate when He was begotten in the flesh into the world. He is the Alpha and Omega, with no severance of position from eternity past to eternity future.

The proof that Jesus of Nazareth was God Incarnate is in many passages such as Malachi 3:1; Luke 3:2–6, 16; John 1:1, 14, 23, 29–31; Colossians 1:19–20; and Colossians 2:9. Perhaps the clearest of all these passages is Colossians 2:9, which says: **For in him dwells all the fullness of the Godhead bodily**.

These verses prove that Jesus was both God and human when He walked on earth. Malachi 3:1 says in part: **And the Lord, whom ye seek, shall suddenly come to his temple, even the messenger of the covenant**. Plainly speaking, this was God Himself, coming in fleshly form to bring a new message of deliverance for humanity as was prophesied. To claim that Jesus the Savior was not begotten of the Father at His birth in the manger is to deny the salvation message of the New Testament.

On page 18 of *The Name of Jesus*, Kenneth Hagin quotes Hebrews 2:9, explaining it to be proof that Jesus died spiritually and was therefore begotten at His resurrection. The verse says: **But we see Jesus who was made a little lower than the angels for the suffering of death, crowned with glory and honour; that he by the grace of God should taste death for every man**.

The first part of this verse is vital to understanding what the writer was trying to convey: **But we see Jesus who was made a little lower than the angels**. This means that Jesus was a human being who suffered death as any other man would, yet He was now **crowned with glory and honour** because prior to coming to earth, He was *higher than the angels*!

It is true that Jesus died so that we would not die spiritually. But Hagin somehow read the verse differently. In exegesis of the text, it does not even allude to the idea that the Spirit of Jesus was separated from the Godhead at His death. Hebrews 2:9 states that Jesus tasted death: it was by His **suffering of death**—meaning an agonizing physical death—whereby He was **crowned with glory and honour**.

Kenneth Hagin, and perhaps many of us, have misinterpreted the last half of Hebrews 2:9 by assuming that Jesus tasted spiritual death so that we wouldn't have to. But considering that the verse declares it was by **the grace of God** that Jesus **should taste death for every man**, we know that the interpretation is that God the Father let His begotten Son taste a torturous physical death because now, He (the Father) is familiar with the suffering of death and the high cost for the redemption of human souls. Though Jesus was fully God, He was also fully human and, unlike the angels, would naturally at some point taste physical death just as any other human would.

Though the Father also required Jesus to shed His blood and greatly suffer at His death, we really don't want to suffer for Jesus like He suffered for us. We want only the benefits of Christian living. Yet in the mindset of shunning Jesus's suffering or our suffering with Him, we have thus opposed the doctrine of Jesus's death, burial, and resurrection. We have theoretically denied Jesus as Lord!

Continuing on page 18 of *The Name of Jesus*, Kenneth Hagin states: "*The death Jesus died was more than a physical death. Jesus tasted death for every man—including spiritual death.*"

Hagin presses his theory of uniting the body, soul, and spirit of Jesus, determining that all of it perished on the cross. Just as the spirit and soul of sinful man is separated from God at death, Hagin taught that the Spirit and soul of Jesus was also severed from righteousness and communion with His Father. This is impossible since Jesus and His Father are of the same Spirit and cannot be separated in that realm—a realm that is different from the physical realm. Jesus said: **I came forth from the Father, and am come into the world: again, I leave the world, and go to the Father** (John 16:28). This single statement from Jesus proves Kenyon and Hagin are not only wrong in their doctrine but are also unwitting apostates for teaching a blasphemous and confusing theory, even though they both taught that Jesus preexisted with the Father. God sacrificed His only begotten Son on the earth, but the union of the Trinity Godhead was not severed at Calvary. To understand why, we must exegete the biblical doctrine and definition of deity: Revelation 1:11 says: **I am Alpha and Omega, the first and the last**. Among many other Bible passages, this proclamation from Jesus makes the conclusion that the position and nature of His divinity could not be lost, gained, or set aside. Deity is perpetual and eternal: it is permanent, with no beginning or ending—a difficult concept for the human mind to engage.

Kenneth Hagin taught that Jesus was indeed God during His earthly ministry—which is contradictory to his "begotten at His resurrection" theory. This theory stems from the equally false theory of Jesus's spiritual death on the cross. Hagin stated: "*Jesus tasted death—spiritual death—for every man. He became what we were, that we might become what He is*" (*The Name of Jesus Legacy Edition*, p. 20).

This was Hagin's touted "*New Revelation Knowledge*"—the spiritual death of Jesus the Savior—which was for the purpose of making man equal with Himself. But it is incorrect and perverted doctrine—even if viewed as metaphoric in nature.

On the following page (21), Hagin highlights Acts 2:25–31 where Peter explained in his sermon about the patriarch David who again spoke in the psalms of the coming Savior. In verse 31, Peter concludes: **He seeing this before spake of the resurrection of Christ, that his soul was not left in hell, neither his flesh did see corruption**.

Had Hagin carefully read Acts 2:31 to see that only the entity of "his soul" was mentioned, and had he looked up the word "hell" in his Concordance, he should have realized that Jesus did not die spiritually. Here, Peter uses the word *hades*, meaning "the grave"—not the word *geenna* (*Gehenna*), "the place of torment." Therefore, Peter spoke only of Jesus's physical condition that could not remain corrupted in the grave.

The Bible tells us that God is spirit, the Holy Spirit is spirit, and Jesus the Son was also spirit until He obtained a physical body for the purpose of saving mankind. Thus, the only part of Jesus that perished on the cross of Calvary was His physical body, which was resurrected back to life and is the evidence of eternal physical life for those who believe in Him.

Jesus speaks of Himself in John 3:16: **For God so loved the world, that he gave his only begotten Son, that whosoever believeth in him should not perish, but have everlasting life**. The Greek word "gave" in this passage is a verb meaning to "bestow," "commit," "bring forth," or "deliver." The term "only begotten" means "uniquely" and "only born." Hence, Jesus was delivered into the world as "uniquely born of the Father."

Since Jesus was the only begotten Son and was a member of the Trinity Godhead, it was impossible for Him to die spiritually. Hence, the "*spiritually born again Jesus*" teaching is, in reality, the cover-up label for the "*human-only Jesus*" *gospel*. This sham of a doctrine totally obliterates the basic salvation message of John 3:16 because it incorrectly asserts that God did not *give* His only begotten Son at His birth but instead gained a Son when Jesus was raised from the dead. This labors against the very basic explanation of how our salvation comes about—which is simply and thoroughly explained within the John 3:15–21 text.

John 3:18 signifies the terms of our faith and belief. Jesus says: **He that believeth in him is not condemned: but he that believeth not is condemned already, because he hath not believed in the name of the only begotten Son of God**. Here, Jesus states that He Himself was "the only begotten Son of God"—meaning the only Incarnation of God in the world. This single verse, John 3:18, is the pivotal Gospel verse upon which the rest of the New Testament hinges. John 3:16 is the initial proclamation of belief for one's own salvation, but verse 18 signifies the name and title by which this belief rests upon. Therefore, contextually speaking, John 3:18 is proof that Jesus was begotten long before His resurrection from death. Jesus had obtained His name as the only begotten Son of God at the moment He was conceived in Mary, and it still held true when He spoke these words recorded in John, chapter 3.

Speaking of Mary, the mother of Jesus, Matthew 1:21 says: **And she shall bring forth a son, and thou shalt call his name Jesus: for he shall save his people from their sins**.

This verse tells of the Son's transfer from heaven to earth and the mighty name He inherited in bodily form. We can then discern the meaning of Revelation 1:5: **And from Jesus Christ, who is the faithful witness, and the first begotten of the dead**. This means Jesus was the first to be resurrected to life eternal—bridging the way for the redeemed to also one day be resurrected from death, incorruptible.

Within the entirety of Kenneth Hagin's book *The Name of Jesus*, he completely ignores John 3:16 and instead highlights the word "begotten" used in other passages to justify his theory of the "begotten at His resurrection" type of Savior. On page 16 of his book, Hagin references Hebrews 1:4 as further evidence that Jesus was not begotten at His birth. It states: **Being made so much better than the angels, as he hath by inheritance obtained a more excellent name than they**.

By itself, this verse does not specify exactly when Jesus obtained His excellent name, and Hagin makes no comment of what follows in Hebrews 1:6; rather, he mistakenly glosses over it—**And again, when he bringeth the first begotten into the world, he saith, and let all the angels of God worship him**.

This verse specifies that Jesus was first begotten into the world at His birth only because within the same line, it says: **And let all the angels of God worship him**. Angels worshipped Jesus only at His birth in the manger according to Luke 2:13–14. No New Testament verse tells that angels worshipped Jesus at His resurrection.

When reading the first chapter of Hebrews, we see the importance of believing in the "first begotten" Son as (technically and uniquely) the only begotten Son at His birth and during His earthly life. Disappointingly, Kenneth Hagin was guilty of picking and choosing, skipping and deleting. But by the full text and comparison of other related passages, we find that Jesus was neither "first begotten" at His resurrection, nor was He *born again* in a spiritual sense.

The Name of Jesus by Kenneth Hagin intertwines E. W. Kenyon's theory of the *spiritually born-again Jesus* with his own "begotten at His resurrection" theory. Hagin states on page 26 that the awareness of "*the authority of that Name is for the benefit of the Church.*" This is true, but nowhere does the New Testament say that believers have an authority to pray for healing because of Jesus's resurrection; rather, it is because of His divinity at His birth and as the only begotten Son, as John 3:16 says. In other words, the text is clear—that God "gave" His only begotten Son: Jesus spoke of it as a past-tense occurrence. The precise wording of John 3:16 also derives that God did not sacrifice His heavenly Son but that His heavenly Son was "begotten in the flesh." Hence, the authority given to the body of Christ is derived from a belief in the "begotten at His birth" kind of Savior. And this is why Kenneth Hagin totally ignored John 3:16 in his book.

When we use the name of Jesus in prayer for healing and restoration, we should know that we have the right and the authority to use it if we are living in righteousness before God. If, however, we have definitively surmised that our righteousness originates from a Christ not "begotten in the flesh" but instead "begotten at His resurrection," we pray to and through a false Christ, and Satan, the counterfeit Christ, takes His place to perform counterfeit healing. Matthew 7:22–23 holds this as unquestionable proof: **Many will say to me in that day, Lord, Lord, have we not prophesied in thy name? and in thy name have cast out devils? and in thy name done many wonderful works? And then I will profess unto them, I never knew you: depart from me, ye that work iniquity**. Yes, healing and wonderful miracles come by the name of Jesus! Though if it's not the Jesus begotten at His birth, we have fallen for a counterfeit Jesus, and it benefits the church nothing.

Conflict of doctrine

Second Timothy 3:1–5 warns us about **blasphemers...having a form of godliness, but denying the power thereof: from such turn away**.

Quite obviously, Kenneth Hagin did not willfully intend to preach blasphemy. However, when one preaches a Jesus who was spiritually defeated at His crucifixion, they are **denying the power thereof**. They are preaching a different gospel—a false Christ.

Nearly in the same breath declaring that Jesus was spiritually *born again*, Hagin is quick to defend the deity of Jesus! An amazing dichotomy! On page 47 of *The Name of Jesus*, he says: "*If Jesus is not virgin born, then He is not deity; He is not God. If He is not God, then His Name means nothing.*" Though Hagin's heart was sincere, he made hideous doctrinal mistakes in his *born-again Jesus* teaching.

On page 53 of *The Name of Jesus,* Hagin presents a brief one-page segment titled "That Name—in Salvation." One of the many reasons Hagin lists as benefit of the powerful name of Jesus is for life eternal, stating: "*There is no other way to Eternal Life—except through Jesus, and through His Name!*"

This, of course, is a doctrinally sound proclamation, but later, on page 107, Hagin states: "*If you study the Scriptures carefully, you will find that nowhere does Jesus mention faith or belief when He talks about using His Name.*"

Amazing! Not only is Hagin contradicting himself, but he continues in his apostasy! Again the doctrine of the salvation Gospel hinges on what Jesus said of Himself in John 3:18: **He that believeth on him is not condemned: but he that believeth not is condemned already, because he hath not believed in the name of the only begotten Son of God**. This applies directly to our faith and belief. In Romans 10:9, the apostle Paul said: **That if thou shalt confess with thy mouth the Lord Jesus, and shalt believe in thine heart that God hath raised him from the dead, thou shalt be saved.** This means we must attest to and believe in the Lord Jesus—the only begotten Son.

Kenneth Hagin didn't seem to make the connection that the specifically stated "birth" of the only begotten Son had at that time generated the title "Lord Jesus," which is synonymous to His name in Scripture. The fact of Jesus's virgin birth and the name which He inherited proved His position as the instigator of our faith and the Author of our salvation. How could Pastor Hagin have missed this? Though Hagin rightly asserts that other passages state how Jesus declared that His name should be used in prayer for healing, there are also many other New Testament verses similar to Romans 10:9 that are easily discerned as relating to the name of Jesus in salvation—none of which speak of healing:

> **That at the name of Jesus every knee should bow—and every tongue should confess that Jesus Christ is Lord**. (Philippians 2:10–11)

> **But as many as received him, to them gave he power to become the sons of God, even to them that believe on his name**. (John 1:12)

> **And this is the commandment, that we should believe on the name of his Son Jesus Christ.** (1 John 3:23)

> **These things I have written unto you that believe on the name of the Son of God; that ye may know that ye have eternal life, and that ye may believe on the name of the Son of God.** (1 John 5:13)

> **And in his name shall the Gentiles trust.** (Matthew 12:21)

Kenneth Hagin's book *The Name of Jesus* deals mainly with the importance of the mighty name of Jesus and that healing of the physical body comes about because of that name. Hagin asserts that because Christians are joint-heirs with Him for the purpose of physical healing—and in a personal acceptance for that healing—that Jesus does indeed heal today because of His mighty name. The follower of Jesus cannot and should not dispute this. Yet the primary focus of the name of Jesus within Scripture is in no wise exclusively applied to physical healing and physical provision only. The initial reason and purpose of the name of Jesus is the apex of New Testament salvation doctrine. But since Hagin misinterpreted the primary cause and doctrine of our salvation for his theory that Jesus was "*spiritually born again*" and "*begotten at His resurrection*," he is miles away from comprehending the real Gospel of the Bible.

Admittedly, Hagin's book is not a thorough explanation of the Gospel of salvation. Yet not once does he mention John 3:16 as a key verse that relates to the reason for Jesus's healing power as the only begotten Son. On pages 143 to 154 of his book, Hagin explains the many passages that use "the Name of Jesus" and what they mean. He does include John 3:18 on page 146, but at the same time, his teaching of the spiritual death of Jesus completely destroys the declaration and interpretation of the John 3:16–18 text as well as most other passages he listed on these pages.

Since much of Hagin's book deals with physical healing, he therefore theorizes that the majority of the work that Christians must do in the earth is to "*heal the sick*" because of our equal power with Jesus—and when we believe on His name. Hagin was adamant that God uses only those who have great faith in the name of Jesus to bring about healing at our command and every time we pray in faith. However, we must think carefully about this theology: if it is true, God the Father is therefore demoted to a level of compliance at our command! He has no sovereignty over us because we are in control! We have thus maligned Scripture...and especially the Gospel message.

Can Jesus still heal through the prayers of them who malign His Gospel? Actually, no. Although healing from the real Jesus can occur when the receiver of healing believes in the correct Jesus—the Son of God, who was begotten at His birth.

We should be cautious and knowledgeable to discern that physical healing can come by another source—from the "father of lies." This issue is addressed later in chapter 10.

Jesus said: **As my Father hath sent me, even so send I you** (John 20:21). Within the context of John, chapter 20, we find no evidence that Jesus was sending out His followers to heal people as He did earlier in His ministry—but only to spread the good news of life eternal. Neither does this passage interpret that believers can acquire an equal divine nature with the Lord Jesus.

Though Essek Kenyon's book *The Wonderful Name of Jesus* and Kenneth Hagin's book *The Name of Jesus* are wonderful teachings on understanding and applying our faith, the doctrine from which they draw that admirable kind of faith is apostate from the Bible's definition of it. Both Kenyon and Hagin defined faith as a belief and trust in a Jesus who was *spiritually born again in Gehenna*—a "doctrine of devils" lie! Had Hagin scripturally scrutinized E. W. Kenyon's theory of the spiritual death of Jesus carefully, he may have come to another conclusion and would not have taught such apostate doctrine himself.

Essek Kenyon died two years before Kenneth Hagin had even heard of him, and Kenyon, being a Baptist pastor, would have likely disagreed with Hagin on certain points such as "speaking in tongues." Yet the teachings of E. W. Kenyon and Kenneth Hagin are one and the same: declaring things into existence, believers being *little gods*, and a Jesus who was *spiritually reborn in hell.* Though these major theological blunders stray far outside the orthodoxy of Christian doctrine, they are embraced by many sincere believers today.

Even though Kenneth Hagin was a great preacher and teacher of the faith in his generation, the basis for his faith rested in a false Christ unbeknownst to him. The disturbing theological heresy within his book *The Name of Jesus*, which was also theorized by E. W. Kenyon some sixty years earlier, was considered *New Revelation* truth, yet both men were blind to the blasphemous theologies they had mistakenly deduced. When Kenneth Hagin's book was published in 1978, it became part of the growing fortification of unperceived heresy and apostasy within Christendom.

Christian author Dan McConnell, a former professor of theology at Oral Roberts University, documents the connection with E. W. Kenyon and Kenneth Hagin and the escalating apostasy within the church in his 1995 book *A Different Gospel*. It is an historical and biblical analysis of the modern Faith movement.

A 1997 book titled *E. W. Kenyon—The True Story* by Pastor Joe McIntyre, Word of His Grace Church in Seattle, also revealed from his research of Essek Kenyon's life...and by analyzing his sermons... that in reality, Kenyon had later rejected the teaching and theologies of any occult beliefs of *New Thought* doctrines or Christian Science teachings, and that they had no place in the orthodoxy of biblical Christianity. Even though it appears Kenyon had changed his mind about some of what he'd written in *The Wonderful Name of Jesus*, it seems he should have made revisions to it or taken measures to end further publishing rights. Yet he never did.

Questionable statements in other books and publications by Kenneth Hagin should give the reader pause. Hagin wrote: "*Spiritual death means having Satan's nature. Therefore, Jesus was the first one who was ever born again*" (*The New Birth*, KH Ministries [Tulsa Oklahoma, 1975], p. 10).

Here Hagin affirms Kenyon's doctrine of Christians having the same *born-again* status and authority as Jesus, only because He, Jesus, was the first to cross over that spiritual threshold in triumph. But it's a concocted mystical type threshold of the philosophical human mind: it is not truth from the Bible. The eternal Son of God couldn't possibly acquire Satan's nature, then become spiritually regenerate from such a fallen state.

A few years later, in Hagin's article "The Incarnation" from *Word of Faith* magazine, December 1980, page 14, he writes: "*The believer is just as much an incarnation as was Jesus of Nazareth.*"

The above two statements by Kenneth Hagin are severely blasphemous. Hagin has wrongly negotiated the union of the divine Jesus with presumed divinity of His followers. Assuming Hagin meant to convey the idea that believers are only figuratively "*an incarnation as was Jesus,*" the issue is still a bit confusing for his particular use of the word "*incarnation,*" which means "manifestation—appearance—materialization of God," implying that believers are of the same nature and have at least a degree of personal power of divinity. According to our Bible, however, a *born-again* believer cannot literally or metaphorically be the same "*incarnation as was Jesus of Nazareth*" simply because He was the only one who could occupy that position.

Though Romans 8:17 reveals that believers are joint-heirs with Jesus, there is no "equal power" also stated. And Paul states that not every believer has been endowed with the gift of healing (1 Corinthians 12:9). When one is healed by a prayer of faith, the healing itself is God's manifestation. Christians therefore are not literal "begotten sons and daughters of God." The salvation message of our Bible totally debunks this current-day teaching. John 1:12 says: **But as many as received him, to them gave he power to become the sons of God, even to them that believe on his name**. In this verse, the word "power" means "privilege," "competency," and "freedom." Replacing the word power with any of these other words brings better clarity to the verse. Those who believe on His name are privileged and competent to spread His Gospel—not to have joint-heir equality of power.

According to exegetical truth of the Bible, the "power" that comes from the particular Jesus who received His excellent name as the only begotten Son also rendered a power that caused physical healing. Yet Kenneth Hagin bestows this very same kind of divine power and authority on all believers, stating: "*Man was created in terms of equality with God—he has made us as much like Himself as possible—he made us the same class of being that He is Himself*" (*The God-Kind of Life*, KH Ministries, 1981, pp. 35–36).

This muddled dubiety should not go unnoticed by the mature Christian reader of Kenneth Hagin's teaching.

Hagin also stated in "The Incarnation" article in the December 1980 *Word of Faith* magazine: "*Jesus needed to be 'born again' because his spirit was estranged from God. He committed sin on the cross when he said 'my God, my God, why hast thou forsaken me?*'" (Matthew 27:46)

To claim that the Lord Jesus ever committed sin is ridiculous and inconceivable; in fact, it is blasphemy. Of course, Jesus cried out such a thing! According to John 1:18, He was **the Only Begotten Son** and had been in the **bosom of the Father** from eternity past. For those many hours Jesus hung on the cross, He was "forsaken," meaning "left behind," as the Concordance explains. He was not spiritually estranged but temporarily severed from His Father in a physical sense—suspended between heaven and earth for six hours. The soul of Jesus was utterly crushed with grief! Though if we believe Jesus committed sin on the cross, we have thus denied Him as the Incarnate God for the assumed fact of His spiritual defeat! These blasphemous teachings remove the core of the Gospel!

The doctrine of the divinity of Jesus and the undermining of it cannot be taught simultaneously. God is not the author of a confused or ineffectual gospel. If He is, then we must biblically extrapolate that God is not as holy as the Bible says He is. And thus, most all humanity will likely gain eternal life in the end because of God's great mercy and leniency against sin: He has no wrath or punishment for unregenerate mankind, only because His stringent Ten Commandments really couldn't be kept by anyone.

Could this be Bible truth? We have already proven it is not.

The keys

Several New Testament verses tell us that Jesus knew beforehand that His physical body would rise from the grave. Then many years after His resurrection, Jesus appeared unto the apostle John on the island of Patmos saying: **I am he that liveth, and was dead; and, behold, I am alive for evermore, Amen; and I have the keys of hell and of death** (Revelation 1:18).

How did Jesus get these keys of hell and of death? Was it by spending a few days duking it out with His new spiritual equal—suffering at the hands of Satan in hell? But then gaining confidence of His true identity, snatched the keys of hell away from Satan to go and release the righteous dead being held captive? No! This imaginary scenario doesn't even make sense according to the words of Jesus in the first chapter of Revelation. Jesus obtained the keys of hell and death because He died, and now He lives forever! Being the only Incarnation of Deity, Jesus had paid the ultimate price by His physical death, then to release the righteous dead held captive—as well as purchasing eternal life for all who would believe on Him in the future. Jesus obtained the keys that locked up hell and death because He raised His own physical body from the grave (John 2:19). This doctrine is proclaimed as a spiritual application for mortal man, which was caused by a common physical condition held by Deity for thirty-three years. Therefore, Jesus did not experience the physical or spiritual torments of Gehenna. Neither were there any literal keys to be grabbed away from Satan.

Chapter 4

Last-Days Deception

The salvation message of our Bible is clear—encompassing the doctrine that Jesus was more than just human: He was God prior to the cross. This core foundation of Jesus's Gospel is why the enemy has plotted to pervert and denigrate it. Hence, spiritual deception is already here: it is not reserved for the final few years of the age. Nearly every book in the New Testament contains warnings against false teachers and false prophets. There are thirty-two warnings in all. Clearly, this is an important area God wants us to be aware of. The Bible calls them false prophets because they lead people away from the Savior and eternal salvation.

Realize that God is not obligated to supervise His sons and daughters in the faith: we should remain in the correct doctrine of salvation on our own and throughout our lifetime by studying God's Word. First Corinthians 10:11 says: **Now all these things happened unto them for ensamples: and they are written for our admonition, upon whom the ends of the world are come**. Then in verse 12, Paul makes the point that we must be vigilant to stay on course: he says, **Wherefore let him that thinks he stands take heed lest he fall**. In other words, if we don't read and study our Bible to discern the correct way of righteousness, we may be deceived by a well-meaning pastor into thinking we are standing firm, doing good, and doing right when in fact, we have fallen!

Our Bible states in several places: **The just shall live by his faith** (Habakkuk 2:4). We who live in the new covenant era should not have to live by God's continual chastisement and correction as the Israelites experienced. Because of the Bible—our instruction manual—we should not require God's supervision: it's all spelled out for us in the book! We remain in faith, and we live by faith by clinging to the sound doctrine of God's Word.

But I observe that some sincere believers wonder why I appear to obsess over deception. I tell them: "*Deception is pervasive, yet not perceived: that's why it's called deception!*"

Am I obsessing over a nonissue for the true followers of Jesus? No! Though you love God and do your best to follow Jesus—and may even have your prayers answered—you are ignorant of Satan's devises if you think that deception cannot touch you. The New Testament is jam-packed with warnings of deception and of the false teachers that will arise in an end-time "deceivableness." To whom are these warnings for? They aren't for unbelievers and skeptics of Christianity but for the followers of Jesus! The enemy is not focused on souls already lost; he is focused on you—the redeemed! If you think you cannot lose your salvation only because of your intimate closeness to Christ Jesus, then the slyness of your own deception has already begun! You have not seen or understood the many Bible passages telling it is possible to lose eternal life, even after you once believed the truth. If we aren't aware of the great potential to doctrinal derailment, we then also have great potential for only an intimate yet ignorant relationship with a god of our imagination. Jesus and the apostles called us to do far more than just an intimacy with God: we must first prayerfully discern biblical truth and knowledge about the Savior we commune with. Proverbs 14:18 says: **The simple inherit folly: but the prudent are crowned with knowledge**. Admiration and worship of Jesus means little if scriptural knowledge of His identity is neglected. In the New Testament gospels, "communing with Jesus" is primarily understood as the communication of the Savior who reveals Himself to us through His Word. In John 10:7, Jesus says: **Verily, verily, I say unto you, I am the door of the sheep**. This "door" is the doctrine of who Christ is. We must gain scriptural knowledge of Jesus and His doctrine of salvation…and of the enemy's strategies against it. When we do this, our intimacy with Jesus becomes much more meaningful: it's an innate confidence of an ongoing relationship with our heavenly Father because of Jesus our Savior.

Wicked teachers among us

The doctrine of Jesus's Gospel is a linear and finite beam of light that cannot be fragmented, twisted, or penetrated with the logic of man. And yet today, the human logic and good intentions of many Christian pastors has overshadowed biblical doctrine. Second Peter 3:16–17 tells that some within the fellowship will bring deception because they do not discern the scriptures; we are thus **led away with the error of the wicked**…as Peter says.

Within the church, a wicked false teacher is one who has either twisted the well-defined doctrine of the Savior, or they will not focus on His redemptive work. An appeal may be given to come to God under false pretense—gaining insight on

- *how to make Jesus your best friend—by sharing your life with Him,*
- *how to gain a positive self-image—by discovering God's unconditional love,*
- *how to gain financial freedom—through generosity and giving to the church,*
- *finding purpose in life—by discovering your gift,*

and a plethora of other ways to make our life pleasing to God with self-improvement and good works.

When attaching these ideologies to the Gospel—or as a benefit of the Gospel, it becomes a type of *self-help gospel*, and we've become guilty of a self-seeking amalgamation of the Spirit and the flesh. We must carefully discern the meaning of Isaiah 64:6: **But we are all as**

an unclean thing, and all our righteousnesses are as filthy rags. Contrary to the natural mind and our own desire to become a better person, the self-generated improvements of which we endeavor mean nothing in the sight of God.

Jesus told us to love God and one another; but His primary command was to go and make more disciples for the sake of the Gospel. Jesus didn't come into the world to give us methods for earthly success…or to show us how to prosper financially…or to give us personal life tools so that we can feel good about ourselves. The destiny God has for each of us begins with responding to His Gospel. If after having confessed our sin, we then focus on ways to improve our life without making the Gospel of Jesus a continuing priority, we have fallen off course! In truth, we stay on course when we continue in the truth of the saving Gospel. Repenting of sin is meaningless unless we stay focused on why we repented from sin in the first place. Career goals, self-improvement goals, relationship goals, and more will all fall into place when we prioritize Jesus the Savior and His Gospel of righteousness. It is Matthew 6:33 in a nutshell: **But seek ye first the Kingdom of God, and his righteousness; and all these things shall be added unto you**.

When our eyes are opened to God's love for us by sending His Son for reconciliation unto Himself, we then have a *born-again* transformation of the mind. God is generous to give most of us time to progress in spiritual growth and maturity. Though if seduced by false teachers into believing condemning false doctrine, or persuaded to cling to the **filthy rags** of self-improvement and good works, we risk losing what God has prepared for us through Christ Jesus. In truth, even though God covers us with His grace, underneath, we remain wretched sinners who need the Savior. Our lifelong need for the Gospel of salvation will not end until the day we die.

A persuasive false teacher (false prophet) pulls us away from the kingdom of God by inviting us to explore the fulfillment of life, rather than seeking His righteousness. Studying our Bible helps determine who a false teacher is for the kind of false doctrine they teach and preach. In New Testament terms, a Christian false teacher is one who

- *neglects or deviates from the Gospel of Jesus;*
- *promotes supposed biblical methods of success and prosperity;*
- *overemphasizes miracles, signs, and wonders;*
- *motivates us to experience God, rather than submit to God;*
- *manipulates Holy Scripture to promote their own doctrine.*

In Matthew 24:3, the disciples asked Jesus: **What shall be the sign of thy coming, and of the end of the world?** Jesus's first response is **Take heed that no man deceive you**.

How does this reply make any sense? How can Christians be deceived? Jesus explains how in verse 5: **For many shall come in my name, saying, I am Christ; and shall deceive many**.

In this verse, both the first word "many" and the last word "many" is *polus*, meaning "great number" or "multitude." Jesus is not referring to only some isolated cult leaders claiming to be Christ Himself or even a few deceived Christian pastors with inflated egos. Rather, He speaks of a great multitude who will say "*I am Christ*," being convinced of their own figurative or literal deity, and will, in turn, convince multitudes more of the very same idea.

Is this a too far-fetched interpretation of Matthew 24:5? No, because Jesus warned of deceivers who will **come in my name**! Outside of the church, we see relatively few cult leaders come and go "in the name of Jesus." But a false teacher within the body of Christ will claim to come "in the name of Jesus" and will deceive many by declaring the new theory of "*I am Christ.*"

At first, this seems logical because metaphorically speaking, Christians are the body of Christ. So why not say, "*I am Christ*"? Yet the particular teaching of Spirit-filled believers being *"born again with Christ"* is directly linked to the doctrine of *"equal power and authority with Christ"*. Think carefully about this concept. In reality, it is Satan's sneaky snare of deception for the purpose of self-righteousness and self-ego. And theologically speaking, it severely diminishes God's sovereignty over us. Seeing how a major segment of the

Evangelical Church has embraced this teaching, we must surmise that Christians caught up in it cannot see the deception.

Jesus continues in Matthew 24:11, saying again: **And many false prophets shall rise, and shall deceive many**. Then just in case the message wasn't quite grasped, He says it a third time in verse 24, explaining in more detail: **For there shall arise false Christs, and false prophets, and shall show great signs and wonders; insomuch that, if it were possible, they shall deceive the very elect**.

How could God's own people—the elect—be so deceived? Jesus tells us how and why: it is for being witness to great signs and wonders—*miracles of healing, miracles of increase*, and even *paranormal or supernatural activity*—all induced by and advocated by false Christs and false prophets as Jesus warned.

The distorted and arrogant teaching of equality with Christ is in great contrast to several passages such as Luke 22:42 where Jesus knelt and prayed: **Father, if thou be willing, remove this cup from me: nevertheless, not my will, but thine be done**. Jesus bore a specific burden of responsibility that none other could bear with Him. If we desire equality with the Savior, we must also be put to death for the sins of others! Does that make any sense? Of course not! Thus, those who teach any level of *equality with Jesus* are indeed false teachers, and the train of thought in Matthew, chapter 24, should prod us to search out just who the false Christs and false prophets are today. Are we immune to their influence simply because we are sincere in our belief in Jesus and remain faithful to our church? No! The false teachers come from within the church! They are seen as good prophets, good pastors, good elders, and good teachers with good hearts. This is why their deceptive teaching is unperceived. Though we may hear Christian terminology used and Bible passages quoted, we should recognize through a personal study of Scripture that the sound doctrine of the Triune God has actually been compromised and redefined.

Both Jesus and the apostle Paul warn us specifically to be on alert in the latter days. In 1 Timothy 4:1 (NKJV), Paul warns: **Now the Spirit speaks expressly, that in the latter times some shall depart from the faith, giving heed to seducing spirits, and doctrines of**

devils; speaking lies in hypocrisy. Notice Paul's careful wording here: he didn't say that some would depart from the fellowship of believers—but that they will give heed to **seducing spirits and doctrines of devils**. This passage warns us of apostasy and deception within the church—a departure from the faith, not departure from church fellowship.

Monotheistic doctrine

The Bible declares a *monotheistic* doctrine—*one Creator God.* Within Christianity, however, the Word of Faith movement unwittingly teaches *monolatrism—the worship of one God without denial of existence of other divine beings*. Though the Word of Faith group may insist they do not believe or teach such a literal doctrine of *monolatrism*, it, even when viewed as figurative in nature, is unharmonious to any Bible passage. Those who raise their voice against this false doctrine are shunned by the Faith movement and accused of unnecessarily splitting doctrinal hairs and of dogmatic rhetoric that divides the church. Yet scripturally, we find that any form of *monolatrism*, or "*equality with God*" type teaching, attacks the heart of the saving Gospel. It theologically dethrones Jesus from His supreme authority in the church.

The first one to suggest that man can be equal to God was Satan himself when he tempted Eve in the garden of Eden. Genesis 3:4–5 states: **And the serpent said unto the woman, Ye shall not surely die: For God knows that in the day ye eat thereof, then your eyes shall be opened and ye shall be as gods, knowing good and evil**.

The "*little gods*" and "*little Christs*" theology now being taught within the church is declared as *New Revelation* from the Holy Spirit. Though according to the Bible, it is the same satanic temptation that beguiled mankind long ago: it desecrates who God is as the Supreme Being. Satan, having his ego deflated for being exiled from heaven, hates God and ever since has attempted to discredit God—spreading lies about His Lordship.

Monolatrism theology is the same doctrine of the Catholic Church and the Mormon Church. For many centuries, Catholicism has taught that man can attain equality with God through Jesus the Son. Teaching number 460 in the *Catechism of the Catholic Church* states: "*The Son of God became man so that we might become God. The only begotten Son of God wanting to make us sharers in his divinity assumed our nature so that he might make men gods*" (The Wanderer Press, 1994, p. 116).

Latter Day Saints (the Mormons) also declare that we can become as God. They teach that there have always been many gods, and there will continue to be more gods created. This opposes many Bible passages, and yet some even within the Evangelical Church tell us: "*God is duplicating Himself in the earth today!*" The late Morris Cerullo, owner of INSP (the Inspiration Network), made this statement many times. Though it may sound innocent, knowing that Christians should naturally demonstrate God's love, it is at the same time perceived as God literally duplicating Himself in humans. Bible truth and the sound doctrine of orthodox Protestant Christianity has thus been weakened and compromised with a slant of false Catholic and Mormon doctrine—a mixture with false doctrine and pagan beliefs.

In the orthodoxy of the Christian faith, we should understand that humans cannot become *little gods* for our good works as Mormons believe. However, many within the Evangelical Church proclaim that because of the single phrase **Let us make man in our image** (Genesis 1:26) and by adding the "*born again with Jesus*" theory, that we have logically become *little gods*. Theologically, we arrive at the very same conclusion as Catholics and Mormons, only via another route.

The late Bishop Earl Paulk, founder of Cathedral of Chapel Hill, a Charismatic-Pentecostal megachurch in Decatur, Georgia, stated on page 4 of his booklet *Unity of Faith*: "*Mormons are brothers and sisters in the faith. For so long we have said: why don't the Mormons change? Perhaps we should be the ones to change. Mormons are Christians too!*"

Was Bishop Paulk correct? Mormonism teaches that God was once as we are now, and that we can become "as God is'" by our good works here on earth. If this doctrine is true, it then discredits Jesus's atonement for our sin! Jesus died so our sins might be forgiven—and now, through added good works, we become equal to the One who has the power to forgive our sin? No! Doctrinally speaking, this is not only a blasphemous teaching but an absurd concept as well! What was God's point of sending a Savior? So that humans could climb the ladder of deity to the highest level of equality with the Creator Himself? Seriously? This goes against the Bible's *monotheistic* doctrine!

Mormons are not true disciples of Jesus if they follow the teachings of their religion. Their theology and doctrines define them as an extreme cult offshoot of Christianity.

The Bible is clear: humans cannot become like God, nor can they even come close—even in an allegorical sense. Our Bible distinctly separates humankind from the Creator:

> **To whom then will ye liken me, or shall I be equal? saith the Holy One**. (Isaiah 40:25)

> **Before me no god was formed, nor will there be one after me**. (Isaiah 43:10 NIV)

> **For thou art great and do wondrous things: thou art God alone**. (Psalm 86:10)

This is truth from the Bible: God is God, and we are not. Jesus is the Mediator between God and man, and none can take His place or be equal to Him in any faction.

(Throughout the remainder of this book are many references from YouTube—an easy access medium through which much biblical and doctrinal misinformation as well as sound biblical doctrine has been posted. How can we know what is true and what is false on YouTube? If the posted sermon or information does not align with Scripture, it is false teaching. Though if we don't study our Bible, anything seen and heard on YouTube becomes believable.)

Blasphemy of the "little Christs" doctrine

Today, we hear pastors preaching the "*little Christs*" doctrine, which seems to have first come from good-hearted Pentecostal/Charismatic pastors years ago. It is now a pervasive teaching throughout much of the church—that every *born-again* believer is a *little Jesus upon the earth*.

Yes, we should want to emulate the love and compassion of Jesus, and metaphorically speaking, Christians are the body of Christ. However, to place the title of "*a little Christ*" on every believer is heading toward blasphemy and is the exact warning from Jesus in Matthew, chapter 24.

A blatant example of this false doctrine comes from Word of Faith pastor Creflo Dollar (Creflo Dollar Ministries, Atlanta, Georgia) who specifically teaches that when a person is *born again*, they become a "*little Jesus.*" Pastor Dollar tells his congregation: "*You are a little Jesus upon the earth—a little god—little 'g'. You are 'gods' because you came from God; the only human part about you is this physical body that you live in. The real me is just like God*" ("Justin Peters Cultic Doctrines, Pagan Practices, and False Prophets," YouTube, 14:52). Pastor Dollar's statement is a perversion of Genesis 1:26—**And God said, Let us make man in our image, after our likeness**, which he refers to as proof that we are of the same makeup as God because we have become His spiritual offspring. Dollar theorizes that since animals produce after their own kind, logically, the Godhead must have done it the same way in the beginning: they got together and produced "*little gods*"—thus causing Adam and Eve, and now Christians, to have the same divine spirit nature as God. Yet in Scripture, any human claiming literal or metaphoric traits of inner divinity is understood as blasphemy. But Pastor Dollar's sermon makes a sort of logical sense, until you listen closely as he further expounded on this theory. He tells his congregation that God intended for Adam and Eve to keep their godlike nature, but when they sinned, they forfeited their divinity. And since we, as their offspring, have also been dethroned from deity because of sin, we now have the opportunity to gain it back. A simple synopsis is this:

> *Mankind needed a Savior to cause a return of divinity and authority to the human race, just as Adam had in the beginning. When Jesus arose from the dead, He became the first born-again man of divinity, thus paving the way for humans to regain their deity and authority through repentance of sin.*

By adopting this extended theological position, we have thus switched from figurative doctrine to literal doctrine—the literal god-like divine nature of every *born-again* Spirit-filled human. Somehow, the spiritual nature of the *born-again* rank is theorized as parallel with the divine nature of God. But just as it was impossible for Adam and Eve to have been divine before they sinned, it is also impossible for Christians to gain a level of divinity today.

The apostle Paul said: **O wretched man that I am! Who shall deliver me from the body of this death?** (Romans 7:24). Was Paul lamenting over the fact of his sick and degenerating body that would one day see death unless his Savior soon returned for him? No! Paul speaks of spiritual things here. He knew of his own tendency toward sin—a corrupt body of death. He therefore couldn't have had God's literal divine nature within himself, even though the Holy Spirit dwelt within him.

Being filled with the Holy Spirit does not prevent us from sinning. The Holy Spirit lives within us to guide us heavenward and to convict of sin. This is a theological topic of New Testament truth that every follower of Jesus must probe and understand. Many books have been written about the Holy Spirit: some are sound New Testament theological truth; others are not. We can discern the truth by using the correct study method of contextual interpretation and searching out juxtaposed Scripture.

If humans can so easily obtain a godlike divine nature when they repent of sin and trust in the Lord Jesus, then there is no need to read most of Paul's New Testament Epistles of spiritual instruction and knowledge. Why? Because according to the "*little gods*" and "*little Christs*" doctrine of indwelt divine nature, we have already arrived at deified perfection at the point of salvation! Yet Paul states in many places that this kind of instant spiritual perfection is not possible. If we are persuaded to believe in a theology of equality with Jesus—even in a metaphoric sense—then multiple passages such as Philippians 3:12 make no sense whatsoever: Paul says, **Not as though I had already attained, either were already perfect: but I follow after, if that I may apprehend of Christ Jesus**.

Yes, even the great apostle Paul knew of his own spiritual imperfection. Nowhere did Paul allude to his equality with the Lord Jesus or of his personal alignment with the power and authority of God the Father.

Though Pastor Creflo Dollar does claim that God is sovereign in the world, his 2012 tweet message on Hootsuite revealed a careless and perverted theory: he stated, "*As spiritual beings who possess the nature of God, we have the ability to speak things into existence just like God did in Genesis 1*" (*Word of Faith Heresies*, YouTube).

This statement is heresy and blasphemy. If it is true, then *born-again* Christians are incarnate just as the Savior Himself, and thus have the ability to empty all hospitals of sick people, eliminate poverty, and speak world peace into reality by their divine authority. The mere fact that this hasn't ever happened within the last two thousand years is proof that the teaching of the divine nature and divine ability of humans is false.

The same perversion of Holy Scripture has also come from Pastor Casey Treat of Christian Faith Center in Seattle. Within a sermon titled "Believing in Yourself," Pastor Treat declares to his congregation of thousands:

> *The Father, the Son and the Holy Ghost had a conference and they said: "Let us make man an exact duplicate of us." —I am an exact duplicate of God! —Say it out loud! —I am an exact duplicate of God! —Come-on, say it! —Shout it! —Since I*

> *am an exact duplicate of God I'm going to act like God!* ("Word of Faith Heresies," YouTube, 22:05)

Here, Casey Treat isolated and completely mangled Genesis 1:26. The nature of Pastor Treat's aberrant doctrine is that God the Creator and His created "man" being classified as the same. This is an assault on and even a rejection of the sovereignty of God and His Gospel of salvation. Whether under the old covenant of millennia ago or under the new covenant of today, those who trust and believe in God and who are obviously created by God can never be "*an exact duplicate of God*" as Pastor Treat proclaimed. When the Trinity Godhead said **Let us make man in our image** (Genesis 1:26), it did not mean that the Godhead was literally duplicating Himself. In this verse, the word "image" (*tselem*) means "resemblance" or "representative." It simply meant that man represented his Creator and, by being the pinnacle of God's creation, also has the ability to now know Him in a personal way through the atoning cross of Christ.

The Bible nowhere tells that those who are *born again unto righteousness* and who have put their faith in Christ are equal with Him in the slightest. God's Holy Spirit lives within us when we abide in His righteousness, but we have no such ability to speak things into existence as only a Divine Creator can do.

Let's back up just a bit… How could Adam have sinned in the first place? Creflo Dollar, Casey Treat, and all within the Word of Faith movement claim that Adam was an exact duplicate of God: he was bestowed the same godlike type of dominion and divinity.

So then…Adam, the perfect man with a perfect divine nature, sinned against his own nature? Righteous perfection committed a sinful and rebellious act? Deity sinned against its own deity for being seduced by a measly serpent? This makes no sense! The Bible makes no such statement.

The idea that Adam and Eve were initially made divine, even in a figurative sense, is completely false. Though Adam and Eve were made perfect in their original physical state, they were not made divinely equal to their Creator. If they were, then why did they sin? This logic fosters the idea that God has a flawed nature and was a bit confused or at least a little uncertain just how His creation of man was going to play out. But Psalm 145:17 is just one of many verses that speak directly against this idea—**The Lord is righteous in all his ways, and holy in all his works**. If God is righteous and holy, He therefore has no flawed nature whatsoever, and His works are perfect in all His creation. Hence, Adam, who was created after God's image, was not a duplicate of God but was God's human creation for the purpose of fellowship.

God was not caught off guard by the sin of Adam and Eve. We see that the Messiah was **slain from the foundation of the world** (Revelation 13:8). This was God's plan to redeem humanity long before Adam was created, yet this redemption required man's choice—to be submissive or insubmissive: God created humans with their own mind and will, not robots without a brain. If Adam was created divinely perfect and was intended to remain perfect, then what would be the purpose for a planned Redeemer prior to the foundation of the world? The supposed "incarnation" of all who are *born again* is arrogant, man-centered doctrine which exalts man and mocks the Creator God.

Nonetheless, by this confused and erroneous theory, many deceived teachers within the body of Christ present this doctrine as Bible truth. In our thought process and in our prideful desire to have this same divine authority, we have not humbled ourselves in the sight of Almighty God: we are not worthy of the grace of salvation only because of our egotism. Isaiah 66:2 describes the great chasm between God and egotistical man: **But to this man I will look, even to him that is poor and of a contrite spirit, and trembleth at my word**. God looks to use those who are humble, not to bestow upon them a divine power but to use their repentant heart and the fear of God for His glory.

Since the *born-again Jesus* doctrine theorizes the believers' equality with Him on a certain level, it therefore and in turn demotes the Savior to a level of equality with man. This interprets Jesus to be "*our elder brother*" as some now teach—a dangerous doctrine that we will later discuss.

The idea of *born-again* humans being equal with the supposed *born-again Jesus* directly stems from the false doctrine that Jesus didn't become totally God until His resurrection. This defines Jesus as human only before the cross or that He lost His divinity through spiritual death at the cross—then gained it back when raised from the dead. Trusting in this false Christ cannot give us eternal salvation according to the New Testament. The **great white throne** judgment described in Revelation 20:11–15 is the final judgment for souls condemned to the lake of fire. These condemned souls did evil and were scoffers of God during their life. When comparing this passage in Revelation to the testimony of Jesus in John 3:16–21, John 6:46–47, and Matthew 7:21–23, we should discern that a belief in the *elder brother/born-again Jesus* concept deduces a belief in a *human-only savior*—which will also condemn us for being scoffers of the divine Savior.

Jesus did not call on and rely on God's power to perform miracles during His ministry: divine power was already within Himself. Though Jesus acquired all resurrection power when raised from the dead, there is no such *elder brother* type of savior described in the New Testament who mentors us in acquiring the same. We must rather be humbled and believe on the Lord Jesus—the Jesus who came as the eternal Lord who saves us from eternal damnation. We can then be united with the Lord Jesus Himself at the great marriage supper of the Lamb event. We will be gathered with all the righteous who ever lived and will have eternal life—being only observers at the **great white throne** judgment a thousand years later. Revelation 20:6 states: **Blessed and holy is he that hath part in the first resurrection: on such the second death hath no power**. Revelation 20:14 then says: **And death and hell were cast into the lake of fire. This is the second death**. All humanity will be gathered at this final great judgment. Only those who had trusted in the Lord Jesus will be rewarded for their belief in sound doctrine. The apostle John then says: **He that overcometh shall inherit all things** (Revelation 21:7). It is only through knowledge of the Scriptures that we easily "overcome" and rise above the unsound doctrine being taught by the false teachers of our day.

When did Jesus become "The Christ"?

When did Jesus obtain the title of "The Christ"? Was it when God touched Him at His baptism as some claim? No. Was it when He performed His first miracle, turning water into wine at a wedding celebration? No. Was it when He arose from the dead? No.

In John 6:46–47, Jesus revealed that His Sonship identity had no beginning: **Not that any man hath seen the Father, save he which is of God, he hath seen the Father. Verily, verily, I say unto you, he that believeth on me hath everlasting life**.

Here, Jesus gives clear evidence that He was the Messiah, the Son of the Trinity from eternity past as well as on the day He spoke these words, prior to the cross and His resurrection. Since Jesus was with the Father before coming to earth, He literally became "The Christ" when born in the manger.

Beside the testimony of Jesus Himself, Acts 4:10–12 perfectly explains it all: **That by the name of Jesus Christ of Nazareth, whom ye crucified, whom God raised from the dead…neither is there salvation in any other**. This is a specific Jesus—not just any Jesus. It is the Jesus who was the Christ of Nazareth even before His ministry began. Jesus did not become a representative of God who acquired a divine help. A belief in this kind of Jesus gives Him no Lordship authority over our life. The only link that justifies us to our Father in heaven is a faith in the Lord Jesus. This means that Jesus was Lord during all of His earthly life, just as Isaiah 7:14 and Matthew 1:23 proclaim: **Behold, a virgin shall be with child, and shall bring forth a son, and they shall call his name Emmanuel, which being interpreted is, God with us**. This is not metaphoric language. The Son of the Trinity Godhead literally came to earth and was "with us" for an appointed time.

If you can't quite wrap your brain around this concept, then you must take it by faith and, as a little child, put your trust and hope in the Lord Jesus. It's so simple. Jesus said: **Except ye be converted, and become as little children, ye shall not enter into the kingdom of heaven** (Matthew 18:3).

Betrayal among brethren

It appears by many signs that we are living in the very last years of this age just before Yeshua (Jesus) returns. In Mark 13:10, Jesus said: **And the gospel must first be published among all nations**. Then in Mark 13:13, He says: **And ye shall be hated of all men for my name sake: but he that shall endure unto the end, the same shall be saved**.

These verses show us that though the Gospel is published and verbally spread throughout the whole earth, it will be an offense to many who hear it and do not accept it.

Going back to Matthew 24, verses 9 through 11, Jesus states the same and then prophesies more detail: **And ye shall be hated of all nations for my name's sake. And then shall many be offended, and shall betray one another, and shall hate one another. And many false prophets shall arise, and shall deceive many**.

Does this sound like a believable conflict within Christianity today? Absolutely! Jesus then continues in Matthew 24:12: **And because iniquity shall abound, the love of many shall wax cold**. Jesus is talking to His disciples here—not to a crowd of skeptics. Therefore, and in context, He is warning the one who preaches the true Gospel to be prepared for persecution—to be hated and ridiculed not only in the secular world but also within the church. Jesus's warning is also a mandate to preach only sound doctrine and to not deviate from it. But a large portion of the church is now turning from the Gospel of the Lord Jesus to a twisted and blasphemous gospel of equality with the risen Savior Himself. In Matthew 24, Jesus is referring to His own future followers: up to a certain time, they would have love toward one another. Then at the time of **the end of the world** (Matthew 24:3), some will so pervert the Gospel of truth that it causes a division and callousness among the brethren. This apostasy from the Gospel began within the church many decades ago, and some have now become offended at other Christians who have revealed the erring brethren. This prophecy of Jesus in Matthew 24 has come to pass in our generation! Those who have deviated from biblical truth have fallen into coldness of heart, just as Jesus prophesied. The *born again with Jesus* teaching, and the *little gods* doctrinal friction among believers is fulfilling Jesus's end-time prophecy of trouble within the church. We are therefore assured that mankind has entered the very final years of this age.

Within much of Christianity, the foundation for faith is no longer understood. To millions of Christians, Jesus has become only a stepping-stone to personal advancement. With little emphasis on acknowledging our sin, many of us are told to only trust in Jesus and thereby receive endless benefits. But where did Jesus state any earthly benefits for trusting in Him? Are they implied somewhere between the lines of Mark 16:16–18 or anywhere else in the New Testament? No! In fact, we should decipher the opposite because of what Jesus says in Matthew 28:18: **All power is given unto me in heaven and in earth**. Who has the power? Jesus the Savior! And what kind of power is He speaking of here? It is spiritual power—not a power that causes earthly benefits—doled out only to the followers of Jesus upon their request.

Moving on, let's look again at Matthew 24:10: Jesus said, **And then shall many be offended, and shall betray one another, and shall hate one another**. Here, the key word for determining that Jesus was referring to His own followers is the word "betray." Unbelievers are opposed from believers: a nonbeliever cannot betray a believer because there is no biblical fellowship or doctrinal comradery between them. We can then understand that this betrayal and hatred among believers toward the end of the Church Age is directly linked to the contrasting views over the interpretation of who Jesus really was and what His Gospel was about. In these opposing views of the doctrine of the Gospel, both sides are fulfilling Matthew 24:10 perfectly. Those who believe Jesus came to save them from their sins are offended at and avoid fellowshipping with those who believe Jesus came also to give them earthly success. And rightly so, according to Paul's words in 2 Corinthians 6 and Ephesians 5. Likewise, those who subscribe to the *born again with Jesus* doctrine steer clear of Christian brothers and sisters who see it as false teaching—that believers have divine authority with Jesus. Yet unless a scriptural investigation of the exact interpretation of this stated "authority" is correctly discerned, the body of Christ will be at odds and divided against each other. Today, adamant believers on both sides of the controversy remain offended, and some are even betraying one another as Jesus prophesied. Evidence of this public betrayal among believers is proven in the following instance:

On the Trinity Broadcast Network, *Praise the Lord* program, dated April 2, 1991, its late founder and host Paul Crouch revealed his frustration with biblical sound doctrine. As he faced the camera, Crouch blasted those who opposed TBN's teaching of the *born-again Jesus* and *little gods* doctrines. He irately exclaimed: "*Let God sort out all this doctrinal doo-doo, I don't care about it! These heretic hunter guys who spend their lives straightening us all out doctrinally, they're gonna go straight to hell*" ("Word of Faith Heresies," YouTube, 04:18)!

On this particularly sad day for Christianity, Paul Crouch, a presumed ambassador for Christ, sneered at Bible doctrine and of its little importance. He also gave no passage to support the fate of his hated "*heretic hunter*" enemies. He continued, saying: "*The world is going to hell, and you are criticizing the gospel we preach? I'm tired of you all splitting doctrinal hairs—get out of my sight! I don't even want to see your ugly face! Get out of God's way; quit blocking God's bridges or God's gonna shoot ya if I don't*" ("Word of Faith Heresies," YouTube)!

Yes, the founder and host of TBN stated this on his own Christian TV Network, a network through which the Gospel of Jesus is supposedly preached—a Gospel of love and forgiveness, a Gospel based on the belief in the Lord Jesus as sovereign Savior. However, Paul Crouch ignorantly denied Jesus Christ as Sovereign simply because he believed Jesus's divinity, or lack thereof, could be manipulated by any interpretation of the Word.

The prophecy of Jesus has come to pass—**And because iniquity shall abound** (iniquity within the body of Christ), **the love of many shall wax cold**.

A main focus of the Faith Movement teaches a Jesus who was *born again* at His resurrection. Therefore, though they would deny it, those who adhere to this theological mistake are actually not subject to God's sovereignty but are instead "*partners with Jesus.*" What's wrong with this theology? Very simply: we cannot partner with Jesus to effectively spread His Gospel if our definition of that Gospel is based on a *spiritually born-again Savior.*

Consider again what 2 Timothy 4:2 says about specific doctrine: **Reprove, rebuke and exhort with all longsuffering and doctrine**. TBN founder Paul Crouch neither considered this admonishment nor was humbled enough to listen to those who reproved the carelessness of his and TBN's doctrinal indolence. In light of Matthew 24:10—**And then shall many be offended, and shall betray one another**—it was obvious that Paul Crouch was offended at and had betrayed other Christians who disagreed with his (severely flawed) interpretation of the Gospel. Paul Crouch and TBN's own "statement of faith" rejects the idea that Jesus was definitively God before the cross, which specifically rejects New Testament statements such as 1 Corinthians 2:2: **For I determine not to know anything among you, save Jesus Christ, and him crucified**. This verse is very clear: it was Jesus the Christ who was crucified. In other words, Jesus most assuredly did not become "the Christ" at His resurrection.

The pathetic rant of Paul Crouch against New Testament doctrine relates directly to Romans 16:17–18:

> **Now I beseech you, brethren, mark them which cause divisions and offences contrary to the doctrine which ye have learned; and avoid them. For they that are such serve not our Lord Jesus Christ, but their own belly; and by good words and fair speeches deceive the hearts of the simple.**

Here, the apostle Paul shows us that "the doctrine" is of utmost importance. What is this doctrine? First Corinthians 15:1–4 tells us it is the death, burial, and resurrection of the Lord Jesus Christ. It is not the death of the man Jesus, who then became our Lord, the Christ. This passage in 1 Corinthians, among others, is the very foundation of the Gospel by which we are saved. And yet Christians argue and debate, becoming angry at one another, and cannot agree on a definitive interpretation. Amazing!

Entitlement theology

Today, New Testament doctrine has been distorted and maligned by many within the faith. On the Jerry Savelle Ministries International website, dated November 19, 2015, Pastor Savelle explained from Romans 8:17 that we are joint-heirs with Christ for the purpose of an earthly benefit. He states: "*As a joint-heir with Jesus, you're entitled to healing—to prosperity—to victory and success; they are your inheritance.*"

Jerry Savelle and many others in the Word of Faith media tell us that our *born-again* position guarantees physical healing and blessings of abundance. The joint-heir theology of Pastor Savelle concludes that the risen and triumphant Jesus now has power over all things, and we as believers have inherited the same power and equality with Him. Is this the meaning of Romans 8:17? If so, Jesus should have triumphed in physical victory over the cross! But He didn't! Rather, Old Testament prophecy was perfectly fulfilled at Calvary, rendering our eternal "joint-heir" spiritual victory—not a physical and earthly victory prior to Christ's Second Coming.

The declaration of guaranteed health, prosperity, and success is nowhere within Romans 8:17 or any surrounding verse or anywhere else in the New Testament. We cannot isolate verse 17 from surrounding verses—we must understand the fullness of Romans 8:16–21 and beyond: **The Spirit itself beareth witness with our spirit, that we are the children of God: and if children, then heirs; heirs of God, and joint-heirs with Christ; if so be that we suffer with him, that we may be also glorified together**.

This passage says nothing of healing, prosperity, and earthly success—but in fact states we must literally suffer to be considered joint-heirs with Jesus. Ultimately, when Christ returns, we are glorified—"exalted to dignity" for suffering as joint-heirs with Him. Paul then explains in verse 18: **For I reckon that the sufferings of this present time are not worthy to be compared with the glory which shall be revealed in us**.

The word "sufferings" in this passage means "hardship," "pain," and "affliction." As believers, this is what we must endure. In all of

Paul's writings, he nowhere promises that our declarations or prayers of faith will permanently relieve the suffering we experience—but that the suffering we endure will one day be changed to the hope of glory as explained in verse 21—**Because the creature itself also shall be delivered from the bondage of corruption into the glorious liberty of the children of God**. Notice Paul's future-tense terminology: **shall be delivered from the bondage of corruption**. When do we realize this glorious liberty? It is after we've been delivered from the bondage of corruption and unto eternal life incorruptible! Christ was resurrected incorruptible, and we as joint-heirs inherit the same when He returns. Before that time, we are united as joint-heirs with Jesus only in the suffering of His affliction—the affliction of rejection, of hardship, and of His cross.

Are you still waiting and believing for your own healing, for your own prosperity, for your own victory, for your own deliverance, for your own success? Since you believe yourself to be a child of the King, have you wondered why it hasn't happened yet? Could it be that you are chasing after a false gospel? Turn from your false indoctrination! The Bible tells us specifically that our joint-heir status with Jesus does not render these earthly benefits prior to Christ's return!

English-born Evangelist Leonard Ravenhill raised a discerning voice in the 1980s when he stated: "*The early Church was married to poverty, prisons, and persecution. Today the Church is married to prosperity, personality, and popularity. If Jesus had preached the same message that ministers preach today, he would never have been crucified*" (Leonard Ravenhill Quotes, Google search).

Carnal Christians

Biblically speaking, there is no such thing as a mature carnal Christian. A heart changed by the love of Jesus the Savior is a heart not focused on earthly things. But Paul uses the term "carnal" in 1 Corinthians 3:1 when referring to Christians who are babes in Christ still tethered to earthly desires and human strife. In addition, one who is fallen into apostasy from the Gospel or is neglectful of the Gospel is also carnality minded. For the sake of understanding this part of the chapter, let's call them carnal Christians because by removing the word Christians, they become only carnal unbelievers.

Carnal Christians have not discerned the words of Jesus and New Testament apostles. In fact, they have not been *born again* of the Spirit of God because they want Jesus to walk beside them only for the purpose of earthly success and what they believe is entitled to them. In 2 Thessalonians 2, the apostle Paul pens words of knowledge and warning directly addressing the fate of many unfocused carnal Christians: in verse 11, he says, **And for this cause God shall send them strong delusion, that they should believe a lie**. Because of today's *born again with Jesus* false doctrine being taught, we now understand that part of this lie of strong delusion is that believers have an element of equality with the Lord Jesus. Is God unjust for allowing Satan to bring this deception upon carnal believers? No! It is a necessary test. Christians not focused on the sound doctrine of "one sovereign God" are thus persuaded to believe in the figurative "plurality of deity" lie. It gives them a sense of control, and of course, it just sounds logical as a lifelong Christian benefit and a presumed vital aspect of the Gospel. Where did these carnal Christians hear such unsound teaching? From their carnally minded pastors of course!

Immaturity among Christians is revealed when they follow after pastors claiming to have a new message from God for the body of Christ. Instead of studying Scripture for themselves, many believers prefer following those who claim to be on the cutting edge of what is claimed to be *New Revelation teaching* or the latest "*wave of the Spirit.*" Though a genuine wave of the Spirit of God is absolutely possible, our tendency is to latch onto our favorite men and women who lead and teach us in their own imagination and agenda or because of their presumed direct divine revelation which they have personally received. In doing this, we have totally neglected the Scriptures and have favored the teaching of man. The personality and charisma of such pastors and teachers within the body of Christ keeps comprehension of vital Bible issue at bay.

He who bore our sins

In crucial Bible doctrine concerning the correct interpretation of the Gospel, wrong theology can lead to unperceived heresy and apostasy. As we have discussed earlier, Jesus bore our sins and paid the price for them only on the cross: He did not also suffer in hell. Look at Psalm 16:10 in particular: referring to the coming Messiah, it says, **For You wilt not leave my soul in Sheol, nor will You allow Your Holy One to see corruption** (NKJV).

In this verse, the original King James uses the word "hell"—"the abode of the dead": "the grave." Hence, we know that Jesus did not descend into Gehenna—a specific location called "the place of torment"—which he warned of many times, such as in Matthew 18:9, calling it "hell fire."

If Jesus became a sinner on the cross, then He naturally had to pay the price for losing His spiritual righteousness—thus causing His descent into "the place of torment."

Right here is the error in this theology: Jesus was not "made to be sin" while on the cross. Rather, Scripture tells us that Jesus "bore" our sins on the cross.

The Old Testament prophesies of the coming Savior: **For he shall bear their iniquities** (Isaiah 53:11). Verse 12 again tells that He would **bare the sin of many**.

In the New Testament, 1 Peter 2:24 says: **Who his own self bare our sins in his own body on the tree**. Also, Hebrews 9:28 states: **So Christ was once offered to bear the sins of many**.

As referenced earlier in chapter 3, the verse that seems to imply Jesus was "made sin" is 2 Corinthians 5:21: **For he hath made him to be sin for us, who knew no sin**. In this King James verse, the Greek word for "made" has several meanings—"to bear," "avenge," "appoint." Therefore, we know Jesus did not "become" sin. If He had, then His Sonship status in the Trinity Godhead was in the grips of spiritual death and loss of divinity between the day of His crucifixion and the day of His resurrection—an impossible theological conclusion. Since according to Scripture, Deity is eternally holy and sinless, Jesus could not have been under a temporarily three-day control of Lucifer. Again, this reckons a *human-only Jesus gospel*—a blasphemous anti-Gospel teaching.

The "born-again Jesus" teaching

Finding the root error of the *born-again Jesus* teaching proves that the Savior did not experience a spiritual rebirth. Jesus, the Son of God, didn't require a spiritual regeneration to connect with His Father in heaven. When applying the New Testament's "*born again*" terminology to Jesus at His resurrection, we have thus tampered with Bible doctrine: we have theologically reasoned that He had no previous spiritual understanding. We have also removed the title Lord Jesus Christ from Him.

At the cross, Jesus did not lose His deity: He was not stripped of unique classification as the "only begotten Son". The twisted *born-again Jesus* doctrine contradicts the simplest of Bible verses such as John 3:3 where Jesus said to Nicodemus the Pharisee: **Except a man be born again, he cannot see the kingdom of God**. He was talking about a new understanding of holiness, proving that man could be spiritually *born again*—even before Jesus's atonement for sin had occurred. Therefore, Jesus could not have been the first spiritually *born-again* man when raised from the dead. In John 3:6, Jesus then explained to Nicodemus saying: **That which is born of the flesh is flesh; and that which is born of the Spirit is spirit**. As such, being *born again* necessitates the inner awakening of unseen spiritual things. Determining that Jesus was the first *born-again* man at His resurrection logically deduces that He must have been clueless about spiritual things prior to the resurrection! Jesus's conversation with Nicodemus could thus stand on its own as proof that the *born-again Jesus* doctrine is false. Though this theory is impossible and untrue, when claiming to have this same born-again status as the risen Lord Jesus Christ, the believer thereby proclaims their own ignorance of Scripture.

The misgiven logic of the *born-again Jesus* theory is this: *Just as we are human, Jesus also became like us—being emptied of His deity for the purpose of our redemption.*

This doctrine lines up with no Bible passage and in fact defeats the entire Gospel message. When He walked the earth, Jesus set aside only His exhalation, not His divinity. After Jesus turned water into wine at a wedding celebration, John 2:11 says: **This beginning of miracles did Jesus in Cana of Galilee, and manifested forth his glory**. This first miracle of Jesus indicates that He humbly exhibited His glory—His divinity. When reading the full story of this wedding event, we see that Jesus didn't ask for any assistance from God to accomplish His first miracle. But neither did He command anyone to bow down and worship Him on that day.

Romans 8:29 says: **For whom he did foreknow, he also did predestinate to be conformed to the image of his Son, that he might be the firstborn among many brethren**.

This passage does not say that a *born-again* person is in the same class of being as Jesus was. The phrase **"the firstborn among many brethren"** has been blown out of proportion by those who twist its meaning. In reality, Paul is simply saying that Jesus's bodily example in His life and His sacrifice in death has caused and defined the saving *born-again* position for man because of His resurrection.

In seeing the biblical evidence of Jesus's divinity prior to the cross, we know that He did not set the standard for us to have equal power with Himself, but by the confidence in His resurrection power, we have the authority to call upon that power. Romans 8:30 says: **Moreover whom he did predestinate, them he also called: and whom he called, them he also justified: and whom he justified, them he also glorified**. Here again (as in Romans 8:17), the word "glorified" is a bit overstated in the King James Version: this Greek word means only "esteemed." We are "esteemed" and celebrated by the angels in heaven when we repent of sin. God calls us, justifies us, and esteems us as righteous because of the sacrifice of His Son.

When carefully reading Scripture, we find that Jesus was not the "firstfruit" (first redeemed) of all who are redeemed. Look carefully at 1 Corinthians 15:20–23: Christ is not referred to as the firstfruit but the "firstfruits" (plural) in verses 20 and 23. Paul was acknowledging the symbolism of Jesus's resurrection as it related to the Feast of Firstfruits celebration. He says in 1 Corinthians 15:20: **But now**

is Christ risen from the dead, and become the firstfruits of them that slept. This refers to the righteous believers who lived before the cross: Jesus released them from their holding place—He **led captivity captive, and gave gifts unto men** (Ephesians 4:8).

In 1 Corinthians 15:23, Paul then says: **But every man in his own order: Christ the firstfruits; afterward they that are Christ's at his coming**. We therefore conclude by a simple comparison of these passages that Jesus was not the spiritually firstborn of a *born-again* people. Instead, the clear emphasis in 1 Corinthians 15:23 especially is that we who believe in Christ and who live after the cross will then belong to Him at His Second Coming.

His blood mocked

Every religious cult claims that the blood of Calvary's cross either meant nothing or that the blood Jesus shed was insufficient in and of itself to take away sin. Christians are misled when taught that Jesus was spiritually born again in hell to finish the atonement, thereby bestowing all power through the spoken word upon His followers. This heretical belief opposes many passages:

> **Being justified freely by his grace through the redemption that is in Christ Jesus: whom God has set forth to be a propitiation through faith in his blood, to declare his righteousness for the remission of sins that are past, through the forbearance of God**. (Romans 3:24–25)

> **And the blood of Jesus Christ his Son cleanseth us from all sin**. (1 John 1:7)

> **In whom we have redemption through his blood, the forgiveness of sins**. (Ephesians 1:7)

> **But with the precious blood of Christ, as of a lamb without blemish and without spot:**

> **who verily was foreordained before the foundation of the world, but was manifest in these last times for you**. (1 Peter 1:19–20)
>
> **They overcame him by the blood of the Lamb and by the word of their testimony**. (Revelation 12:11)
>
> **By the which we are sanctified through the offering of the body of Jesus Christ once for all**. (Hebrews 10:10)

These passages are concise, and they agree with each other. They explain the truth of exactly what happened at the atonement of Jesus; none of them mention a sacrifice of His Spirit or His deity, which would have concluded a void and defunct gospel message.

But you might ask, can't the Gospel message be legitimately tweaked just a little to justify our equality on some level with the Savior? If so, this could be God's best-kept secret, intended only for those who find the divine key of authority to overcome all earthly things. In the discernment of New Testament exegesis, this is impossible; God has no secrets regarding His Gospel. As shown above, Hebrews 10:10 is clear: we have become separated unto God the Father—"sanctified unto righteousness" by the bodily atonement of Jesus. Thereby, believers have authority to stand against evil; there is no additional divine power within us to "*speak things into existence*" as the Word of Faith camp theorizes. When believing we possess this kind of power, we have mocked the atoning blood of Jesus.

Second Corinthians 4:18 (NIV) says: **So we fix our eyes not on what is seen, but on what is unseen. For what is seen is temporary, but what is unseen is eternal**.

According to this simple verse, it is easily understood that the indoctrination of one's own authoritative spoken words—for the result of earthly benefit—has no eternal value. The unbiblical "power in words" teaching has morphed out of skillful yet deceived false teachers within the church, just as Jesus, Paul, and Peter warned us of.

The apostles did not teach the early church that they possessed any divine power in their spoken words. Rather, they were taught an authority to proclaim the Gospel of salvation, which was backed by the resurrection power of Jesus and merged with submission to God's sovereignty. If seduced to believe we have the same power as the resurrected Savior, we have theologically deduced that God has no sovereignty over us. In our mind, we become the final authority and rulership in our own world.

According to this "spoken word" doctrine, the apostle Paul could have spoken and proclaimed his way out of all the trouble and distress he had to endure throughout the remainder of his life. So why didn't he? Or why couldn't he? Paul's own words inform us exactly why. He said to Timothy: **Remember that Jesus Christ of the seed of David was raised from the dead according to my gospel: wherein I suffer trouble, as an evildoer, even unto bonds** (2 Timothy 2:8–9). Think of the profoundness of Paul's words here. He was seen as an evildoer among the religious and governing rulers—and therefore endured trouble and distress because of the Gospel he preached! He didn't acquire a life of ease and material abundance for believing an authoritative and earthly dominion-oriented gospel. Yet today, this type of false gospel is being taught to the body of Christ!

A serious warning to all believers

In Matthew 7:15–27, the words of Jesus are specifically meant for professing believers. In verse 21, He says: **Not everyone that saith unto me, Lord, Lord, shall enter into the kingdom of heaven; but he that doeth the will of my Father which is in heaven**.

A nonbeliever does not call Jesus their own personal "Lord"; therefore, Jesus is addressing only Christians here. He tells that those who enter the kingdom of heaven will have done **the will of my Father**. The Greek interpretation here is "purpose of the Father." It is the Father's purpose and plan that mankind believe in Jesus as His Son and to keep His commandments.

Jesus continues in Matthew 7:22: **Many will say to me in that day, Lord, Lord, have we not prophesied in thy name? ...and in thy name have cast out devils? ...and in thy name done many wonderful works?**

This event will be an ominous spectacle: Jesus is not talking about the judgment seat of Christ event, where all believers in the saving power of Jesus will be rewarded. Rather, it is the great white throne judgment at the end of the millennial reign of Christ. Jesus speaks to those who thought they were on their way to heaven; instead, they have been gathered in a designated place—on the left hand of God's throne (Matthew 25:41). According to Revelation 20:5, it is deduced that the souls of these professed Christians have spent at least a thousand years in the torment of hell but have now been resurrected back to physical life. They have long since realized their sin of rebellion against the real Gospel and are now gathered in a specific place for a soon departure to the lake of fire, which Revelation 20:15 then tells of. They know of their guilt—they know of their theological and doctrinal mistakes they made during their lifetime on earth. They are frightened and begin to remind Jesus of their many good deeds they had done, hoping He would have mercy on them. But Jesus—both Savior and Judge—cannot have mercy for their slothful neglect in the doctrine of the saving Gospel that the Scriptures had spoken of.

Here in Matthew 7:22, Jesus reveals that some of them had cast out devils during their lifetime. They must have had confidence enough to do miracles in the name of Jesus! Yet these believers had missed the mark! Even though they had prophesied, performed miracles, and had their prayers answered, none of it was a valid sign that they knew and served Him.

In this great final judgment, God the Father lets Jesus the Son be judge over it all, but His love and grace cannot cover their doctrinal mistakes and misapplication of His Gospel. Many in this group didn't realize they had not sought the kingdom of God and His righteousness but instead had focused on many other good things such as their works of generosity to help support the church—which actually did produce miracles of financial increase for them. Despite that, these miracles of increase were satanically induced through **lying signs and wonders** (2 Thessalonians 2:9) because of their love of money. Their generous deeds had become a means to an end for a selfish and carnal benefit. They believed what they were told by the prosperity preachers—that their generous giving toward spreading the gospel would bring them financial increase from God. In reality, it created a carnal-based preoccupation and a double standard against the Gospel. Jesus said: **You cannot serve God and mammon** (Matthew 6:24).

Others in this condemned great judgment gathering had sought the *miracles and manifestations of the Spirit*, which they thought were foremost to advance God's kingdom in the earth. These efforts had replaced the saving Gospel by rerouting the focus to miraculous signs only. Many more in this gathering didn't believe Jesus to be the eternal Son of God, even though they believed in the saving power of Jesus. How is this even possible? In the very next sentence (Matthew 7:23), Jesus states: **And then I will profess unto them, I never knew you: depart from me, ye that work iniquity**. These people had seemingly done many wonderful works, but because they had focused on a perverted gospel during their lifetime, they had actually been functioning under a false power and false authority that rejected the deity of Jesus. Jesus then informs them that their deeds were sinful, and it was all for naught!

Just prior, in verses 16 through 20, Jesus tells what will happen to those who had good fruit versus those that produced evil fruit: **Every tree that bringeth not forth good fruit is hewn down, and cast into the fire** (verse 19). After a full explanation of what this meant, Jesus then tells them: **I never knew you** in verse 23. The Greek word "knew" here is *ginosko*, which is translated to "have knowledge of," "aware of," "perceive," and "understand." By using this particular word, Jesus is in essence saying: "*You never knew Me because you misunderstood and perverted My teaching.*" This is very intimate terminology and refers to the type of bad fruit the believer bears in the false gospel they had followed. Paul's warning against another gospel to the churches at Galatia and Corinth aligns perfectly with Jesus's words here—declaring that our brand of faith was ineffectual because we had perceived a different Jesus, a Jesus who gave earthly success, abundance, and equal power and authority with Himself. This in turn rendered a gospel not centered on the sacrifice and suffering of the Savior. The seduction of false prophecy and false teaching had thereby produced evil fruit—spiritually unbeneficial fruit. According to Matthew 7, the evil fruit of these sincere Christians has brought them to a frightful end. The good deeds they pursued were not perceived as evil but necessary to prove God's power, provision, and blessing. Yet they were worthless good deeds in an eternal sense. They believed in Jesus, but it was not the Jesus who bought their salvation. Instead, they had trusted in a Jesus who granted miracles on demand and a Jesus who gave them the prosperous good life. They had misunderstood and perverted the sole purpose and doctrine of the saving Gospel—**the will of my Father**, as Jesus explained in Matthew 7:21.

When we read Matthew 7 carefully and seeing how Jesus say's **depart from me, ye that work iniquity** (verse 23), we know this is another clue, seeing that the word "iniquity" means "wickedness" and "unrighteousness." It is the condemning unrighteousness of not making Jesus one's Lord. This correlation is seen in many other New Testament passages: Jesus said that though we may call Him Lord, it will not count because we gave Him only lip service during our life—calling him Lord yet contradicting and eradicating His Lordship in our personal lives.

In Matthew 7:26–27, Jesus continues, speaking of those who believed in a false teaching of His Gospel, saying: **And every one that heareth these sayings of mine, and doeth them not, shall be likened unto a foolish man, which built his house upon the sand... and the winds blew, and beat upon that house; and it fell: and great was the fall of it**.

Christians who build their spiritual house upon unsound doctrine will be greatly disappointed in the end. Jesus conveys the idea of discerning good fruit from bad fruit—which renders two totally opposing outcomes. It is the crucial difference in believing sound doctrine versus believing unsound doctrine.

Both Matthew 12:31–32 and Mark 3:28–29 records a stern message from Jesus: **But he that shall blaspheme against the Holy Ghost…is in danger of eternal damnation**.

This is the unpardonable sin, not only referring to a lifetime of rejecting God and His free gift of eternal life, but in the context of how Jesus is speaking to the Pharisees who accused Him of casting out devils by the prince of devils (Matthew 12:24), here, it is referenced as a specific sin. The Pharisees rejected the authority of Jesus and so committed the unpardonable sin. It is the rejection of the clearly revealed knowledge of who Christ is and that the Holy Spirit works exclusively through Him. Thus, Matthew 12:31–32 and Mark 3:28–29 shows the connection to Jesus's warning in Matthew 7:21–23, and we know exactly why those who professed to be Christian will lose eternal life. It is only because they favored good works and neglected the saving Gospel.

Chapter 5

False Teachers Exposed

In Matthew 7:15–16 (NIV), just before pronouncing the ill-fate of many believers, Jesus said: **Watch out for false prophets. They come to you in sheep's clothing, but inwardly they are ferocious wolves. By their fruit you will recognize them**.

Notice how Jesus didn't say that a false prophet would have no fruit. They do have fruit. But what kind? He goes on in verses 17–19 (NKJV) to explain: **Even so, every good tree bears good fruit, but a bad tree bears bad fruit. A good tree cannot bear bad fruit, nor can a bad tree bear good fruit. Every tree that does not bear good fruit is cut down and thrown into the fire**. There are different kinds of fruit—spiritual good fruit that remains and carnal bad fruit that is burned up.

Today, in much of the church, the warning from the apostle John has been ignored: **Beloved, believe not every spirit, but try the spirits whether they are of God: because many false prophets are gone out into the world** (1 John 4:1).

Why would John say this unless it was important to a particular true Gospel? There are several variations of the gospel being preached today, but only one is the truth. A loving pastor may appear to have God's anointing, but Jesus gave us clear warning in advance about wolves in sheep's clothing. If we're not first grounded in the sound doctrine of the new covenant Gospel, we may be prone to blindly follow false teachers for their smooth speech and perceived great love.

Many peripheral topics mostly unrelated to the Gospel of salvation can cause division within the church. But what severs us from righteousness in Christ will readily come through deceptive doctrines of the false teachers among us.

Naming the false prophets

If there is no association between false doctrine and naming the person or church that teaches it, the warning may be obscured in generality, resulting in blindness to the wolves in sheep clothing. In Matthew 23, Jesus named the false prophets of His time—the scribes, Sadducees, and Pharisees—informing the people that they were blind fools and hypocritical snakes. In verses 13–14 (NIV), He said: **Woe to you teachers of the law and Pharisees, you hypocrites! You shut the kingdom of heaven in men's faces. You yourselves do not enter, nor will you let those enter who are trying to**.

The Sadducees were strict teachers of the Mosaic Law; the Pharisees were a bit more liberal in their interpretation of it, but Jesus called them both hypocrites, not mincing any words in His accusations. By exposing these religious leaders and teachers, He was actually naming precisely who the false prophets were. Today, however, we feel intimidated or that we should be more loving, polite, and politically correct. But why? Jesus certainly wasn't! Second Timothy 4:2 gives a scriptural mandate to rebuke and reprove any false doctrine. Though by avoiding offensive accusations or not wishing to cause discord, we are guilty of subduing the one true Gospel message! Wouldn't it behoove us to discover who's right and who's wrong according to the Scriptures? It is not divisive to call out a false teacher by name: the body of Christ benefits from this kind of division—separating truth from error. In 1 Timothy 1:20 and 2 Timothy 2:17, Paul named Hymenaeus, Philetus, and Alexander who had shipwrecked concerning the faith: they had become false prophets and antagonists against sound doctrine within the church, leading many astray. Today, we hear the same deviation from scriptural truth as exampled in the following instances:

In the late 1980s, a TBN aired sermon titled "Our Position in Christ" (tape number A031190-1), "faith healer" Benny Hinn stated: "*Are you ready for some real revelation knowledge? You are God! Within me is a God-man—I am a God-man*" ("Word of Faith Heresies," YouTube, 04:44).

To this day, Benny Hinn still declares that believers have a level of equality with God, though to the one who knows and discerns the Scriptures, Hinn's statement sounds quite arrogant, ignorant, and even stupid. We need only to read Genesis 1:1—**In the beginning God created**—to know that Benny Hinn can be classified as a false teacher, until or unless he recants from this and other false teachings.

TBN's late founder, Paul Crouch, proclaimed: "*Humans become part of the Trinity Godhead—God opens up that union of the very Godhead and brings us into it*" ("Praise the Lord" broadcast, TBN, November 15, 1990; "Word of Faith Heresies," YouTube).

The only passage that distantly resembles this theology is Ephesians 2:6, which says: **And hath raised us up together, and made us sit together in heavenly places in Christ Jesus**.

To clarify, the verse does not say that Christians are equal with Christ Jesus; rather, it says, **In Christ Jesus**, we are **raised up together** because we are redeemed by Him. Hence, Paul Crouch's false belief and declaration led the gullible listener into scriptural disconnect.

Texas Pastor Kenneth Copeland has also made many erroneous and apostate statements within his sermons. In his message titled "The Force of Love" (Kenneth Copeland Ministries, audio tape number 02-0028), Pastor Copeland states: "*We are a class of gods… God Himself spawned us from His innermost being. You don't have God in you. You are one*" ("False Teachers Exposed," Justin Peters, YouTube).

Even in a theologically abstract or figurative sense, Christians cannot be "*a class of gods.*" When humans respond to the real Gospel message, they are admitting to their sinfulness. If, however, there is no struggle against sin (for a false conversion), there may be no presence of the Spirit in our lives! In Romans 7:17, Paul tells of his own sinful nature, and 1 John 1:8–10 reveals the same. Hence, our sinful human nature cannot be mysteriously replaced with an inner divine nature, even after we've accepted Jesus as our Savior. Kenneth Copeland's statement is therefore blasphemy and has come from his misinterpretation of the Gospel of salvation.

In Kenneth Copeland's sermon titled "What Happened from the Cross to the Throne" (tape number 00-0303), he says: "*Jesus's death on the cross was not enough to save us. The physical death of Jesus didn't pay for your sin. Anyone could do that*" ("False Teachers Exposed," Justin Peters, YouTube)!

Copeland's gospel theology is warped beyond recognition. If anyone could pay for their own sin by being martyred, then Peter was sorely mistaken when he wrote: **For Christ also hath once suffered for sins…that he might bring us to God, being put to death in the flesh, but quickened by the Spirit** (1 Peter 3:18). This simple verse states that the physical death of Jesus most assuredly paid for our sin! Pastor Copeland's heretical statement attacking the deity of Jesus aligns perfectly with Essek Kenyon's apostate teaching in *The Wonderful Name of Jesus*. Jesus, who is both God and Savior, to date, is the only One whose flesh of death was quickened by the Spirit. And sadly, Kenneth Copeland deceives the gullible Christian masses by preaching a false gospel message.

Is this too judgmental? Not according to Jesus's instruction when He said: **Judge not according to the appearance, but judge righteous judgment** (John 7:24).

Declaring the original divine state of man, Kenneth Copeland stated: "*God's reason for creating Adam was his desire to reproduce Himself. Adam in the Garden of Eden was God manifested in the flesh*" (1989 K C Ministries, audio tape number 01-3001, "Following the Faith of Abraham," "Word of Faith Heresies," YouTube).

All the above statements by Pastor Kenneth Copeland are directly opposed to the biblical text, which nowhere states that *born-again* humans are a "class of gods"; neither could Adam have been a duplicate of God Himself. If Adam was an exact duplicate of God, how could he have sinned?

Kenneth Copeland plainly announced his theology of who Jesus was by stating: "*He hadn't come to earth as God. He'd come as man*" ("Jesus Our Lord of Glory," *Believers Voice of Victory* magazine, April 1982, page 2).

This statement sounds somewhat justifiable because Jesus was obviously a man. However, Copeland strongly implies in this article that Jesus was only a man. But in John 4:24, Jesus said: **God is a Spirit**. Therefore, the Second Person in the Trinity Godhead did indeed come as a man! What else? How could He make His presence known and do the things He came to do in spirit form only? Nobody would see Him! Is the idea of a Savior who is human and God at the same time so incomprehensible or unimaginable? No! We must believe it is factual because the Bible tells us so!

Justifying that Jesus was human only while on earth is denial of the Son of God.

> **Who is a liar but he that denieth that Jesus is the Christ? He is "anti-christ" that denieth the Father and the Son. Whosoever denieth the Son, the same hath not the Father.** (1 John 2:22)

> **Whosoever shall confess that Jesus is the Son of God, God dwelleth in him and he in God.** (1 John 4:15)

> **Who is he that overcometh the world but he that believeth that Jesus is the Son of God.** (1 John 5:5)

Consider Hebrews 2:14: **Forasmuch then as the children are partakers of flesh and blood, he also himself likewise took part of the same; that through death he might destroy him that had the power of death, that is the devil.**

Here in this single verse is the crystal clear explanation: it was through death of His flesh and blood that Jesus destroyed the power of Satan who, at one time, had the power of death over us. This is yet another verse revealing that the eternal Son, who **took part of the same**, and by death of His physical body, paid the price for our salvation. The heretical doctrine of Kenneth Copeland leads to the understanding of why he stated in logical conclusion to his congregation: "*Jesus volunteered to go to hell! I want you to know somethin'—ain't nobody ever got outta there*" (2004 sermon excerpt from Eagle Mountain Church, Newark, Texas, "Word of Faith Heresies," YouTube)!

Pastor Copeland's theory was obvious: Jesus had no idea if He would ever get out of hell or that He had any authority to raise Himself from the dead but—was resigned to stay there for eternity for the sake of mankind's eternal salvation. What preposterous nonsense!

Kenneth Copeland claims Jesus didn't discover that He was the Messiah until He stood and read aloud from the book of Isaiah that day in the temple. In a blasphemous sermon posted on YouTube, Copeland said: "*The only thing Jesus had to go on was the promises of God in Scripture! He didn't have some special revelation from heaven between He and God the Father. He found himself in The Word*" ("Word of Faith Heresies," YouTube)!

Copeland's statement would be humorous if it wasn't so pathetic. Was Jesus really clueless about His identity prior to addressing the temple crowd on that day—reading aloud from a passage prophesying of Himself? Or perhaps by studying the Torah and Talmud, Jesus had discovered He was the Chosen One by the time He entered His ministry at age thirty? No! Early in His ministry, Jesus told the Jews who questioned His authority: **Destroy this temple, and in three days I will raise it up** (John 2:19). Here, Jesus spoke of the temple of His own body, stating: **I will raise it up**! Yes, Jesus raised Himself from the grave! How? Because He was God! If Jesus wasn't aware of His own divinity and wasn't certain that His own body would be resurrected, then why would He make this statement at the beginning of His ministry?

In Luke 2:49 (AKJV), Jesus, at age twelve, replies to His parents who found Him at the Temple: **How is it that you sought me? Knew you not that I must be about my Father's business?**

Even from a young age, Jesus had a relationship with His Father in heaven, which indicates He did have special revelation from heaven between the Father and Himself.

In addition, even before Jesus performed any miracles, He knew of His own spiritual authority as the Savior of mankind. In Matthew 4:8–11, the devil offered to Jesus **the kingdoms of the world, and the glory of them...if thou wilt fall down and worship me**. If Jesus didn't know of His position of authority at that time, then why did He tell the devil: **Get thee hence, Satan**? And what did Satan do next? He left! By Jesus's divine authority, the devil obeyed Him! Prior to His earthly ministry, Jesus did indeed know of His spiritual authority, and Satan knew of it too!

During a 1988 TBN Praise the Lord telecast, Kenneth Copeland, while in conversation with hosts Paul and Jan Crouch, ignorantly stated: "*Jesus never actually claimed to be God*" ("Word of Faith Heresies," YouTube).

We can prove Kenneth Copeland is wrong in more than a dozen passages specifically proclaiming the eternal deity of Jesus.

In John 3:13 (NIV), Jesus said: **No one has ever gone into heaven except the one who came from heaven...the Son of Man**.

This verse unequivocally states Jesus's uninterrupted divinity—before and after His earthly life.

John 8:58 gives nearly the same thought. Jesus said: **Before Abraham was, I am**.

Here, Jesus says that He existed before Abraham, who lived nearly two thousand years earlier.

Jesus also said: **I and my Father are one** (John 10:30).

The ultimate statement from Jesus proving that He was God Incarnate is John 17:5: Jesus, while in prayer, said, **And now, Oh Father, glorify thou me with thine own self with the glory which I had with thee before the world was**.

Isaiah 43:25 states that only God can forgive sins: **I am he that blotteth out thy transgressions**. And in Mark 2:5, Jesus said to a man with palsy: **Son, thy sins be forgiven thee**. Because Jesus had power to forgive sins, He was God while on earth.

In Mark 2:10 and Luke 5:24, Jesus tells the scribes and Pharisees: **The Son of man has power upon earth to forgive sins**. Here Jesus says that even His human side (the Son of man) had the same power as the Father to forgive sins.

In John 14:9, Jesus asks Philip: **Have I been so long time with you and yet hast thou not known me? He that hath seen me hath seen the Father**.

John 16:27–31 records the conversation between Jesus and His disciples: He said, **For the Father himself loves you, because you have loved me, and have believed that I came out from God**. Then the disciples said to Him: **Now we are sure that you know all things, and…that thou came forth from God**. **Jesus answered them, Do you now believe?**—meaning, "Do you now believe in My deity?"

John 1:10 says of Jesus: **He was in the world, and the world was made by him, and the world knew him not**.

This single verse could stand on its own as perfect confirmation that Jesus was the Creator of the world.

In John 5:18, we read: **Therefore the Jews sought the more to kill him, because he not only had broken the Sabbath, but said also that God was his Father, making himself equal with God**.

John 10:33 (NASB) also tells that the Jews replied to Jesus: **For a good work we do not stone you, but for blasphemy; and because you being a man make yourself out to be God**.

By this text we conclude that Jesus assuredly claimed to be God. In Judaism, the doctrine of the Trinity is considered idolatry: Deuteronomy 6:4 states God is **one Lord**, so any man calling himself God is, by definition, blaspheming. Since, however, the New Testament states Jesus was the Second Person of the Trinity Godhead, He was not a blasphemer. In Mathew 12:29, Jesus quotes Deuteronomy 6:4, saying: **The Lord our God is one Lord**.

In John 6:62, Jesus said: **What if ye shall see the Son of man ascend up where he was before?** When reading the many previous statements leading up to verse 62, we see how Jesus is directly speaking of His eternal divinity. Then in verses 63–64, He says: **The**

words that I speak unto you are spirit, and they are life. But there are some of you that believe not. According to the text, Jesus is talking to His disciples, and that some of them shall **believe not**—just as Pastor Kenneth Copeland of Eagle Mountain International Church also "believes not."

As of this writing, Kenneth Copeland, age eighty-six, is still a front-runner in the Charismatic/Word of Faith movement. The listener should be warned that much of his teaching pertaining to the Gospel strays far outside the orthodoxy of Scripture. Galatians 5:9 states that a little leaven (of false doctrine) sours the whole lump.

The late Fredrick Price, former pastor of Crenshaw Christian Center in Los Angeles, stated: "*Jesus upon the earth was just a man, not the Son of God*" (Fred Price, tape RP19, May 1993, "Word of Faith Heresies," YouTube).

Sadly, heretic Pastor Fred Price had not discerned the salvation message of the Bible. An eye-opening verse in Luke 4:41 tells that when Jesus delivered many from demon spirits who possessed them, they cried out: **Thou art Christ the Son of God**. Here it is recorded that demonic fallen angels recognized Jesus as the Incarnation—the Son of God. But Christian Pastor Fred Price did not.

The apostasy—the falling away—is not a future event for the church. It began long ago under the deception of false prophets.

From his home church in Atlanta, Georgia, Pastor Creflo Dollar preached a blasphemous sermon on December 8 and 15, 2002, titled "Jesus' Growth into Sonship." Pastor Dollar stated:

> *If Jesus came as God, then why did God have to anoint him? Jesus came as a man, that's why it was legal to anoint him! Jesus came as a man, and at age thirty, God is now getting ready to demonstrate to us, and give us an example of what a man with the anointing can do. Jesus didn't show up per-*

> *fect, he grew into his perfection.* ("Word of Faith Heresies," YouTube)

The heresy preached by Creflo Dollar is revealed in Revelation 13:8, stating that Jesus was the Lamb slain from the foundation of the world. This means Jesus was prepared to be the Incarnation of God upon the earth before the world was created. We read in the account of Jesus's baptism at the age of thirty, when the Holy Ghost descends on Him, God speaks audibly, saying: **Thou art my beloved Son; in thee I am well pleased** (Luke 3:22). Notice that God did not say, "*Thou hast become my beloved Son*" or "*Thou art now my beloved Son.*" No! Jesus had always been the acceptable and sinless Son of the Triune Godhead. In contrast, Pastor Dollar states Jesus was not perfect but "*grew into his perfection.*" Astounding!

Sadly, Paul Crouch, Benny Hinn, Kenneth Copeland, Fred Price, Creflo Dollar, and many other Word of Faith teachers have not discerned the truth of the Gospel they claim to believe in. In fact, they have dismissed it. Their doctrine of the *born-again/human-only Jesus* is a denial of His Lordship. They believe in and teach a Jesus not described in the Bible—a Jesus that was not the Son of God at his birth, before his baptism, or before the cross—but only after His resurrection. They are Bible-illiterate apostates and heretics. These are just a few of the many false prophets among us.

Tampering with the Gospel

Understanding through the infallibility of Scripture regarding the nature and divinity of God, such as Malachi 3:6 and Revelation 1:8, we determine that divinity cannot be gained or lost or set aside. Divinity is perpetual—from eternity past to eternity future. It is timeless and unwavering in its position. The distinction of Jesus's eternal deity is the Gospel's foundation. Though many devout Christians have not discerned that a false gospel message is now being preached, the Bible clearly warns us that eternal life is impossible if we follow a different gospel. The spiritually "*born again at His resurrection"* kind of Jesus is decisively *another gospel.* Looking at the full context of 2 Corinthians 11:3–4 (NKJV), Paul states:

> **But I fear, lest by any means, as the serpent beguiled Eve through his subtlety, so your minds should be corrupted from the simplicity that is in Christ. For if he that comes preaches another Jesus, whom we have not preached, or if ye receive another spirit, which ye have not received, or another gospel, which you have not accepted, you might well bear with him**.

Here, Paul is stating the obvious: it is the simplicity that is in Christ of which corrupted minds have perverted. The last phrase in verse 4, **you might well bear with him**, indicates there will be some sincere and devoted believers who, for a time, will ignorantly cling to another Jesus, another spirit, or another gospel. But the cure for ignorance is knowledge—a knowledge that comes from balancing scripture against scripture to discern the truth. Again Galatians 1:9 (NKJV) says: **If any *man* preach any other gospel unto you than that you have received, let him be accursed**. And 2 John 1:7 says: **For many deceivers are entered into the world, who confess not that Christ Jesus is come in the flesh**.

To believe that Jesus was *begotten of the Father at His resurrection* or was *spiritually born again at His resurrection* is to believe unequivocally that Christ did not come in the flesh at His birth in the manger but instead morphed into deity by the right choices He made during His life. This is not only Bible contradiction but is hideous blasphemy.

The watchmen ignored

Decades ago, there were just a few men who raised concern over the apostate direction the church was taking. The late Christian apologist Dr. Walter Martin, founder of the Christian Research Institute, was one such person. He ruffled a few feathers within Christianity by warning of the heretical teaching of many well-known Christian pastors. Though Martin was largely shunned and ignored for daring to raise such controversy within the body of Christ, he often replied: "*There is nothing wrong with controversy for the sake of truth!*"

Walter Martin's statement made a lot of biblical sense. Hosea 4:1 says: **Hear the word of the Lord...for the Lord hath a controversy with the inhabitants of the land, because there is no truth, nor mercy, nor knowledge of God in the land**.

Even though these words were written before the Savior came to earth, shouldn't we also address any controversy God has with us today? In this passage, God calls it *His controversy* with men who ignore truth, mercy, and knowledge of God. Hence, if there must be controversy within the body of Christ to define and enlighten biblical truth, then so be it!

In a 1985 hour-long interview on the Trinity Broadcast Network *Praise the Lord* broadcast, guest host Pastor Doug Clarke questioned Walter Martin on his views. The program, which can be found on YouTube, was aptly titled "Apostasy Alert," in which Dr. Martin warned of those within the church who were straying from biblical sound doctrine—in that their views of Jesus were dangerously similar to those of "*the theologically bankrupt cults of Mormonism, Jehovah's Witness, Christian Science, and liberal Catholicism.*" He then said: "*The Evangelical/Charismatic Church has also theologically deviated in a massive way from its beginning*" (Walter Martin's Last Time on TBN, YouTube, 06:56).

During the interview, Walter Martin defended the deity of Jesus as the focal point of the Gospel and exposed in detail the doctrinal error of two men greatly loved by the TBN ministry—Kenneth Hagin and Kenneth Copeland—who taught the *human-only Jesus* theory for the presumed fact that He was spiritually *born again* out of hell. Martin exposed them by name and stated that their teaching labored against the sound doctrine of the Gospel of Christ Jesus. He said these men were great preachers and had good intentions but that they erred in this blasphemous kind of doctrine.

In the beginning of TBN's television ministry in 1973, its founders Paul and Jan Crouch initially declared the sound doctrine of the deity of Jesus. But they soon compromised with an ecumenical agenda and an anti-scriptural interpretation of a gospel heavily influenced with Word of Faith's apostate theology.

Today, TBN's continued apostasy is within God's divine purposes to perpetuate the end-time deception of those who pursue any teaching and doctrine for personal benefit. Since the *born-again Jesus* theory logically leads to one's own equality with the resurrected Savior, its convincing seduction remains as the perversion of a false Christ portrayed to millions of believers worldwide. Because of Satan's last-days deception within the church and in order to preserve the Father's true Gospel of salvation, He must divide the church over differences of doctrine rather than unite them. As shown in many New Testament passages, it is God's necessary plan and purpose to separate carnal believers from the true disciples of Yeshua.

Chapter 6

Mind-Boggling Simplicity

Though the purpose of the heart of God is made easy for man to comprehend, our general intellectualism and the knowledge of and academic devotion to biological science can hinder the Gospel message. Since the virgin birth of Jesus was unnatural in a physiological sense, it takes a simple kind of faith to believe this salvation scenario is true. Thus, one must, in a sense, reject their own natural intellect and believe from the heart in surrender to a higher power than science and physiology. Even still, many who have accepted Jesus as their Savior have also let their intellect get in the way, spending too much time analyzing, theorizing, and twisting Scripture to find a doctrine more believable or beneficial in an earthly sense. It is these who have fallen off the simple narrow path of salvation into the theological ditch: they are **ever learning, but never able to come to the knowledge of the truth**, as 2 Timothy 3:7 says. But the path to eternal life, though it may not be easy for some, is astoundingly uncomplicated. Paul then gives further insight as to why many believers cannot accept the simple Gospel message but are enticed away from it. He says in 2 Timothy 4:2–4 (NIV): **For the time will come when men will not endure sound doctrine. Instead to suit their own desires, they will gather around them a great number of teachers to say what their itching ears want to**

hear. They will turn their ears away from the truth and turn aside to myths.

Paul earlier wrote of those who would pervert Scripture in their search for a more earthly beneficial gospel: in Acts 20:29, he said, **I know this, that after I depart shall grievous wolves enter in among you, not sparing the flock.** We are now witnessing in full scale Paul's prophecy of apostasy.

Many Christians don't listen carefully when the *born-again Jesus* doctrine is taught. It goes over their heads, and they hear only the wonderful *New Revelation Knowledge* proclaiming their imparted power and authority with Jesus. In this belief, they believe that God has not lost His sovereignty for the justification that it's always His will for believers to triumph in perfect health and successful victorious living.

So…what should we do with Bible verses stating the opposite? **Yea, and all that will live godly in Christ Jesus shall suffer persecution** (2 Timothy 3:12). And Philippians 1:29 says: **For unto you it is given in the behalf of Christ, not only to believe on him, but also to suffer for his sake.**

Notice how these passages speak of the Christian's conviction and lifestyle yet do not mention prosperity and perfect health as part of it or as a byproduct of following the Savior and His Gospel message.

We as Christians are to be salt and light to unbelievers—to show the way of eternal life. We intermingle with them and can still be successful in business and career just as they are. But we cannot biblically determine that our financial success or good health is a result of our devotion to Jesus the Savior. Many of the ungodly and wicked are also physically healthy and successful in economic endeavors. New Testament passages distinctively separates the desire for health and wealth from a desire for God, for righteousness, and for eternal matters.

At the time when Christ returns to earth, those who have done the will of the Father **shall receive a crown of glory that fadeth not away** (1 Peter 5:4). But Jesus must withhold the anticipated crown many Christians think they will receive: as Paul said, **For we must all appear before the judgment seat of Christ; that every one may receive the things done in his body, according to that he hath done, whether it be good or bad** (2 Corinthians 5:10).

Here, Paul is not speaking of believers versus nonbelievers. Rather, he speaks of varying degrees of reward for every believer in Christ. All believers who repented of their sin and trusted in the Jesus of the Bible will gain eternal life. But those who additionally sought to profit the flesh in earthly gain—**for filthy lucre** (1 Peter 5:2)—will not receive **a crown of glory** (1 Peter 5:4). Though heaven's entrance may be gained, it would seem unwise to test God's grace in our desire for financial gain or a questionable belief of metaphoric equality with His Son—which, exegetically speaking, would be the cancelation of one's eternal crown of glory.

Here's why: In Revelation 3:11–12, Jesus states, **Behold, I come quickly: hold that fast which thou hast, that no man take thy crown**.

We read here that it's possible for men to take your crown through unsound doctrinal teaching. This aligns perfectly with 1 Peter 5:4 and also Jesus's warning in Matthew 24:4—**Take heed that no man deceive you**.

For many believers, the teaching of Jesus seems so basic and simple that the enemy effortlessly convinces that they must further probe and acquisition some sort of secret scriptural knowledge and mastery. But in truth, the Lord Jesus Christ cannot be our Savior if we deviate from His simple Gospel. Believing that you are *born again just as Jesus* may not sever you from eternal life—that is, if you retain the conviction that Jesus was literally God before the cross. It only reveals that you haven't discerned how being *born again with Jesus* theologically renders a blasphemous deduction. If these last few chapters haven't convinced you to turn from this false belief, then hopefully God will have mercy on your ignorant theology. If, however, you are convinced of the lie that Jesus was not literally and fully God prior to the cross, then neither can you biblically justify such a feeble foundation for gaining eternal life.

Chapter 7

What Is Faith?

In scriptural terms, "faith" is the absolute trust and belief in God the Father and Jesus the Son. It is complete confidence in the atoning work of Jesus's death, burial, and resurrection, which will give us eternal life.

But how do we apply our faith now—before we enter eternal life? What is its benefit in an earthly sense? Can we think of our faith as a cure-all remedy that will gradually and mysteriously decrease all problems we face? Did Jesus tell us to put faith in God so that toward the end of our life, we can experience a few good years of contentment and comfort—free from physical ailments? No, that's not what our faith is for!

In addition, our faith is no excuse for foolishness. We cannot eat poorly and neglect physical exercise, then expect our faith in Christ to protect us from stroke or heart disease. If you were a smoker for many years, will your faith in the blood of Christ now prevent you from getting lung cancer? Of course not! Neither can our faith in God reduce the chances of getting a cold or the flu. Our faith is spiritual and has an eternal purpose. Faith in God and in the blood of Christ brings the assurance of righteousness before God, which causes inner peace. Even though we biblically discern that this faith cannot provide earthly comfort or relief from sickness and disease, it is nonetheless by this faith that miracles of provision and physical healing are possible.

Faith for healing

Word of Faith pastors proclaim that physical healing is always God's will for every believer and that if we abide in Jesus, but we are not healed from sickness or disease, we lack enough faith to believe for it. This is a cruel weight of condemnation from those teaching the *positive confession* doctrine. How can we have faith enough to believe we are saved unto eternal life yet not have enough faith for physical healing? This makes no sense considering how our intellect has difficulty rationalizing a belief in something unseen…or in trying to figure out how our physical bodies could possibly live forever in heaven.

But we must wonder…why doesn't God heal every disease or sickness by our prayers of faith? Once again, turning to the Bible, we find clues.

In 2 Samuel 12, we see how King David prayed and fasted for his sick son—yet he died. Did David not have enough faith? Or maybe he didn't fast long enough or pray hard enough—none of which is the case.

In 2 Kings 2:9, we read that Elisha received a "double portion" of his predecessor Elijah's anointing and went on to do many miracles during his life. In 2 Kings 4:34, Elisha had faith enough to bring the son of the Shunamite woman back to life. But in 2 Kings 13:14, we read that **Elisha had fallen sick and died from his sickness**! What happened? Didn't this mighty man of God have enough faith for his own healing? Instead of living longer and dying from old age, he died from a sickness!

In Galatians 4:13, Paul tells that he preached the Gospel despite his…**infirmity of the flesh**! Why didn't Paul, the great apostle for Christ, have enough faith for his own perfect health and dominance over his physical frailty? It is because he knew there was no such promise provided by his faith.

In Philippians 2:27, Paul writes that Epaphroditus, his companion and coworker in the faith...**was sick and near death**! But the surrounding text reveals that God used Epaphroditus in spite of his sickness!

In 2 Timothy 4:20, Paul says: **Erastus abode at Corinth: but Trophimus have I left at Miletum sick.** Prior to this, when Paul was with brother Trophimus for a period of time, did he forget to pray for him? It's not likely, considering Paul's great faith. So what happened? Had God's healing power now run dry? Just three decades earlier, Acts 5:16 records that all were healed by the apostles. Later in Acts 28:8, we read that Paul laid his hands on a man and prayed, and he was totally healed. But years later, when mentoring Timothy, Paul advised him to...**use a little wine for your stomach's sake and for your often infirmities** (1 Timothy 5:23).

Why wasn't Timothy's stomach ailment healed? Why wasn't Trophimus healed of his sickness? Why wasn't Epaphroditus healed so that he could better preach the Gospel? Why didn't the prophet Elisha's faith in God keep him from sickness and death? According to Old Testament passages such as Genesis 20:1–18; 1 Samuel 1:9–20; 1 Kings 17:17–24; and many more, God healed people before the appearance of Jesus the Messiah on the earth. So why did the prophet Isaiah need to declare in Isaiah 53:5: **And with his stripes we are healed**—a perceived prophecy about physical healing that would one day come? It is because Isaiah 53 does not speak of future physical healing but of the fallen spiritual condition of man and how the coming Savior would remedy it. Isaiah 53:4–5 says:

> **Surely he hath borne our griefs, and carried our sorrows: yet we did esteem him stricken, smitten of God, and afflicted. But he was wounded for our transgressions, he was bruised for our iniquities: the chastisement of our peace was upon him; and with his stripes we are healed.**

Isaiah is specifically referring to spiritual healing and forgiveness of sins. Isaiah 53:6 continues: **All we like sheep have gone astray; we have turned every one to his own way; and the Lord hath laid on him the iniquity of us all**. The entire context speaks of the coming Savior who would one day replace the old system of animal sacrifice for sin, which would heal humanity's alienation from God by a different method. Yes, we are healed—from sin! Physical healing was therefore not a guaranteed provision by the cross of Christ. This conclusion is not drawn from an unbelief that physical healing isn't possible, nor is it by neglect of Scripture—but by the exact opposite! It is through great faith in a sovereign God and exegesis of the biblical text.

The New Testament reveals the real meaning of the Isaiah 53:5 phrase **with his stripes we are healed**. In Matthew 8:16–17, after Jesus had cast out devils and healed many that were sick, Matthew explained how this was the fulfillment of Isaiah's prophecy of the coming Savior: **That it might be fulfilled which was spoken by Isaiah the prophet, saying, Himself took our infirmities, and bare our sicknesses**. Matthew refers only to the miracles which Jesus performed during His earthly ministry and as evidence that Isaiah's prophecy had come to pass. Matthew specifically did not say that Jesus bore our sicknesses "on His cross." We must carefully read and compare Isaiah 53 with Matthew 8. Jesus bore the infirmities of humanity during His earthly ministry because of His common human condition: He observed with compassion and healed their infirmities—bearing them upon Himself. In the context of Matthew's explanation of Isaiah 53:5, we then discern that the "stripes" that Jesus bore were of His wounded spirit: **Surely he hath borne our griefs, and carried our sorrows** (Isaiah 53:4).

In the Church Age we live in, we are guaranteed only to be healed from sin, just as Isaiah prophesied. A promise of physical healing because of Jesus's atonement on the cross cannot be interpreted from Isaiah 53:5. As other passages also indicate, perfect healing and health is guaranteed only in a future tense—at the resurrection of the dead. Before that time, we will be physically healed only if it is the Father's divine will. We cannot claim or command physical healing because of the cross of Calvary. Rather, we ask for healing according to the will of the Father. We should not doubt but ask in faith because we believe that God *is able* to heal.

In truth, our universe is directed and governed by the sovereignty of our Father in heaven. Our own declarations and prayers of faith cannot demand God's power over us. If they could, God has then lost His sovereignty for our assumed position and chieftain of divine command. This belief theoretically nullifies His Lordship. Unfortunately, this concept is what the Faith teachers of *positive confession* don't seem to grasp.

We see in the New Testament that at times, Jesus and His disciples imparted immediate and complete healing to people who were sick or infirmed. In Luke 9:1, we read: **Then he called his twelve disciples together, and gave them power and authority over all devils, and to cure diseases**. Jesus has not since bestowed this same power and authority on every Christian. Again this is not doubt or disbelief that divine healing can happen but is discernment of what the text does not say. If we apply this divine power of Luke 9:1 to every believer today, we must also apply what follows in Luke 9:2–3 (NIV) as well: **He sent them out to preach the Kingdom of God and to heal the sick. He told them: Take nothing for the journey…no staff, no bag, no bread, no money**. Since no subsequent text tells that every believer has this same power or the same command to give up their livelihood to go and preach the Gospel—and to heal afflicted people and to take no food or money—we know that this was a divine power that Jesus gave at a specific time…and only to specific people.

After this, Jesus sent out another seventy to prepare the way before Him. When the seventy returned, they gave a great report, saying: **Even the devils are subject unto us through thy name** (Luke 10:17). Jesus said to them: **Behold, I give you power to tread on serpents and scorpions, and over all the power of the enemy: and nothing shall by any means hurt you** (Luke 10:19). These seventy had power over devils only because Jesus had given it to them in particular.

Today, God's healing power has not run dry. Contrary to the teachers of total cessationism, the apostolic gift of healing has not ceased or waned but remains upon those who have been given this particular gift, just as the first twelve apostles experienced for a time. It is God's divine will to either heal or not to heal at a particular moment in time. Jesus understood this: He didn't just go around healing everyone who needed it but was sensitive to His Father's will. In John, chapter 5, there were many infirmed people lying beside Jerusalem's Pool of Bethesda, but Jesus healed only one man! Though miracles of healing still happen just as in the days of Jesus and the apostles, we must discern and test the spirits. A spirit of false prophecy will say, "*It is always God's will to heal.*" A spirit of Bible truth will say, "*Thy will be done.*"

In reality, God allows sickness and disease to happen—probably to remind us of our humanity or to slow us down, among many other reasons. Yet some do not receive total healing though great prayers of faith are sent up to the throne of God. Why? It is for God's glory! God is lifted up in the eyes of unbelievers when they see the faith and steadfastness of Christians who are persecuted or remain sick and diseased: they are in distress yet still trusting in God! Though God's healing power is a witness to the unbeliever, remaining faithful to Christ, even though one is diseased or distressed, is an even greater witness to the authority of God and heaven's hope. When we are distressed with the adversity of life's circumstances, it is synonymous to physical suffering. Second Corinthians 1:5–7 (NIV) explains much: Paul says, **For just as the sufferings of Christ flow over into our lives, so also through Christ our comfort overflows. If we are distressed, it is for your comfort and salvation...because we know that just as you share in our sufferings, so also you share in our comfort.**

The King James Version also uses the word "sufferings" here, which is described in Strong's Concordance as "hardship," "pain," and "affliction." If a prayer of faith can relieve physical suffering, then couldn't it also relieve any other kind of hardship? Surely it could! So why doesn't it always? Simply because all the distress we experience in life was the very same distress Jesus Himself either had to endure or was in acquaintance with when He lived among us.

Why does a disease such as cancer not always stay in retreat or be totally removed even when we pray in great faith? The reason is this: Jesus said, **Ye are the salt of the earth...Ye are the light of the world... Let your light shine before men, that they may see your good works, and glorify your Father which is in heaven** (Matthew 5:13–16). The salt, light, and good works Jesus spoke of here is the faithfulness and steadfast trust in God through all of life's circumstances—even amidst the adversity of sickness and disease. These good works are not inferred as acts of healing by believers but that daily time spent with God produces love and good works, giving God glory and honor to those around us.

We as humans have inherited Adam and Eve's sin: we have reaped the consequence of listening to the deceiver, which ultimately has led to physical infirmities. When Jesus lived among humanity, He had compassion on this condition of suffering. Yet the New Testament reveals that Jesus didn't heal everyone who needed it—sometimes for their unbelief and other times for the fact that it was not His Father's will.

But wait! What about James 5:14–15? **Is any sick among you? Let him call for the elders of the church; and let them pray over him, anointing him with oil in the name of the Lord. And the prayer of faith shall save the sick, and the Lord shall raise him up**.

Shouldn't we determine from this passage that sickness must always flee if we use the name of the Lord? No, we must know the meaning of key words in this passage. In verse 14, the Greek word for "sick" is "diseased," "feeble," or "weak," but in verse 15, the word for "sick" means "faint" or "wearied." When inserting these words in place of only "sick," we come away with a slightly different view—especially when reading the rest of verse 15: **And if he have committed sins, they shall be forgiven him**. Meditating on the fullness of verse 15 alone and replacing the word "sick" with "faint," we see how the apostle James is trying to encourage those who are weak and weary in the faith to continue on, even if they have fallen back into sin.

(The King James translators perhaps assumed a continuation of the same thought from verse 14 into verse 15 and therefore used the word "sick" again. But Strong's Concordance, among other resources for understanding the Hebrew and Greek lexicons, clarifies seemingly incongruent or confusing issues for us.)

The Bible answers our questions about why physical healing does not always happen. In the documentation of the life of Jesus, we find that whenever he healed someone, the Greek word used was either *therapeuo* or *iaomai*, meaning "cure" or "make whole": in other words, "completely healed." In Matthew 10:1, Jesus gives His disciples power to go out and *therapeuo* all who were sick. But in Mark 16:17–18, just before He ascended into heaven, Jesus tells His disciples: **And these signs shall follow them that believe; In my name they shall cast out devils; they shall speak with new tongues;… they shall lay hands on the sick, and they shall recover**. Here Jesus said that those who follow Him would do great wonders, including casting out devils! But when He said that the sick shall "recover," the Greek word used was *kalos*, meaning "to make well" or "begin to amend." This word has a technically different inference from *therapeuo*, which means "perfectly cured and restored from disease."

This seems to be an obscured detail—a point that the Faith teachers have somehow missed. It may be disappointing to learn, but in fact, Jesus didn't say that the sick would always be totally healed or made whole unto perfect physical restoration in the same way that He healed the sick during His ministry. There are times, when in God's Sovereignty, that one is totally healed and may live many years afterward in perfect health. But this is not what Jesus promised for every prayer of faith for the sick. I have observed many times in my own life that through prayers of faith, the sick or diseased person may recover from their illness for a time; however, the reality is that most people will get sick and die from an illness or a degenerating condition. We have no promise in Scripture for perfect health until the end of our days. This isn't a negative unbelief that total and miraculous healing cannot occur—because certainly it can! However, we must align our understanding with Scripture. It's not a defeating blow for them that are sick but of hope for at least a period of relief and perhaps of total restoration. If you've been totally healed for many years from a disease such as cancer, which should have taken your life long ago, then you are among the very fortunate whom God has chosen to "make whole." However, we will all someday lose our mortal body to death, unless we are alive at the return of Jesus.

Jesus stated: **These things I have spoken unto you, that in me you might have peace. In the world you shall have tribulation; but be of good cheer, I have overcome the world** (John 16:33 NKJV).

The word "tribulation" here not only means "trouble" and "distress" but also "affliction." Is the trouble and distress we experience in life always removed when we pray a prayer of faith over that circumstance? No. Then why would physical affliction always be completely and permanently removed? All things are subject to God's divine will. Yes, we should pray for healing and for relief from suffering. But we should also consider what Jesus stated in John 16:33—that the joy and peace we gain from abiding in Him overcomes in the midst of trouble, distress, and even physical affliction.

Paul spoke of his **thorn in the flesh** in 2 Corinthians 12:7. His infirmities, reproaches, and necessities, as he says, were to emphasize his own weakness and feebleness in himself...and so were to the glory of God.

In Dr. Walter Martin's excellent teaching sermon titled "Does God Always Heal?" (YouTube), the apologist for Bible truth said:

> *There has arisen in our day, a whole new school of people teaching doctrine that is partially true, and partially false. What is true will bless you...what is false can become a cruel imposition of an authority which is not based in Scripture, but in emotion, and in ignorance, and misinterpretation of the Scriptures.* (27:15)

Martin stated he would likely be accused of being hostile toward other brethren who had opposing biblical views on healing. He said: "*That's right...I am eternally hostile to false teachings!*" Dr. Martin explained that he still loved and accepted his Christian brethren who taught falsely and then added: "*But we must test every doctrine according to the Scriptures.*"

In this particular sermon by Walter Martin, he spent a great deal of time in 1 Peter 2:21–25 as the perfect example of why the context of thought is so vital for understanding Scripture. Here Peter is in no wise referring to physical healing as a promised benefit of the cross of Christ. Rather, the clear emphasis in context is spiritual healing through Christ's suffering and that we must at times suffer for His sake as well. In 1 Peter 2:24, we see Peter's reference to Isaiah 53:5: **By whose stripes you were healed**. By neglecting Peter's narrative prior to verse 24 and immediately after in verse 25, we've missed the point of Christ's suffering and atonement for our salvation. But by reading the full text, we find that when **returning unto the Shepherd and Bishop of your souls** (verse 25), we become healed only spiritually. But today's "*name it and claim it*" pastors have twisted the text to say that Jesus purchased our salvation *and* our perfect physical health—only because they saw the word "healed" in verse 24. Easily discovering that the Concordance reveals this word means only a generic "cure," we must establish by the context of Isaiah 53 and 1 Peter 2 that both Peter and Isaiah are focused on spiritual healing only.

If physical healing is guaranteed for every Christian—only for believing it—then why do so many Christians die from sickness and disease? In his sermon "Does God Always Heal?" Dr. Walter Martin stated profoundly:

> ***There is one illness from which you will never recover. Your last one.***

First John 5:14 makes it very clear that God's will supersedes our will: **And this is the confidence that we have in him, that, if we ask any thing according to his will, he heareth us**. We cannot assume therefore that it is God's obligation to do anything we ask simply because we pray in faith for it. It is only according to His will that we receive. God does as He pleases in our lives—**God has mercy on whom He will have mercy** (Romans 9:18 BSV).

Realize also, it is the mercy and compassion of God to send a terminal disease on the sinner, for the simple reason that it forces them to consider the Gospel and respond to it—knowing that eternity is just around the corner. God's love and perseverance compels us to think beyond this life.

In 1 Corinthians 1:5, Paul tells what to do with an immoral brother who does not repent: **To deliver such an one unto Satan for the destruction of the flesh, that the spirit may be saved in the day of the Lord Jesus**. Is this Paul's wish for cruel treatment of the sinner? No! It is his proclamation of God's compassion!

In the atonement that Jesus made for us, the promised benefits are forgiveness of sins, freedom form sickness and disease, and an eternal glorified body. But no one here on earth has yet received a glorified immortal body. We therefore cannot expect to have total freedom from sickness and disease before our entrance into heaven. The only part of the atonement that we are assured of in this life is forgiveness of sins.

Since we live in a fallen world, sickness and disease is part of it. For the most part, it's not an attack from the devil as some believe. Rather, it is the natural result of the fall of Adam and Eve. Nonetheless, infirmities and shortcomings are used by God to glorify Himself. When Moses complained to God that he could not talk to the people because his speech was not eloquent enough, God replied to him: **Who makes the dumb, or the deaf, or the seeing, or the blind? Have not I the Lord**? (Exodus 4:11).

In Deuteronomy 32:39, God says: **I kill, and I make alive; I wound, and I heal: neither is there any that can deliver out of my hand**.

We also read in Isaiah 45:7 that God says: **I form the light and create darkness: I make peace, and create evil: I the Lord do all these things**.

When we consider that it was man who first sinned, we know exactly why God kills, wounds, causes sickness and death, and creates evil. It is because of our own rebellion and the sin of pride.

Job 42:11 shows us where Job's affliction came from: **Then came there unto him all his brethren...and comforted him over all the evil that the Lord had brought upon him**. It was the Lord who tested Job with affliction!

These verses are clear evidence that sickness, disease, infirmity, distress, and loss are allowed by and at times caused by God.

We are, however, responsible for one thing: 1 Corinthians 11:26–30 states that we are condemned for not having a contrite and repentant heart before God when partaking the "cup" of His blood poured out for us and in the "bread" of His body broken for us. Verse 30 says: **For this cause many are weak and sickly among you, and many sleep**. God allows some to become sick or infirmed—sometimes unto death. We bring it on by our own sin and disobedience to the one true Gospel.

Putting faith in faith?

Within some Christian circles, it is now commonly taught that faith is a "substance" or "force" through which reality is birthed. But there is great error in this teaching, leading to a self-centered kind of supernatural supply of heaven's resource for any child of God who just believes for it. This is not the biblical Gospel of faith.

Here is where the Faith teachers err: The King James Version of Hebrews 11:1 says, **Now faith is the substance of things hoped for, the evidence of things not seen**.

The Concordance reveals the word "faith" is a common noun, and the word "substance" means "assurance" or "confidence"—an adjective. Rereading the verse with this insight, we see it takes on a different meaning: **Now faith is the [assurance] of things hoped for**. The adjective applies to the noun, even though the noun is stated first. The King James translators used the word "substance" to describe "faith," which causes some readers to synonymize both words—that our "faith" is a "substance" (both words being nouns), which is improper and confusing within the structure of written communication. Rather, our faith is "a faith of confidence," not a "force" that brings to pass whatever we desire: our faith is not a tangible resource we tap into. This verse therefore cannot be interpreted to say that our faith causes reality but that our faith is described as "our confidence."

Hebrews 11:1 has been perverted by carnal Christians as a pivotal power point for success and the abundantly blessed life. In reality, the writer's thought here is that our faith is simply the assurance of God, heaven, and eternal life. God Himself is our confidence: He is the "substance" of our faith.

Having great faith is not praying hard enough and believing hard enough to make something happen. If we could make something happen by only believing hard enough, then this faith is indeed a tangible substance, and we therefore don't need God in our lives! Instead, we need only the faith of believe-ism optimism for whatever we need or want. Obviously, this is not the thought behind Hebrews 11:1, especially when reading just a few verses later that our faith should encourage us to put confidence in the Lord—**Looking unto Jesus the author and finisher of our faith** (Hebrews 12:2). Our faith and hope is in God alone. There is no such thing as putting faith in faith. Doing this leaves God out of the equation.

Luke 18:35–43 tells of a blind man who needed only to ask Jesus for his sight. Jesus replied: **Receive thy sight: thy faith hath saved thee**.

Did the man's blind eyes become seeing eyes only because he had confidence that he would one day see? No! The man had heard that the Great Healer, Jesus of Nazareth, was approaching, and he cried out: **Thou son of David, have mercy on me!** The man knew that Jesus had the power to heal him because He was the Son of God. Jesus not only granted sight to the man but also told him that his faith had saved him—he gained eternal life! The blind man happened to be in the right place at the right time—when the Son of God was passing by. If this blind man had never met Jesus, would he have ever received his sight for putting faith in his faith that it would one day happen? No! He needed to have a personal spiritual "faith encounter" with the Savior Himself.

Chapter 8

The Prosperity Doctrine

In the last many decades, we in America and other affluent countries around the world have in general enjoyed the abundance of prosperity and "the good life." Is it for having believed in Jesus and His Gospel? Of course not! The majority of low-income, middle-class, moderately successful, and the affluent have no interest in the Gospel Jesus preached. Most in society are either trapped in false religions or give no attention to spiritual things whatsoever. But when the Gospel is accurately shared with them, and they are drawn to the Savior—being convicted of their sin—the realization of spiritual things comes alive, leaving social classification, ethnicity, or personal status and accomplishments irrelevant. **There is neither Jew nor Greek, neither bond nor free, neither male nor female: for ye are all one in Christ Jesus** (Galatians 3:28).

As time passes, the deception of apostasy (the unperceived departure from sound doctrine) comes in diverse manner and in waves of ignorant enthusiasm. The *prosperity gospel* is a major form of apostasy that has crippled the testimony of Jesus within the church today. A vast number of Christians now believe that Christianity and prosperity go hand in hand. However, the New Testament does not unite the Gospel of salvation with financial prosperity, except by the twisting of Scripture.

The excitement of financial gain will naturally overtake the heart of the believer if the Gospel is not prioritized. When a pastor convinces the congregation of God's supposed great plan to prosper His people, our spiritual eyes become unfocused and lured to carnal things. This false-teaching pastor may not divulge the many Bible passages warning of the snares of riches. Why? Because he himself is snared with deception: he has become an apostate pastor for not discerning any distinction between a "spiritual Gospel" and a "material gospel." We therefore cannot treat the *prosperity gospel* as having any part of the Gospel of salvation.

Proverbs 1:22 says: **How long, ye simple ones, will ye love simplicity? and the scorners delight in their scorning, and fools hate knowledge?**

Do you think Solomon's proverb might have been intended only for the foolish, unregenerate, and unbelieving mocker of God? Not necessarily. Read Solomon's very next words in verse 23: **Turn you at my reproof: behold, I will pour out my spirit unto you, I will make known my words unto you**.

The warning in verse 22 is followed by wise counsel in verse 23: it was meant for those who have at least some awareness of an Almighty God. If you keep reading all the way to verse 33, you'll be astonished: every sentence is a warning to any who scoff at searching for God's wisdom. This would include today's deceived Christians who inwardly mock those who proclaim the importance of biblical knowledge and doctrine. A knowledge of God's love, which provides only for the material and financial blessings of life, is ignorance of the scriptures and has no merit over the spiritual Gospel. Seeing God's love only through His material blessings disparages spiritual wisdom. With eternity in mind, spiritual wisdom should far supersede any benefit of material gain in this short life we live. Jesus stated in Luke 12:15 (NKJV): **Take heed and beware of covetousness: for a man's life consists not in the abundance of the things which he possesses**.

Though the Gospel of the Great Commission is simple, it also requires wisdom to share it. When sharing with others a gospel that includes additional earthly benefits, we are guilty of perverting God's Word. Proverbs 1:32 states: **For the turning away of the simple shall slay them, and the prosperity of fools shall destroy them**.

Can this proverb apply to believers in Jesus? Yes! Are there any foolish Christians today? Yes! In Proverbs 1:32, the word "simple" means "seducible." The seducible Christian who turns from the wisdom and knowledge of the one true Gospel will eternally weep in sorrow, just as Jesus warned. They will be in no better condition than the sinner who never accepted Jesus as Savior—eternally gnashing their teeth in anger against God.

Connecting two theological myths

The supposed spiritual victory of the *born-again Jesus* is directly linked to the doctrine of Christian prosperity. As some say, "*Jesus lost it all so that we might gain it all.*" This justifies why Jesus was spiritually *born again* and that Christian prosperity is the result. Seduced carnally minded Christians see these two theological myths as biblical truth. But false doctrine linked with more false doctrine results in acute false doctrine.

Those who preach the authoritative and financially triumphant *prosperity gospel* are esteemed and revered for revealing the supposed truth of what is contained in God's Word. Rarely are these pastors scorned or restrained within their own church but are greatly loved and admired for bringing the hope of financial security and a sense of control over adverse circumstances. Therefore, the listener who believes these doctrinal lies doesn't want to investigate any further. Why should they? They have all the dynamic tools and potential needed for getting everything they want in life—the promise of perfect health, a declaration of success, prosperity, and a better future. But in blindsided ignorance, these tools for earthly success and good health—extracted from misapplied and misunderstood passages—actually remove us far from the Christ-centered saving doctrine of the real Gospel. The health and prosperity doctrine seems to accommodate our need for earthly survival and success. Yet if Jesus had taught such an earthly advantageous Gospel, for what would He have been crucified?

The teachings of the apostle Paul oppose any such doctrine of financial abundance and material gain. He tells the body of Christ at Rome to be **patient in tribulation** (Romans 12:12). Here, the word "tribulation" means "affliction," "persecution," and "trouble." The church at Rome was under great persecution at that time. Today, in free countries around the world, the church is not under any such distress, and because of this, a concocted gospel rendering a successful, happy, and contented earthly life thrives in that environment. We therefore cannot relate to the affliction of the first-century church at Rome, and we might rationally conclude that those poor Christians who lived in Rome long ago just couldn't muster the same kind of faith we have today. Or they simply weren't aware of the *New Revelation* of Jesus the Savior we now have. Right? If so, we have a dichotomy against Scripture: the Faith teachers continue to preach repentance from sin but with a direct association to the *born-again Jesus* and the *prosperity doctrine* also preached alongside it. To them, there is no disconnect between salvation and prosperity: there is no severance of the Gospel of Jesus, from perfect health and financially favorable circumstances. All are linked together as the totality of a biblical gospel that makes sense—mainly because of the tactful method used to fuse them together. And yet Paul told the Philippian church: **I count all things but loss for the excellency of the knowledge of Christ Jesus my Lord: for whom I have suffered the loss of all things** (Philippians 3:8).

Yes, the great man of faith, Paul the apostle, deemed the loss of every material thing, career advancement, and all earthly satisfaction as meaningless in exchange for the knowledge of Christ Jesus. Paul's conviction and perspective is an astounding contrast to today's gospel of earthly benefits still being preached in the Christian media and in many churches.

Seeds of money and tithing

In these last years of the Church Age, God has allowed Satan to deceive the seducible Christian, thus causing a distinctive contrast of belief between those focused only on the Gospel of Jesus from those who justify an added prosperity theology to it. Christians swayed by this wonderful prosperity plan are bound to the false works of mandated tithing and generous perpetually planted "money seeds" to reap a future harvest of financial blessing for themselves. It's a kind of side-gig benefit—a *"give to get"* welfare security.

The entirety of the *prosperity doctrine* begins with and leans heavily on tithing. For well over a century, much of the church has heard "*we should tithe because God commands it.*" According to the doctrine of New Testament faith, this is false teaching and has now digressed farther down the road to "*If you want to prosper and be successful in the kingdom of God, you must begin tithing.*" Nowhere does the New Testament state this. The Gospel of salvation is clearly separated from possessions, money, and especially mandated tithing, as we will soon prove.

There's nothing wrong with giving 10 percent to your Gospel-preaching church, but by carefully calculating the amount to make sure of your blessing—or that God isn't offended—you have thus procured your own false blessing! You have placed yourself under the curse of the old Mosaic Law just as Galatians 3:10 (NIV) states: **All who rely on observing the law are under a curse**. Why can't tithe pastors understand this simple verse? It plainly states we cannot add any works to the new covenant to gain favor with God. If we do, we are cursed!

The New Testament gives clear direction to today's Christian regarding our deeds: we are no longer vindicated for our sin by sacrificing animals, and neither is tithing to the Lord required. Paul says we are cursed when relying on any performance of the old law. It's a curse caused by ignorance of the simple Gospel of salvation, propagated by the false teachers of our day. We have bought into the lie of Satan, the deceiver, who hates what Jesus did. But the bondage of ignorant works is easily removed by knowledge—the knowledge that comes from studying God's Word. Read the New Testament! Don't add any "works" to the Gospel of Jesus! The supposed "tithing command" is not a test from God to see if you can be obedient every payday. The doctrine of tithing is the statutes of the Mosaic Law!

In Matthew 13, Jesus speaks directly against wealth procured by money management and manipulation in direct association with the Gospel. He said: **He that also received the seed among the thorns is he that hears the word; and the care of this world; and the deceitfulness of riches, choke the word, and he becomes unfruitful** (Matthew 13:22 NKJV).

When carefully discerning the words of Jesus, we realize they very much apply to the false prosperity teaching we hear today. A prosperity doctrine applied to the Gospel of salvation becomes our personal monetary investment in the kingdom of God. It sounds somewhat justifiable, though in reality, the Savior exposes it as our "unfruitful" works for the ulterior motive of financial gain. The manipulative Christian prosperity mindset rapidly leads us into the deceitfulness of riches, as Jesus warned in Matthew 13:22 and also Mark 4:19.

Nowhere in the New Testament is seed referred to as money. Especially here in Matthew 13:22, we know that "the seed" Jesus speaks of is only the spiritual Gospel. The simple phrase **he that hears the word** explains it perfectly: the **seed** is the spoken word; it does not refer to tangible things or money. Jesus said that though the seed of the Gospel is at first gladly received, a deceitfulness of wealth can in many ways highjack our righteous intent. The prosperity doctrine has accomplished exactly this. We hear from the pulpit that "*tithing is obedience to the gospel*" and that our financial struggle will be relieved because God will prosper and bless us if we follow this biblical method. If we believe it and follow the direction of the false teachers, we have fallen prey to the ear ticklers of our time, and it will produce nothing more than the **unfruitful deceitfulness of riches**, as Jesus said.

This single verse, Matthew 13:22, perfectly severs the seed of the spiritual Gospel from the seed for earthly prosperity: there is no such union of the two. These disjoined ideals actually offend each other. To the mature believer who is sanctified unto Christ, this isn't an issue to consider or worry about because they've long since relinquished all their finances unto the Lord and are happy to give a general tithe amount to their church if able. But to the undiscerning ear and to carnal immature Christians, the pastors' stated tithe proposition of a *planted money seed* into the Gospel is easily rerouted in the mind as the method to reap a selfish financial harvest. And for some, the tithing and seed-giving strategy does provide prosperity for them! It works because Satan the deceiver wants to separate Christians from the one true Gospel. He has succeeded through the seductive idea that tithing and generous giving justifies the *prosperity doctrine*. If riches increase, you're hooked! If riches do not increase, the prosperity preacher tells you, "*Be patient—God is testing you to see if you can remain faithful and obedient to Him.*" But again Jesus said in Matthew 13:22: **The care of this world, and the deceitfulness of riches, choke the word**. When the manipulation of our money takes precedence—being used in double standard toward a spiritual Gospel and a material gospel simultaneously—we thereby choke the Word of God, becoming spiritually unfruitful.

Delusions of grandeur and the promise of economic ease are sought after by carnal Christians for thinking they have found the key to God's promise of increase. In discernment of the New Testament, however, we find that prosperity is not a promise from God but, in many cases, is actually a curse from God for believing in a different gospel. It's a similar analogy to the homosexual insight given in Romans 1:26—**For this cause God gave them up unto vile affections**. Just as "gay Christians" are deceived with no conviction of their sin, so also is the "prospering Christian" deceived when, for the sake of personal benefit, they ignore or do not discern the warning from Jesus about linking spiritual seed with earthly riches. God gives them up to their vile affections for money, and they wallow in its filth—all the while believing they have found the biblical principles of prosperity through tithing and generous giving. Christians have been duped by the imaginations of *New Revelation* prosperity teaching—and further supported by tithe testimonials of the "*miracles of increase*" façade.

Financial seed sowing is not the teaching of Galatians 6:7–8: this passage indicates the kind of seed that will produce spiritual fruitfulness or spiritual unfruitfulness—a seed of the flesh versus a seed of the spirit. In no wise does Paul speak of a physical seed, such as money, that can produce a spiritual harvest—but only a harvest to the flesh…reaping corruption. **For he that soweth to his flesh shall of the flesh reap corruption; but he that soweth to the Spirit shall of the Spirit reap life everlasting** (Galatians 6:8). We can apply "seeds of money" to the first part of this passage but not to the last part. In a literal sense, a physical seed sown produces more of the same kind of seed. Likewise, when carnally minded believers are lured by the false "money seed" teaching of prosperity preachers, they begin sowing seeds of money into their church or a ministry, expecting their financial future to be brighter. Yet they have perpetuated their own love of money! If a money tithe is a seed, it then should produce a money harvest, just as grain seed produces more grain. This is why Jesus referred to "the seed" as the Gospel: it is the spiritual and intangible Word of eternal life. The currency of heaven is righteousness, peace, and joy. It is produced by the "seed of the Gospel message" which is planted in the hearts of men and women.

In Acts 20:35, Paul says: **Remember the words of the Lord Jesus, when he said, It is more blessed to give than to receive**. When applying the concept of "seeds of money" to this verse, we know that we should not and cannot give money to any worthy cause with the expectancy of getting more money in return. This is why the *prosperity gospel* does not work as a legitimate gospel that produces a harvest of souls: the kingdom of God does not operate in the physical realm of money. In today's structure of the church, money seems to be needed to aid in spreading the sincere Gospel message. But the seeds of money given toward the preaching of a *prosperity gospel* will produce only the nurturing of more prosperity teaching, rather than a harvest of souls who seek eternal life through righteousness in Christ. Jesus explained it is impossible to serve two masters; hence, the Gospel of the Bible and a Christian prosperity doctrine do not mix. Souls are purchased only with the "seed of the gospel"—the knowledge of the Gospel of salvation.

The Old Testament speaks of "seed" as literal grain. The New Testament identifies "seed" in metaphoric terms only:

- Jesus—in Galatians 3:16, Jesus, **which is Christ**, was the seed of Abraham.
- God's Word—in Luke 8:11, Jesus said: **The seed is the word of God**—sown in the hearts of men.
- God's chosen—in Matthew 13:38, Jesus said: **The field is the world, and the good seed represents the sons of the kingdom**.
- Giving to the poor—in 2 Corinthians 9:10–11, Paul says: **He has given to the poor: his righteousness remains forever. He that ministers seed to the sower both minister bread for your food, and multiply your seed sown, and increase the fruits of your righteousness**.

In the last passage, the seed could be thought of as money given to the poor to buy food: hence, the seed sown is then multiplied and actually becomes the fruits of your righteousness. This passage would also indicate that giving money to facilitate the organization of our church has nothing to do with our righteousness. The main theme of the full passage (2 Corinthians 9:5–12) is not so much about sowing the Gospel seed but is an encouragement to not be hesitant to help others—especially the poor.

Nowhere does the Bible refer to seed as money. We cannot bargain for God's favor: it cannot be purchased with money given to your church or a Christian ministry or a televangelist. This is manipulation of Holy Scripture and has led to deception and sin within the body of Christ. The New Testament calls us to be generous with our money yet discerning as well. Bogus charlatans of scam and greed are everywhere—especially on Christian television. Many phony "Christian ministries" do not prioritize the saving Gospel but spend airtime asking for money. Viewers desperate for financial relief or physical healing are coerced to "*call or go online right now and plant that seed to receive your blessing!*" We hear them say: "*Don't delay because delayed obedience is disobedience.*" This is part of their deceitful tactic; they know that if you delay sending them money, you will surely have enough time to realize the stupidity of what you were about to do.

However, giving a *firstfruits* offering unto the Lord is still an appropriate way to give in the new covenant era. The biblical *firstfruits* concept is to thank and honor God (Proverbs 3:9–10)—different from the tithing command, which was to provide food for festival feasts and to feed the poor.

When verbally stating that you are giving "*a seed offering,*" it then becomes idolatry because it places the act of giving a money seed as means to an end and thus justifies an expectancy of future material increase and success. Instead, we should give solely for the benefit of the receiver and to help spread the Gospel. Once given, it should be forgotten. In Matthew 6:3, Jesus said: **Do not let your left hand know what your right hand is doing**. When reading this verse within its context, we see how Jesus was talking about giving to the needs of the poor. And when we sow the seed of the Gospel—the Word of God—into someone's life (Luke 8:11), a harvest of souls—not money—is then reaped through prayer.

In truth, the Bible simply states that the believer should give their life unto God, with the hope and promise of eternal life in return. The New Testament's strong suggestion of generosity does not imply that future prosperity or a financial breakthrough will follow…but simply that our own needs will be met if we are generous to others.

> **Give and it shall be given unto you; good measure pressed down and shaken together and running over shall men give into your bosom. For with the same measure that ye mete withal it shall be measured to you again.** (Luke 6:38)

This indicates that God will take abundant care of us if we practice generosity—that whatever we give away will be meted back to us. Notice that Jesus says nothing about giving money specifically here. There are many ways to give other than financially. We have all been given certain gifts and abilities. Giving from the abundance of one's gift and ability should be the lifestyle of a believer. Yet Luke 6:38 is often applied by carnally minded Christians as a component of a biblical gospel that brings wealth—a continuous pursuit of maintaining financial security by giving more and more money to the church. Considering what Jesus said about the love of money in other passages, we know this was not His intended message here in Luke 6:38.

The new covenant of grace

In the Old Testament, God's laws of obedience given to Moses are referred to as "ordinances"—a duty of works. These commanded laws showed the Israelites that they were unrighteous before God unless these ordinances were performed and until the Messiah would come. When the Messiah did come, the Jews didn't recognize Him because they were anticipating a mighty leader from the line of King David who would rule with an iron fist, crushing the Roman Empire. Since, however, Jesus was overpowered by Roman rule, even His own people, as a whole, rejected Him as the Messiah. A handful of Jesus's disciples and those who later believed on Him wrote our New Testament which, in perfect exegetical debate, should change every religious preconception about the former Mosaic laws within Judaism. Jesus the Messiah, the High Priest of a new covenant, which is offered to all mankind, replaced the old Mosaic covenant by His death on the cross. Though all ordinances of the Old Testament's Levitical-Mosaic laws remain as a record of indictment against sin, the New Testament tells us they are now replaced with simple trust in the death, burial, and resurrection of the Lord Jesus Christ to cancel the debt of sin.

The Israelites' tithe laws were part of the ordinances of commanded sacrifice. Today these ordinances have disappeared because of the new covenant. Colossians 2:13–14 says: **And you, being dead**

in your sins and the uncircumcision of your flesh, hath he quickened together with him, having forgiven you all trespasses; blotting out the handwriting of ordinances that was against us, and took it out of the way, nailing it to his cross.

Correctly interpreting this passage, we find that our sins, in addition to the old laws, were nailed to the cross of Christ. But just as we must forsake our sin to be forgiven it, we must also change our understanding of the ordinances of the old law. We must turn from all past works and accept the full blessing and freedom of a new day in Jesus the Savior.

An amazingly straightforward passage is Acts 13:39: Paul says, **And by him all that believe are justified from all things from which ye could not be justified by the laws of Moses.**

You can't get any clearer than that. If we believe in the necessity of any part of the old covenant law, we have justified it in spite of the redemptive work of Jesus! We have retained the mindset of old covenant law, just as do current-day Jews who reject Jesus the Messiah. Most tithers haven't considered this; they think that both a belief in Jesus and tithing are necessary, primarily because of what is written in Malachi, chapter 3. But as we have seen in New Testament passages, this is frustrating the work of the Holy Spirit, simply because it is a defunct method of obedience to God. Tithing is not a new covenant law or a kingdom law.

In Matthew 5:18, Jesus said: **I have not come to destroy the law…but to fulfill. Till heaven and earth pass, one jot or one tittle shall in no wise pass from the law till all be fulfilled.**

In other words, by His life, death, and resurrection, Jesus, the new High Priest, removed the Mosaic laws, severing them from the Ten Commandments till the end of human history.

Romans 3:20 states: **Therefore by the deeds of the law there shall no flesh be justified in his sight: for by the law is the knowledge of sin.**

Here, Paul is speaking of the entire law, including the Ten Commandments. But because the commandments are not something we perform as deeds, this understandably separated them from the additional ordinances of Moses.

Romans 3:26–28 explains further about discerning these laws: **That he might be just, and the justifier of him that believeth in Jesus. Where is boasting then? It is excluded. By what law? Of works? Nay: but by the law of faith. Therefore we conclude that a man is justified by faith without the deeds of the law**.

The text is easy to understand: the "law of faith" replaces the "law of works"! We are not justified or blessed in the slightest by doing any works of the old law!

Paul then says in Romans 4:4: **Now to him that worketh is the reward not reckoned of grace, but of debt**. What he means is when a man labors, he is justified to be paid for that labor; but when he labors for something that is a free gift, he labors in vain. Romans 4:5 then says: **But to him that worketh not, but believeth on him that justifieth the ungodly, his faith is counted for righteousness**. Therefore, we need not labor in tithing to gain God's favor.

Reading Romans 10:1 and beyond, grasping the significance of each statement leading into the next, we find it is to the believer's detriment to **have a zeal of God, but not according to knowledge**—which happens by **being ignorant of God's righteousness, and going about to establish their own righteousness, have not submitted themselves unto the righteousness of God**.

Paul's Letter to the church at Rome states many times that we cannot establish our own righteousness by performing any part of the law. As Romans 10:4 then indicates, **For Christ is the end of the law for righteousness to every one that believeth**. In the mindset that God is pleased when we "bring a tithe" or "pay the tithe," we pay the price for our ignorance of not understanding Paul's proclamation of faith! We are either "in Christ Jesus" or we are "in the law." We cannot be in both. Because of Christ, all works have ended! Jesus only is the new covenant of grace.

The Bible tells us we cannot be focused on two opposing realms at the same time. Jesus stated: **For where your treasure is, there will your heart be also. If therefore thine eye be single, thy whole body shall be full of light** (Matthew 6:21–22). Prayerfully meditate on the great wisdom Jesus gives us in surrounding text as well. Our financial success cannot possibly depend on tithing; when we believe it does, we sink into relentless anxiety—thinking that God will not or cannot provide for us unless we sacrifice the proper dollar amount! This strikes a chord, doesn't it? Stop focusing on the wrong thing! Peace and contentment is our reward when we separate our career and financial goals from the spiritual Gospel we believe in. Though God directs our steps in business and career, we must give higher prime concern to eternal matters. Jesus tells us we cannot unite an earthly prospering stratagem with the Gospel of eternal salvation. Neither can we unite Old Testament law with New Testament grace.

In Paul's Second Letter to the church at Corinth, he says:

> **To this day the same veil remains when the old covenant is read. It has not been removed, because only in Christ is it taken away. Even to this day when Moses is read, a veil covers their hearts. But whenever anyone turns to the Lord, the veil is taken away. Now the Lord is that Spirit, and where the Spirit of the Lord is, there is freedom**. (2 Corinthians 3:14–17 NIV)

Think of the severity of this passage. The synopsis here is that we are not in Christ because we are hindered by not fully accepting Jesus as our personal Lord, only because the old covenant is read in our congregations and proclaimed as truth for today—primary in Malachi 3:8–11, a pre-Messiah passage. The veil of the law has thus overshadowed our hearts! When a tithe pastor convinces you that the Israelites' food tithe has now become a money tithe within the church, in essence, the veil of the old law is fortified, separating us farther from the Gospel of the Savior.

Looking again at Galatians 3:10–11, the apostle Paul said: **For as many as are of the works of the law are under the curse...but that no man is justified by the law in the sight of God**. When reading the fullness of surrounding context, we see Paul is speaking of all works of the Mosaic law, which would include the responsibility of paying a calculated tithe amount.

Another fascinating fact is revealed when searching the Old Testament to find that Israelite laborers such as the blacksmith, ironsmith, silversmith, goldsmith, masons, and carpenters were not commanded to tithe from their earned income of money. Nowhere in Scripture do we find that money was a tithed commodity for the Israelites. This fact alone is enough to obliterate the doctrine that God has ever required anyone to give Him a tithe of money from their increase or income…proving that a mandated money tithe is a doctrine of man. This is not meant to be an antagonistic retort against those who teach tithing but a factual conclusion from Scripture to show just how far removed today's doctrine of tithing is in relation to the old covenant ordinances.

Obedience to the **tithes and offerings** ordinances stated in Malachi 3:8–10 is profoundly opposed in the straightforwardness of many passages in the book of Hebrews. Hebrews 7:18 (NIV) states: **The former regulation is set aside because it was weak and useless**. Hebrews 8:13 (NIV) says: **By calling this covenant "new," he has made the first one obsolete**. Hebrews 10:1–2 (NIV) also says: **The law is only a shadow of the good things that are coming—not the realities themselves. For this reason, it can never, by the same sacrifices repeated endlessly year after year, make perfect those who draw near to worship. If it could, would they not have stopped being offered?**

Particularly, in Hebrews, chapter 7, the writer states: **For the law made nothing perfect, but the bringing in of a better hope; by the which we draw nigh unto God** (Hebrews 7:19). Hebrews 7:22 then further clarifies: **By so much was Jesus made a surety of a better testament**.

If a technical tweak of the old tithing law thus defined and declared that we should now "tithe to Jesus" in the new covenant age, it would logically be stated as such within verse 22 or very near to it. Since it is not, we know that this **better testament** is distinctively referring to the rejection of all regulations, including tithing, within the Mosaic laws—which are expounded upon in Hebrews chapters 7 through 10. We therefore see something very wrong with today's teaching of mandated tithing as the means by which God will bless us. Being swayed by this false teaching as the method for gaining financial abundance, we have given no heed to the warning from Jesus in Matthew 6:24 and Luke 16:13 when he said: **Ye cannot serve God and mammon**. This word "serve" means "be in bondage to." Think carefully and seriously about this insight.

Within many mainstream denominations, tithing is commonly taught. In a 2012 *Signs of the Times* telecast aired on Better Life Broadcasting Network, a segment titled "Tithing Plain and Simple" was posted on YouTube. The half-hour program was an interview between host Willard Regester, MD, lay evangelist, and Adventist Stewardship Ministry director, G. Edward Reid, who explained and supported tithing from his perspective. When Dr. Regester asked Pastor Reid whether a Christian should tithe on their net income or their gross income, Reid answered: "*Well, that depends—do you want a net blessing or a gross blessing?*" Pastor Reid's answer was precisely what the prosperity doctrine is all about. It is giving more to God for the sake of receiving more from God. Near the end of the program, the two elderly gentlemen concurred between themselves saying, "*The poor are poor probably because they don't tithe.*" This is the most foolish and biblically ignorant statement I've ever heard in attestation of tithing. What about people in third world countries who are fortunate enough to have a job paying a dollar a day? Are they poor because they don't tithe to the Lord from that dollar? Hardly! God has placed the poor and the needy all over the world because those who are blessed with abundance need to learn compassion. Jesus said: **The poor you will always have with you, and you can help them any time you want** (Mark 14:7 NIV). If the poor remain poor because they don't tithe, Jesus would have emphatically stated: "*You will always have the poor with you—unless you teach them the laws of obedience.*"

Mandated tithing and generous giving for the purpose of blessing is works, and any law of works labors against the Gospel of salvation.

The Malachi connection

We can discern much wisdom and insight for living today's Christian life from the minor prophets of the Old Testament. The book of Malachi is no different. The basic theme of this last book of the Old Testament was in rebuking the people for having lost their first love. They had become lazy, bemoaning the ordinances that their ancestors were instructed in centuries earlier. But they were clueless and questioned: **Wherein have we despised thy name?** (Malachi 1:6)—which indicated the careless condition of their heart. It can be the same for us today: a selfish carelessness takes over when we become unfocused on spiritual things.

Nearly the entire book of Malachi is a warning only to the Levite priests—not to every Israelite. Today we've made the error of isolating a few verses from Malachi to rationalize that God still demands certain works of obedience. But Malachi's exact physiological instructions, such as not offering polluted bread upon the altar and not offering the lame and the sick animals for sacrifice (Malachi 1:7–8), makes no sense in the new covenant we now live under. Yet today, Malachi 3:8–11 is pinpointed as God's precise 10 percent formula for blessing His people. How so? In the same manner as the prophet Malachi exposed the condition of the priests' heart by their lackadaisical efforts, devout tithers must also be rebuked for insincerity toward and ignorance of the Gospel that Jesus preached. We must renew our first love with the God of our salvation. According to the correct understanding of the Malachi text, the Israelites were tithing the full amount, yet they were told it was insufficient. What was happening? Why was God so displeased?

First we should understand that the book of Malachi was written about four hundred years before Jesus came. The prophet warned of God's displeasure with the Levite priests because they were not performing the fullness of the laws. They were scolded in several areas, including their neglect to bring the "whole tithes." This didn't refer to a full 10 percent but referred to the pureness of the offering in sacrificing the unblemished of the herd and the freshest from the crops. The result of their deceit was a warning from God: **Neither will I**

accept an offering at your hand (Malachi 1:10). God accepted nothing they offered because it was not the very best. Today, living under God's new covenant, what we glean from the entirety of the book of Malachi is that God will not honor anything we give if not given with a pure heart and unselfish motive. When told that we must simply give 10 percent to be blessed, many of us give out of the boredom of thoughtless necessity. But by proper interpretation of the Malachi text, we see that this thoughtless way of giving becomes an insufficient offering—a "polluted offering"—the meaningless works of religion.

Beginning with Malachi 2:1, the entire following text specifically addresses only the Levite priests. Then according to Malachi 3:8–9, the Levite priests (and the whole nation of Israel) were cursed if the priests did not observe the prescribed tithe laws by keeping them "unblemished." Malachi 2:2 then becomes a favorite of tithe teachers to show how God will "curse your blessings" if you don't tithe. But once again, we need to read within the context: when seeing what comes before this warning, we find that this "curse" happened because they did not "take it to heart." To find out what Malachi was talking about, we need to back up even further. In Malachi 1:12–14, we see the reason for the curse was their carelessness in thinking a spotless sacrifice was not important. Since these ordinances have now disappeared, we should discern that it's not a specific 10 percent that God blesses but the mindset in which we give: it must be pure and spotless. When interpreting the 10 percent amount as the only requirement of the "tithes" of the Mosaic ordinances, we greatly err. We must read other passages from Malachi, chapters 2 and 3, and discover why this kind of instruction for blessing is here in this last book of the Old Testament. Malachi 2:9 states: **According as ye have not kept my ways but have been partial in the law**. The Levite priests addressed here were not keeping the fullness of the law. Then in verse 10, it says: **Why do we deal treacherously every man against his brother by profaning the covenant of our fathers?** It's interesting to see that this word "treacherously" in the Hebrew language is *bagad*, meaning "unfaithful," "to pillage," or "deal deceitfully"—against our fellow man. Here in the second chapter of Malachi, a theme is developing in the pillaging of God's best portion and also the portion meant for the needy—the fatherless, widows, and aliens—to **deal treacherously every man against his brother**. This wasn't the fault of Israelite farmers and ranchers who gave the required tithes; the fault lay with the Levite priests who were deceitful with the tithes collected—keeping the best for themselves and sacrificing the blemished animals unto the Lord.

Then in the middle of all these rebukes is the announcement of a coming deliverer—"the Messenger" of a coming new covenant. Malachi 3:1 begins by saying: **Behold I will send my messenger and he shall prepare the way before me: and the Lord whom ye seek shall suddenly come to his temple, even the messenger of the covenant.**

Jesus specifically refers to this passage in Matthew 11:10: John the Baptist is the first "messenger" spoken of in Malachi 3:1. But the prophet then states, **The Lord whom ye seek—the Messenger of the covenant** would soon come: it is Jesus the Messiah. This word "messenger" means "prophet" or "priest"; we therefore know that Jesus then became the Prophet of the new covenant: He alone is the new High Priest.

In Malachi 3:3–4, we see that the Messenger will **purge the sons of Levi...that they may offer unto the Lord an offering in righteousness**. How would this happen? Would the prophesied Messenger to come force the Levites to do their task of properly offering undefiled bread and sacrificing spotless animals and to enforce the proper distribution among the poor? No! In discerning the New Testament, we now know that the sons of Levi were purged by completely removing these tasks altogether, which makes the offering righteous by an entirely different method! It is the "offering of the Messenger"—the sacrifice of Jesus the Savior, who now gives all men the ability to offer our righteousness unto the Lord—without works.

In Malachi 3:5, we find another clue leading up to the curse for abusing the tithe: it says, **And I will come near to you to judgment; and I will be a swift witness against...those that oppress the hireling in his wages, the widow and the fatherless and that turn aside the stranger from his right, and fear not me, saith the Lord of hosts**.

This directly relates to the tithe of food that rightfully belonged to the poor (the fatherless, widows, and stranger) who lived in the land. Generosity to the poor and needy was a strong command to the Israelites according to Deuteronomy 15:11 and Proverbs 19:17.

We then arrive at Malachi 3:8–10 (NKJV), which in a nutshell states: **You have robbed me…in tithes and offerings… You are cursed with a curse… Bring all the tithes into the storehouse that there may be meat in my house**.

In verse 10, there are several meanings for the word "all" in the Hebrew language: one of these interpretations is "enough." This may indicate to the reader that the Israelites were giving less than 10 percent, and this was the reason for the rebuke from the prophet Malachi. But this is not the case: the first chapter of Malachi tells that not enough of the freshest and unblemished was offered unto the Lord. Thus the phrase **all the tithes** in Malachi 3:10 refers to not enough of the freshest and unblemished tithe. It was not only a full 10 percent but the pureness and quality of that amount. When we compare all of these rebuking statements in sequence, we determine exactly what the problem was. The people were tithing the right amount, but the Levite priests were deceitful by not presenting enough of an acceptable offering unto the Lord. The lame or sick animal was offered in place of a spotless and healthy animal. Therefore, this old covenant type of sacrificial giving, including the method for determining the tithe amount, is now gone away! Jesus, the Messenger of Malachi 3:1, has become the acceptable sacrificial offering that replaced all of it!

In John 6:51, Jesus stated: **I am the bread which came down from heaven…which I will give for the life of the world**. Jesus, the spotless Lamb of God, has become the perfect sacrifice—replacing the unacceptable polluted offering with His sacrificed body—the bread of life. Today, when we bring a "mandated 10 percent" to the Lord (especially with impure motives), it then replaces the perfect sacrifice of Jesus, and we have given a polluted offering.

The overlooked verse

Even though we discern that tithing is not a new covenant edict, God made sure we would clue in by driving one last nail in the tithe coffin. A single verse, purposely and strategically placed in the book of Malachi, reveals the fullness of New Testament truth. God doesn't want us to stay in the bondage of works: He needs us to see the importance of His only begotten Son who became the sacrifice for our reconciliation unto Himself. This is the most blatantly clear verse in the Bible revealing that God no longer demands a tithe from anyone. And can you believe it's in the Old Testament? Fasten your seatbelt…

Immediately prior to the condemnation for robbing God of tithes and offerings in Malachi 3:8–9, we find an eye-opening revelation in the previous verse. Malachi 3:7 states: **Even from the days of your fathers ye are gone away from mine ordinances, and have not kept them. Return unto me, and I will return unto you, saith the Lord of hosts**.

This profound verse is ironically hidden from tithe pastors: they are blind to Malachi 3:7 because they either don't connect the dots or they skim over it or they pervert the verse to justify that tithing is still commanded by God in the Church Age. But we cannot separate Malachi 3:7 from verses 8–10: we need to compare the whole passage with the New Testament. In the King James Version of Malachi 3:7, the word "ordinances" is stated for a reason—to help us make the connection and comparison with the new covenant of grace. Because the Levite priests thought they were doing a pretty good job with their tasks, they couldn't comprehend why the prophet scolded them. In the last sentence of Malachi 3:7, they questioned: **Wherein shall we return?** Then the answer in verse 8: by returning to the prescribed ordinances for **tithes and offerings**. Here in the very next verse (Malachi 3:8), we see that the priests were guilty of robbing God and neglecting the whole law by failing at one point—a point that related to honor and respect of God's instruction. They had shunned the proper commanded tithing methods and had scorned the required pure sacrificial offerings—all stated as "ordinances" in Malachi 3:7.

Should we who live under the new covenant also "return" to the old covenant ordinances as Malachi 3:7 commands? No! The Messenger (Jesus) removed these ordinances! He destroyed all ritual laws! In understanding the importance of the message of the

Messenger in Malachi 3:1, we know this does not remove any admonition to consider the poor or to give to the Lord in general, but it removes the ordinances of obligation in "offerings for sin" and "tithe duty," just to name a few. The Messenger has set us free!

The absolute profoundness of Malachi 3:7 is this: since every aspect of the tithe laws were contained within these ordinances, we are now precisely informed here in this verse that the entire command and method of tithing, which was the immediate focus in Malachi 3:8–10, was completely cancelled by the work of the Messenger of the new covenant! God has orchestrated the placement of this statement very carefully in our Bible so there would be no question—even about the easiest of works of the old law.

Malachi 3:7 still applies to us today—only in a much different way. We should also return unto the Lord, as it says, but to do so by returning to the laws of *animal sacrifice* for sin or *burnt offerings* of devotion or *circumcision* or *food restrictions* or *tithing from ones' increase*...all in an attempt to make us righteous and blessed, actually brings a curse on us according to many New Testament passages. Rather, we return to the One who bought our salvation—the Messenger of the new covenant!

Christians have been put under unnecessary fear and bondage because Malachi 3:8–10 has been so isolated and expounded upon instead of considering the primary thought and warning contained within the whole book of Malachi.

This insight regarding the importance of Malachi 3:7 is not what a tithe pastor wants you to hear. What he doesn't realize is that when people discover biblical truth about tithing, they would then be released from their bondage and free to give in their own Spirit-led way. Think of the psychological effect of being released from this 10 percent law to receive God's favor. For many Christians, giving to their church would increase! Why? Because...

> ***Freedom produces joy—and joy kindles generosity.***

Only the Israelites were required to tithe from their crop and herd; there was no such command for the fatherless, widows, and the poor living within Israel's border. Instead, they received part of the food tithes given. Therefore, should the Mosaic tithe laws apply to all believers today—including those within the church who are financially challenged? A tithe pastor encourages his whole congregation to give a tithe, but is one-third of the collected tithe going back to the poorest within the congregation as the Mosaic law would seemingly instruct? Not likely. Yet today, more than a few ministers continually quote Malachi 3:8—accusing their parishioners of robbing God if they don't tithe! Such a travesty!

Misguided motivations

Just as giving is manipulated in many churches today, it was manipulated two thousand years ago as well. We know this is true by the example of the widow's mite story in Mark 12:41–44. The primary reason this incident was recorded in Scripture has not been perceived by most. Here we read that Jesus and some of His disciples were observing people giving money into the temple treasury. When the widow came to put in her two pennies, she seemed to be sincere in her love for God and wanted to give as much as she could. But let's dig a little deeper into this story and its strategic placement in Scripture. What Jesus says and doesn't say is insightful. After commenting to His disciples about the widow's great sacrifice and comparing it to the great amounts of money being given by the wealthy—which had little value in the eyes of God—it's interesting to note that Jesus made no reference to the presumed importance of giving money to the synagogue where the laws of God were taught. When the widow came to put in her **two mites**, Jesus instantly knew of her situation and seemed to be sympathetic—stating that she had **cast in all that she had, even all her living** (translated as "the means of livelihood"). Because of her sacrificial act, she had just given away all the money she had to live on at the time. But Jesus, neither condoning nor condemning her verbally, seemed concerned and may have been justifiably grieved and angered that she was giving to a corrupt religious system that would nail Him to a cross just a few days later.

The Pharisees and scribes were surely guilty of manipulating offerings even from the poor. Why else would a widow with little or no income be so compelled to give all the money she had? This widow may have loved God with all her heart but must have been coerced in some way because the placement of this story in both Mark's gospel and Luke's gospel is between two powerful statements made by Jesus. In Mark 12:38–40, just before Jesus's observation of the widow at the temple treasury, He warned of the hypocrisy of the scribes and that they **devour widows' houses**. Jesus wasn't pleased with the religious manipulators. He warned the people to beware of those who take advantage of the poor and that they **shall receive greater damnation** (verse 40). Then in Mark 13:2, immediately after the story of the widow's sacrifice, Jesus prophesies the coming destruction of the temple she was giving to!

In both Mark's and Luke's accounts of this incident, Jesus made no mention that the widow would be blessed for the sacrifice she made. Yet some pastors interpret this story as meaning that the widow was justified in giving out of her want because she would get far more in return for the few pennies she gave. If that was her motive, then she was wrong and had obviously been persuaded by the religious exploiters of the day. In the case of this poor widow, though her heart may have been right, I would also speculate she was rather foolish for letting the religious scribes and Pharisees govern her financial decision-making. There is no record of Jesus telling the disciples present that God would supply for this widow's needs after having given all she had. This is profound because many Old Testament passages tell that God provides for those who love Him.

The conclusion we draw here is that though God will indeed supply for our needs, our obedience to Him has little to do with giving money to them that preach the Gospel but has everything to do with obedience to the Gospel itself and to the Holy Spirit—and to be wise with our money, time, and talent. We should see the foolishness of giving above our means of livelihood and that we can become corrupt in our giving if we've been seduced by the teachers of false doctrine.

First Timothy 6:5 perfectly refutes today's *prosperity gospel*, saying: **Perverse disputings of men of corrupt minds, and destitute of the truth, supposing that gain is godliness: from such withdraw thyself.**

The Greek word for "gain" in this verse is *porismos*, meaning "money-getting" or "acquisition." Paul instructs believers to withdraw from any who preach and teach the gaining of possessions and wealth as having any part of the Gospel. Pastors who preach tithing seem to ignore 1 Timothy 6:5 and instead tell us it is God's will for Christians to prosper because He wants to bless them with abundance just as the Israelites were blessed when they obeyed God's ordinances. Though because the Mosaic ordinances cannot be the laws of the new covenant, this leads millions into a snare of deception. The real purpose for prosperity is to help those in need and to help spread the Gospel of salvation—not the gospel of abundance. Can we thus excuse an obfuscation of tithing as God's current-day method to gain prosperity and financial surplus? Surely not!

Continuing in 1 Timothy 6:8–9, Paul says: **And having food and raiment, let us be therewith content. But they that will be rich fall into temptation and a snare, and into many foolish and hurtful lusts, which drown men in destruction and perdition**.

The phrase **they that will be rich** is interpreted as **they that [intend to] be rich**: it is only these who will **fall into temptation**. This passage is not a warning to those who are already rich or to those who might inherit riches, but it's a warning to those who seek to become rich. For many seduced Christians, the motive for tithing is driven out of the pursuit of wealth…or from a fearful doubt that God may not supply our financial needs unless we are "obedient to the sacrifice." The fear of our own human frailty is somehow relieved through the act of prescribed works. Even though God promises to supply all our needs when we trust in Him, tithe promoters keep us in the bondage of ignorance by telling us, "*Financial blessing and provision will be yours if you give God the first 10 percent.*" Does this make sense when comparing multiple New Testament passages on the subject of giving? No! It is manipulation! We are free to give God the first 10 percent if we choose, but we must also carefully budget for family provision at the same time. First Timothy 5:8 tells us: **But if any provide not for his own, and specially for those of his own house, he hath denied the faith, and is worse than an infidel**.

Wisdom, prudence, and obedience is not found in blindly tithing—assuming that God will take care of the rest of our financial needs if we just do our part to give Him the appropriate amount. Surely we are more accountable than that. In Luke 14:28–29, Jesus said to count the cost of everything before proceeding; otherwise, we risk being mocked if we cannot fulfill our commitment to the project or our commitment to the faith. Low-income tithers who struggle financially are poor witnesses for the faith. Rather, God promises provision for all who trust in Him—not provision for tithers only.

Romans 9:31–33 (NIV) is another very clear passage:

> **But Israel, who pursued a law of righteousness, has not attained it. Why not? Because they pursued it not by faith, but as if it were by works. They stumbled over the "stumbling stone." As it is written: "I lay in Zion a stone that causes men to stumble and a rock that makes them fall, and the one who trusts in Him will never be put to shame."**

Since tithing was a major portion of the law and if Israel pursued a law of righteousness but has not attained it because it was by works, then by definition, all facets of these laws are now insufficient to obtain righteousness and blessing—all because of Christ, the stumbling stone! Any good works we perform has the potential to theologically dismisses our faith in Christ—the One who was deliberately sent for the religious to stumble over. This travail of love by Jesus the Savior is brazenly contradictory to the old covenant law. Jesus is **a rock that makes them fall** (Romans 9:33), simply for believing that appeasing God through works is more sustainable than accepting His free gift of total liberty from the law.

Even though 2 Corinthians 9:6 (NIV) says, **Whoever sows sparingly will also reap sparingly, and whoever sows generously will also reap generously**, we cannot diagnose this verse as a *give-to-get* method for personal financial gain. Rather, it's an encouragement for compassion to those in need and to shun covetousness, thereby reaping a spirit of generosity. The next verse explains this freedom in generosity. In 2 Corinthians 9:7, it says: **Each man should give what he has decided in his heart to give, not reluctantly or under compulsion, for God loves a cheerful giver.** This passage also explains how Christians are not under the obligated necessity to tithe but to be contented and joyous when giving.

Taxes, taxes, and more taxes

Becoming further educated in Old Testament laws, we find that if we tithed in accordance with the fullness of all requirements of the Mosaic ordinances, we must pay a full 23 percent to remain under God's blessing. We must pay the "income tax tithe" (Numbers 18:21); we must pay the "festival tax tithe" (Deuteronomy 14:22); and every third year, we must pay a "welfare tax tithe" (Deuteronomy 14:28–29). This totaled a 23 percent annual average tax required from the crop and herd. Of course, tithe pastors don't reveal this scriptural detail to their congregations because, after all, 23 percent of one's income is a rather high price to pay for God's blessing, right? It may also dissuade church attendance! So it is rationalized that the basic 10 percent theme will suffice to keep God's provision and financial increase on the agenda.

But shouldn't we do as Jesus did? First John 2:6 (NIV) says: **Whoever claims to live in Him must walk as Jesus did**. As followers of Jesus, we should walk as He walked—in His humble attributes and His example of fasting and prayer. But nowhere do we read that Jesus systematically gave a tithe of His carpenter's income to the temple: He was not required by Levitical law to tithe from His income of money. The only law that required a payment of money was the annual tribute tax to the temple. This pittance of a tax, which Jesus showed contempt for, was part of the Mosaic law as described in Exodus 30:13–16. The account of what Jesus said about the temple tribute is in Matthew 17:24–27: when the time came for this annual payment, instead of paying the tax from their own purse, Jesus told Peter to go fishing! Peter then found a coin in the mouth of the first fish he caught to pay the tax for them both—**lest we offend them**, Jesus said. Jesus was in a delicate position knowing that the Mosaic law was no longer in effect but was constrained to openly comply to the old religious statutes, only because all things were not yet fulfilled concerning Himself and the atonement. Exodus 30:13–16 reveals this tribute of offering unto the Lord was to make an atonement for your souls. We therefore understand why Jesus, who Himself would be the replacement for this monetary atonement, naturally disqualified it as a legitimate payment. In the same manner, any monetary payment made to today's religious system is also disqualified as legitimate for salvation or to procure an earthly blessing from God. Yet today, there are a few well-known false-teaching pastors who claim: "*Your salvation is in the tithe*" ("Tithing—World's Best Explanation," Myles Munroe, YouTube, 05:55).

Manipulative prosperity preachers

The perverted *prosperity gospel* message has flooded Christian television and a majority of megachurches in America and around the world. Prosperity principles found in the Old Testament have no connection with New Testament humbleness of heart, repentance, and the need for spiritual regeneration. Yet these new covenant admonishments become overtly overshadowed by the spiritually dysfunctional prosperity message.

The Old Testament contains many "promises of prosperity" passages. Psalm 35:27 says: **The Lord hath pleasure in the prosperity of his servant**. Here, the word "prosperity" means "well-being," not financial prosperity only. The words "prosperity" and "prosperous" appear frequently in the Old Testament: it encompassed the general welfare of life—health, long life, peace, and sometimes a pledge of material wealth—a general "well-being," if God's commands were obeyed. Today, especially in money-hungry America, it seems the only notion we have for the word "prosperity" is financial wealth. Yet many pastors continue to promote prosperity principles not found in the New Testament. Pastor John Hagee of Cornerstone Church in San Antonio, Texas, concisely summed up his ideology of the apostate prosperity doctrine when he stated: "*You determine the size of your harvest when the offering pen comes by. You plant your seed according to your need. Attack the lack with the seedtime and harvest principle. Your prosperity gives God pleasure*" ("Mega Church—the Gospel of Prosperity Pimping," YouTube, 01:16).

In the Evangelical Church of today, the seed of greed has replaced the seed of the Gospel message. Congregational manipulation continues by megachurch moguls who twist their tale of perverted Scripture to sustain the business institution of "church."

One might think this is sharp and uncalled for accusation. But...if Jesus, the righteous Savior, who paid for our sin by His own death on a torturous Roman cross, had sat in Pastor Hagee's congregation that day listening to such an off-based, unfocused, trivial, and perverted gospel message, he likely wouldn't be silent. Yet today, Jesus can do nothing above what he's already done. The hearts of the people have been turned far from the true Gospel message to a gospel of worthless tares. Jesus can only leave them alone to follow after their carnal lusts. If seduced to drift off the Gospel course set out for us, it's our own fault. Jesus does not force His Gospel on anyone.

Shameless false doctrines denouncing the teaching of Jesus now run rampant within the church, yet Christians listen carefully when such an influential voice speaks. Whether they speak truth, subtle doctrinal discord, or profound lies opposing the Gospel, the listener is brainwashed to think they always hear the truth because of the pastors' popularity and the megachurch Sunday crowd. The "safety in numbers" nature has powerful impact on the human psyche. Not only did Jesus warn of such propensity in human nature, but even in the secular world, we hear warnings against a "going with the crowd" mentality. It is exposed as potentially detrimental, as exampled by the mind-bending control Adolph Hitler had over the German masses.

That is why we must walk in the truth of Scripture in personal conviction and discernment.

Most tithe-teaching pastors have misconstrued the blessings and material abundance of Abraham, our patriarch of the faith. Many Christians are told that they are in a "covenant relationship with God" when they tithe just as Abraham did. But there is a disconnect here: Though Abraham's tithe (Genesis 14:20) was given to the High Priest Melchizedek, it was not a payment from his personal increase nor was it a covenant act between him and God. It was his pledge to Melchizedek from the plunder of war, and it is not recorded that he ever tithed again from his personal wealth. We are, therefore, not in a covenant relationship with God when we give Him a tithe. Further evidence of this is found when carefully comparing Genesis chapter 17 with Galatians chapter 3. **The promise by faith of Jesus Christ** (Galatians 3:22) is not the same promise (**covenant**) to Abraham in Genesis 17:10, which was based on circumcision—a precursor to the Mosaic laws. If we are **Abraham's seed, and heirs according to the promise** (Galatians 3:29) because of our faith in Christ, then how could the subsequent laws of additional ordinances given through Moses 430 years later (which included the covenant of tithing) also be the same laws of obedience for the believer today? According to Galatians 3:18, they weren't! **For if the inheritance be of the law, it is no more of promise**!

Currently on Daystar and TBN, we find the persuasive Pastor Robert Morris of Gateway Church in Dallas, Texas, preaching on the subject of prosperity and tithing about twice yearly. He tells his congregation of tens of thousands that God removes His blessing and curses your whole family if you don't tithe from your income. Morris states that God is "*released to bless you*" when you give a tithe. Yet there are many instances of tithing Christians who have had much adversity, such as losing all their possessions in a fire or suddenly becoming unemployed or suffering a terminal illness, among a list of many other life-altering circumstances.

In Robert Morris's book titled *The Blessed Life*, he teaches that the abundant and blessed life begins with one's obedience to tithe to the Lord. A key passage he refers to in supporting this idea is Exodus 13:12–13. Morris claims this passage proves his doctrine of tithing because it states that the firstborn of beast and man shall be "redeemed" unto the Lord and that this refers to the subsequent tithe command given to the Israelites. But we find that Pastor Morris has made a theological mistake: this passage refers to a completely different ordinance, having nothing to do with the tithing ordinances that were later given by Moses. Morris ironically neglects the preceding verse (Exodus 13:11), which says: **When the Lord shall bring thee into the land of the Canaanites…then…the firstborn shalt thou redeem**. This clearly speaks of the beginning of the old covenant laws for the Israelites, which are precisely stated in the book of Hebrews as **vanished away** and **unprofitable** in the new covenant age.

In every one of his tithe sermons, Robert Morris expounds on Malachi 3:8–11 but misquotes it by changing the word "tithes" to "*tithe,*" making it appear as a single 10 percent requirement for blessing. He then paraphrases: "*But if you will bring the tithe to the storehouse, I will rebuke the devourer for your sake! The storehouse is the Church!*" Yet the New Testament does not reveal any connection between the Israelites' literal storehouse for food and the new covenant church—which was not a constructed building (a storehouse), but was an organization of Christians. Neither is the new covenant church required to literally eat their tithe in celebration as the Mosaic ordinances commanded.

In Pastor Morris' "Principle of First" seminars (posted on the Gateway Church website in 2017), he states: "*If we don't tithe, we rob God of the opportunity to bless us.*" Morris presumes that God's hands are tied: He wants to bless us, but He can't unless we tithe. In fact, Pastor Morris went so far to say that God is "*incapable of blessing us unless we tithe.*"

We must sadly conclude that Pastor Robert Morris of Gateway Church not only serves a very weak and restrained god—limited by the works and actions of man—but he also has not biblically discerned that the statutes of the Mosaic covenant have been totally destroyed by Jesus the Savior. The principle of making God first in our lives does not begin with literally bringing Him the first portion of anything, as was with the old covenant. Rather, when God is first in our heart, we should understand that all that we have belongs to Him.

Though Robert Morris reveals correct Bible insight on other subjects, he has also mastered the art of mangling Scripture to fit his own theology on tithing. In his 2013 sermon titled "The First Open Door" (posted on YouTube), Morris made a feeble attempt to put his congregation under the bondage of tithing by reading from Matthew 26 and 27—the story of Judas receiving thirty pieces of silver to betray Jesus. Morris stated: *"Judas stole the tithe…that's why Satan entered into him. So when you steal the tithe by not bringing it to the House of God, you have an open door to demons in your life"* ("The First Open Door," Robert Morris, YouTube, 27:10).

When reading the full story of Judas's betrayal, we see Pastor Morris's ridiculous embellishment of the text easily proves he is not reading the Bible for all its worth. Yes, Satan entered Judas, as Luke also accounts in Luke 22:3, but Morris attempts to prove that it was only because he "*stole the tithe*"! In a lengthy interpretation, Morris goes on to explain that the priests paid Judas thirty pieces of silver from the temple treasury consisting of the tithes from which people had given. This is not possible: there was no such money tithe stated within the ordinances but only of meat and grain. The silver within the temple treasury was from freewill offerings only. In addition, Morris is assuming too much: Matthew 26:15 only states, **And they covenanted with him for thirty pieces of silver**. The narrative doesn't say that the silver originally came from the temple treasury but only that the priests didn't want to put the money into the treasury after Judas had returned it. Hence, Judas did not steal the tithe as Pastor Morris claims, and this is not why Satan entered into him. Neither do Christians come under demonic oppression for not tithing.

Among the many other prosperity preachers of our time is Word of Faith Pastor Jesse Duplantis who teaches that "tithing" and "seed giving" brings the giver financial abundance. While speaking at the

Southwest Believers Conference in Fort Worth, Texas, in July 2012, Jesse Duplantis, while making a few comments on tithing, stated: "*Every time you give less, you receive less.*"

This is an incorrect interpretation of Luke 6:38—**Give and it shall be given unto you**. When magnifying this verse as a method for achieving financial gain and by further distorting many other verses, Jesse Duplantis gives wrong theology and manipulative false doctrine. His declaration is very clear: that God's blessing and favor can be bought with money! If you want a bigger blessing, give more money to the Lord!

During this particular annual Southwest Believers Conference in 2012 (posted on YouTube), Jesse Duplantis highlighted Luke 4:16–21 where Jesus comes to Nazareth and, on the Sabbath, stood up in the synagogue and read from Isaiah 61 which prophesied of Himself. He read aloud: **The Spirit of the Lord is upon me because he hath anointed me to preach the gospel to the poor**.

In his explanation of why Jesus chose to read this passage, Duplantis stated: "*Jesus preached to the poor so they could get out of their poverty!*"

Surely Duplantis can't be serious! Was the Gospel Jesus preached a way to escape poverty? No! Matthew 5:3 tells that Jesus revealed the light of truth to the humble—the poor in spirit—to give them hope: **for theirs is the kingdom of heaven**, He said. When we repent of our sin and trust in Jesus as our personal Savior, we escape God's wrath and gain eternal life. This is the only Gospel.

Philippians 4:19 states: **God shall supply all your need according to His riches in glory by Christ Jesus**. Notice in this passage who has the riches and who has their needs supplied by those riches. It says **your needs** are supplied by **His riches...by Christ Jesus**. If we twist Philippians 4:19 to say that God provides earthly riches *because* of faith in Christ Jesus, then why hasn't every believer become wealthy for abiding in the righteousness of Christ? Our Bible indicates that being poor does not mean God has forgotten about us. Proverbs 22:2 tells us who makes the rich and who makes the poor. You guessed it—it is God Himself!

The apostle Paul was inflexible to add anything to the Gospel he preached. In Galatians 1:10, he says: **For if I yet pleased men, I should not be the servant of Christ**.

Think of it! The *prosperity gospel* pleases and tickles the ears of men! How could it not? And Paul, the great apostle for Christ, entertains none of it! He was a servant of Christ, not a servant of men.

Jeremiah 5:26 warns: **For among my people are found wicked men: they lay wait, as he that setteth snares; they set a trap, they catch men**. Unfortunately, Jesse Duplantis falls into this category of "wicked men" who "set a trap" for the gullible listener to fall into.

Within his prosperity sermons, Jesse Duplantis often quotes Mark 11:24 where Jesus said: **Therefore I say unto you, what things soever ye desire, when ye pray believe that ye receive *them* and ye shall have *them***.

Duplantis claims this verse is proof that we can have whatever thing we desire by simply asking and believing in prayer. However, we must carefully analyze this passage. In the King James Version, the word "*them*," mentioned two times, was not in the original Greek text. These words should technically be omitted, which derives a different interpretation of the verse. Also, the Concordance describes the word "desire" in this verse as a verb meaning "to ask" or "require." Therefore, this type of "desire" cannot apply to a "want" or "claim" of a tangible substance.

The word "things" in the verse means "a matter," "a possibility," or "an uncertainty." The "desire" of or the request of material "things" is therefore impossible to deduce according to the text: it cannot refer to possessions or money.

Pastor Duplantis hasn't considered the previous verse (23) where Jesus says: **For verily I say unto you, that whosoever shall say unto this mountain, Be thou removed, and be thou cast into the sea; and shall not doubt in his heart but shall believe that those things which he saith shall come to pass; he shall have whatsoever he saith.**

By first reading and understanding verse 23, we can correctly interpret what Jesus was talking about in verse 24. The **mountain** in verse 23 refers to the **things** in verse 24 such as "an event" or "an occurrence" of distress or uncertainty. Jesus is telling us that the uncertainty and distress (a mountain of distress in the mind) can be **removed** when we doubt not that God can resolve it from happening or that it may have any consequence for us. In verse 24, the metaphoric theme in Jesus's terminology shows us what will happen in the opposite situation. The **things** which are "a matter" or "a possibility" will **come to pass** when we pray and believe that we will receive. Therefore, the **things** stated in verses 23 and 24, of which we "desire" or "say" cannot possibly be any physical or tangible thing that **come to pass** or is **removed**. In other words, only an occurrence of a situation or the possibility of an event will **come to pass** or the distress of an uncertain and stressful situation will **be removed**.

From the Greek lexicon, the exact translation of Mark 11:24 reads:

> **Therefore I say unto you, that whatever matter or possibility you require, when you pray, believe that you receive, and you shall have.**

This correct interpretation of Mark 11:24, with the words "*them*" properly omitted, says nothing about receiving possessions or money just for the asking. Other Bible translations also mangle this verse.

We cannot isolate verse 24 from its surrounding context. In verse 22, Jesus begins by saying: **Have faith in God**. When reading all that follows in sequence, we see how Jesus encourages us to have faith in God when we face a difficult situation described as **this mountain**. Jesus said it can be **removed** when we **have faith in God** for a solution. When we pray, **believing that you receive**, the worrisome and anxious thoughts which occupy the mind vanish! Jesus didn't infer that our trials and tribulations would, of necessity, be removed by prayer but that through our faith and confidence that God cares for us, we are assured that He is in control—thereby bringing peace of mind.

Psalm 37:4–5 says: **Delight thyself also in the Lord; and he shall give thee the desires of thine heart. Commit thy way unto the Lord; trust also in him; and he shall bring it to pass**.

Yes, the Lord will give you what you desire, but you must first **delight thyself also in the Lord**. If you do this, then your own desires will become the right desires.

Jesse Duplantis boasts that his own personal wealth has come about because he tithes and sows seeds of money and because he believes for anything he desires as he perceives Mark 11:24 to say. However, by blatantly proclaiming that wealth is attainable for all believers who practice tithing and seed giving, he sidesteps and completely perverts the primary focus of the Gospel Jesus told of. Even though he believes in the saving power of Jesus, his version of the gospel also includes the self-generated *give-to-get* method of prospering and of bargaining with God. Proverbs 30:6 says: **Add thou not unto his words, lest he reprove thee, and thou be found a liar**.

Sadly, we must conclude that Pastor Jesse Duplantis and Pastor Robert Morris are just two of the many current-day corrupt false prophets leading the body of Christ astray.

Romans 1:18 (NIV) says: **The wrath of God is being revealed from heaven against all the godlessness and wickedness of men who suppress the truth by their wickedness**. In regard to the *prosperity gospel* in particular, this prophecy is now being fulfilled—applying to the wickedness within the church—revealed by distinguishing false doctrine from truthful doctrine.

Jesus's words on tithing

Jesus never told His followers to pay tithes, as some pastors tell their congregation. Rather, He condemned the Pharisees for their practice of tithing because they preferred works above weightier matters. In Matthew 23:23; Luke 11:42; and Luke 18:12, Jesus warned: **But woe unto you Pharisees! For ye tithe mint and rue and all manner of herbs, and pass over judgment and the love of God**.

Jesus rebuked them for their lack of judgment, mercy, and faith, even though they did tithe. It's the same today: if we've not been regenerated unto righteousness with a heart intent on the true Gospel, a tithe given to our church has no merit in the eyes of God. We are no better than the slothful Levite priests in the prophet Malachi's time who assumed they were performing the proper motions of tithing but lacked a heart of contrition.

Among the many Bible translations that twist Scripture, the Living Bible incorrectly states Jesus's ridicule of the Pharisees in Luke 18:12, saying: *I fast twice a week and I give to God a tenth of everything I earn.* Since earning and income are synonymous, this version of the verse implies that the Pharisees tithed on their income of money. However, the original Greek and King James text tells that they gave only a tithe of the spices they grew, which was the only requirement of the law. If God required a money tithe from our income today, there is then a significantly missing statement within these passages. First, we must understand that the Pharisees loved money as Luke 16:14 tells. Yet Jesus didn't scold them for not tithing on their money. Why? By the law, there was no command to tithe from one's income of money! However, it would have been the perfect opportunity for Jesus to implore them to begin tithing on what they held dear! Jesus could have then turned to His disciples and declared a transfer of the solemnity of the food-tithe laws into a new divine order of a money tithe to financially establish His church, thereby continuing in obedience to God. But He didn't do it! So did Jesus just not think of it? Did He blow the opportunity? Or just maybe, since His Gospel dealt only with spiritual heart issues, He knew that all the laws of Moses must of necessity be overturned!

Some think that because Jesus mentioned the tithe in Matthew 23, Luke 11, and Luke 18, that it is still required by God today because these verses are contained within the New Testament. But in a sense, Matthew, Mark, Luke, and John would be better understood if they were more distinguishable from the rest of the New Testament. The cross of Christ severed the old covenant from the new covenant, and the book of Acts documents the beginning of the Church Age. But Jesus lived during the time when Jewish people still observed the old laws; that's why He mentioned the tithe here, though He never told his disciples and followers to tithe. Why would He? He wouldn't have proclaimed any validity to the Mosaic ordinances because by the time Jesus began His ministry, these ordinances had technically already been removed. In Luke 16:16, Jesus said: **The law and the prophets were until John: since that time the kingdom of God is preached**. Here in this single sentence, Jesus tells that the law, which included all tithing ordinances, is now replaced with the preaching of the Gospel of the kingdom. Since the coming of John the Baptist, the kingdom of God is not found by performing any laws but is found by repenting from sin and placing trust in Christ Jesus. This is why we cannot legitimately repent and believe as Mark 1:15 says as well as perform any works of the law.

Kenneth Hagin's prosperity teaching

In chapter 3, we exposed the heretical doctrine about Jesus the Savior taught by Pastor Kenneth Hagin. But to his credit, Hagin taught a gentler and less dogmatic concept of Christian prosperity than do the many who mentored under him.

In 2000, three years before his death, Kenneth Hagin met with some close followers he had mentored. The meeting was held at his Rhema Bible Training Center in Tulsa, Oklahoma. In attendance were Kenneth Copeland, Jesse Duplantis, Creflo Dollar, Charles Capps, Jerry Savelle, Mac Hammond, and a few others who Hagin knew had perverted his teaching on giving and prosperity. Though this meeting was not recorded, it is reported that Hagin warned these men specifically against the *prosperity gospel* by name and the extreme off-base doctrine that was being spread under that heading. Hagin was incensed and rebuked them sharply for perverting Scripture. "Dad Hagin," as he was affectionately called, gave each one in attendance a copy of his latest and final book titled *The Midas Touch*. In the book, Hagin declared that financial prosperity itself was not a sign of one's spirituality or of God's blessing. He states on page 116: "*If wealth alone were a sign of spirituality, then drug traffickers and crime bosses would be spiritual giants.*" He also warned of the dangers of greed and explained that the purpose of financial blessing should only be for funding the work of the Gospel.

Hagin clarified in the book that he believed the Bible, as a whole, encouraged God's people to tithe to support the church and its ministry, but he also warned against the too strong emphasis on tithing as a way to secure God's blessing. He states on page 79: "*Through tithing to our local church and giving offerings to other worthy ministries, we can be part of what God is doing in the world today. Our motivation and purpose for giving should be pure and unselfish.*" Hagin then makes a distinction on page 88, saying: "*But there is no curse today for not tithing*"—noting that it was an old covenant law for the Israelites only. He stated that though giving 10 percent can be theorized as a suggested biblical amount, he also emphasized that this concept easily morphs into manipulation from the pulpit as legalism.

Kenneth Hagin adamantly states in *The Midas Touch* that there should be a balance of understanding biblical prosperity and that "*people should not give to get.*" On pages 120–131, he gave many insights on particular issues, declaring that "*naming your seed when giving an offering*" was an unbiblical concept. He also stated that the "*'thirty-sixty-hundred-fold' return in dollars*" was also unbiblical; though if it were a divine edict that directly produced wealth, the majority of Christians who consistently gave tithes and offerings would be billionaires and trillionaires by the end of their life. Hagin also stated that the "*supernatural cancellation of debt*" (that one can give their way out of debt) acclaimed by past "*specialist fundraiser*" preachers was also unbiblical.

To this day, all of Kenneth Hagin's protégés who met with him in Tulsa on that day have not heeded his warning. Through the Christian media and to their congregations, these influential pastors continue to emphasize tithing and generous giving as a means of prospering the believer.

Though Kenneth Hagin seemed to have cleared his conscience—trying to right the wrongs of past misunderstandings of prosperity teaching—his book *The Midas Touch*, published in 1999, has already been forgotten, and the prosperity preachers of today continue tugging at the wallets of gullible believers to help spread a gospel of wealth and earthly abundance instead of the Gospel of salvation.

The pull of escapism

Those who accept Jesus as their Savior but haven't made Him Lord of their lives remain schizophrenic and are pulled in every direction. Religious duties and traditions become mingled with concerns over the world's problems of war, terrorism, financial crisis, doom, gloom, and corruption in government being hurled at them every day through the media. Hence, many Christians have escaped into the pursuit of riches and pleasure. Pastors who once proclaimed the Gospel of repentance from sin have now been replaced with those who profess positive thinking, self-fulfillment, and prosperity as the way to please God. This misguided self-seeking quest, which many have been seduced by, is totally foreign to the Bible's message of salvation. But the attempt to walk in the world's system and in the kingdom of God simultaneously will not be tolerated much longer. Revelation 3:16–17 was a warning to the first-century church at Laodicea but can also be applied to many unfocused Christians today: **So then because thou art lukewarm, and neither cold nor hot, I will spew thee out of my mouth. Because thou sayest, I am rich, and increased with goods, I have need of nothing; and knowest not that thou art wretched, and miserable, and poor, and blind, and naked.**

This warning from Jesus is to any who think they have arrived at the contentment of self-sufficiency for their church attendance, tithing, and an artificial "*give to get*" kind of stability. If these words make you bristle, the warning is for you. It is a warning not from the writer of this book but directly from the Lord Jesus in Revelation 3:16–17.

Tithing—a Catholic institution

When studying the first few hundred years of church history, we find in the writings of Bishop Irenaeus and Bishop Epiphanius that there was no admonition from church clergy for the systematic giving of tithes. Rather, freedom in giving was emphasized, and offerings to the church were entirely voluntary. As time passed, church councils tried to enforce a tithe tax but with little success until the year 585 when the church Council of Macon first ordered payment of tithes from the people to support the church system. Ten years later, in 595, the Council of Macon threatened excommunication to those who refused to pay tithes. Nearly two centuries later, Pope Leo III crowned Charlemagne as Holy Roman Emperor, and in the year 777 during his reign, Charlemagne implemented tithing as civil law within the church. Tithing from parishioners continued primarily as a food tithe until the sixteenth century when Catholic churches in Germany and England converted it to money. Later in that century, the Council of Trent also reiterated the call to tithe. Protestant churches in Europe adopted the Catholic tithing law for a time, but its mandate was abolished in most countries by the mid-nineteenth century, mainly because it was seen as manipulative dogma that was not based in New Testament Scripture.

Tithing in America

The Pilgrims found truth in the Scriptures over the issue of tithing. When they colonized in America, they adopted no such doctrine of church tithing. They left behind the Protestant Church of England, which ignorantly retained some of the religious influence of Catholic bondage. These new colonists in America set up their government whereby taxes supported their churches. Nearly two centuries passed, and in 1789, the First Amendment to the Constitution was ratified and then adopted in 1791. It was later coined "The Separation of Church and State" by President Thomas Jefferson in 1802. The language of this First Amendment simply stated that government cannot prohibit free exercise of religion. The only thing it meant to President Jefferson was that Christians would now have free choice to be involved in education, religion, and government. But in passing this amendment, churches in America then became privatized, losing their funding from taxation. Consequently, many local churches became financially strained, and as the years passed, the idea of renting pews to pay for church facilitation and wages of the clergy became popular. In time, this plan was a failure, and passing a collection plate eventually became customary. By the 1870s, even this was not raising enough money, and the word was again sent out for suggestions as to how churchgoers could be persuaded to give more. By the 1890s, the concept of tithing (a Catholic institution) became accepted and popular in most Protestant denominations. Even into the twenty-first century, Evangelical churches in America and around the world continue to be influenced by the demands of Catholicism's bondage, producing hundreds of megachurches preaching the prosperity doctrine.

It is reasonable to deduce that the Separation of Church and State Amendment of 1789 was the initial cause of financially failing Protestant churches in America in the years that followed. It is, however, a biblical ideology that government and religion do not mix well in a diverse society. But fear not! Man's devises have triumphed once again over heaven's instruction manual. Though to a certain extent, our forefathers removed the means by which Protestant churches were supported, Christian pastors have now twisted Holy Scripture to concoct what they believe is the biblical answer to this dilemma. It is the manipulation of Scripture to guilt Christians into giving a tenth of their income. It is the reinstatement of old covenant bondage—falling under the guise of "obedience" and "faithfulness."

The tithing scam has been revived, repackaged, repurposed, and presented to ignorant and fearful congregations by equally ignorant and fearful pastors who teach it as truth. They are fearful and in doubt that God's people won't provide for the church's financial needs unless they are told that tithing enacts God's blessing. But when comprehending the real Gospel taught by Jesus and in realizing the joy of our own salvation, we wouldn't need to be taught how to give. The freewill generosity of happily redeemed people will provide for this need. In many churches, however, this is not the case because the congregation has been weighed down with a burden of the old law they are commanded to perform to avoid being cursed. After one gives their life to Christ, they find out that God also requires a specific tax of their income. The 10 percent requirement strains the already financially strapped believer, and it becomes a loathsome drudgery of necessity, as the Levite priests could attest to in Malachi's day. Therefore, more than a few Christians are not happily redeemed people for now having a tithe tax burden for being a successful and prosperous member of the family of God. People are blessed and set free by the liberating Gospel of the Savior…yet God curses or withholds from them if they don't tithe? Such befuddlement of new covenant doctrine!

The follower of Jesus who views this tithe amount as only a general guideline for giving and with no expectancy of any return has comprehended the New Testament Gospel. But seduced Christians indoctrinated with the tithe command have difficulty focusing on anything else. They've got to get that tithe paid on Sunday if they want to be blessed during the week!

Today, in the new covenant age, tithing to the Lord is not an obedient act. Tithe teaching pastors have proclaimed their own mangled message of bondage instead of preaching the true Gospel message of freedom *from* bondage.

My personal experience

A few years ago, I presented the biblical evidence I had found against mandated tithing to the pastors at the Charismatic Church where I was a member. The leadership of the church claimed to have read everything you have just read in this chapter, but it was quickly dismissed, and it even caused alarm. In an email from the assistant pastor, I was told: "It is clear that we see differently on this matter, but please don't share your views with anyone else; we don't want to create discord within the church."

As is typical in many churches, my pastors had mistakenly isolated selected passages of Scripture and removed them out of context to defend their preconceived assumptions. Their tithing doctrine stemmed from what they had been taught from the previous generation of church leadership. My attempt was to warn of this false doctrine that labored against the Gospel. Instead, they seemed to have dug in their heels even deeper. Yet I was not deterred because I not only had solid scriptural proof of my findings but also the personal experience of what happens when we align our lives with Bible doctrine.

When my wife and I discovered Bible truth and ceased our "tithe mindset" in January of 2013, there was an immediate increase of revenue in my art business—nearly five times what the annual average had been for the previous three years. This abundance of income continued for the year but dropped off again in 2014. Nonetheless, the increase occurred immediately after we acted on Bible truth. I believe God blessed us financially, partly because we no longer bowed to a law of prescribed works for our Christian walk. Though if it was only coincidental that halting our tithe routine was soon followed by a sharp increase of income, it made no difference! God blessed us even though we were not giving a precise 10 percent! We are now free from the bondage of tithing even if our finances fluctuate. We determine monthly what we can give according to our budget and in the leading of the Holy Spirit.

In 2014, we became aware of someone who needed a medical procedure but could not afford it because she had no medical coverage. The cost of her procedure was about 10 percent of the yearly income of the blue-collar job I also had. But we felt that paying for her need was the right thing to do. Because of this and after carefully analyzing our budget, we determined we should give about 2 percent of our income to our church for the remainder of that year.

What was the result? Our family is blessed with peace, God still provides for our financial needs, and to this day, we haven't yet come under any such curse for giving less than 10 percent.

I'm not advising Christians to give only 2 percent of their income to the church they attend. But listen to the Holy Spirit and be sensitive to the needs of those around you. We can determine the amount of our own giving according to 2nd Corinthians 9:7. This is the freedom Jesus the Savior has provided for us.

The tithing mandate mistake my pastors had made was very similar to other ridiculous cultlike beliefs assessed when isolating certain Bible passages. For instance, shouldn't anyone who works on the Sabbath Day be put to death? Wasn't this the punishment for breaking the Sabbath rules in Numbers, chapter 15? What happened to this strict law against breaking the Sabbath? We find the answer in the New Testament!

Or we could deduce that Jesus came to save only the Jews! In Matthew 15:24, Jesus said: ***I am not sent but unto the lost sheep of the house of Israel****. Should we stop reading right there—assuming that the rest of us non-Jews are just out of luck? Of course not! We keep reading to find the full truth! Jesus made this statement because at that moment of His ministry, He was sent to first redeem within Israel those who would listen. But in John 4:14, Jesus told the Samaritan woman at the well:* ***Whosoever drinks of the water that I shall give him shall never thirst****. "Whosoever" means Jews and gentiles alike! We cannot isolate any passage and make a doctrine of it: we must keep reading, and compare Scripture against itself.*

Thus far in our expository journey, we find that whether presented figuratively or literally, *the human-only Jesus* teaching (shrouded under the *born-again Jesus* doctrine) and the preaching of the *prosperity gospel* are directly linked in the apostasy of the church today. Over a century ago, Essek W. Kenyon made the mistake of twisting Scripture to unwittingly theorize a Jesus far more human than divine, which has evolved into the teaching of Christians having equal authority and power with the risen Savior. Even though Kenyon didn't realize it and would have denied such association with a *human-only Jesus* doctrine, his book *The Wonderful Name of Jesus* had become the spark plug for the modern Faith movement. The transmogrification of the *born-again Jesus* doctrine, merging into *Christian prosperity theology*, has rendered the justification for earthly Christian domination and success. Is it reality? Or have we been scammed? The answer becomes obvious through a more careful study of Scripture.

Chapter 9

Signs, Wonders, and Dominionism

In this chapter, we explore a growing movement birthed out of Pentecostal and Charismatic churches known as New Apostolic Reformation (NAR). These independent dynamic churches have become part of the Signs and Wonders Movement for their emphasis on manifestations, miracles of healing, and spiritual gifts—similar to the teaching in Vineyard churches begun by Pastor John Wimber in 1977.

NAR churches are focused on uniting all believers desirous to be used of God to manifest His power within society. Because of this, Bible passages are twisted to place great priority on the miracles and mystical experiences they believe every believer should participate in as part of the Christian lifestyle and to coordinate the entire body of Christ toward unity.

The New Apostolic Reformation movement—stemming from Pentecostalism—is the rebirth and continuation of the former Latter Rain Movement, which had the same ecclesiastic teaching. The Latter Rain Movement (New Order of the Latter Rain) began in North Battleford, Saskatchewan, in 1948. It soon moved to the United States, birthing the Shepherding Movement in 1970—later known as the Charismatic Movement. This transitioned many believers into the Word of Faith

Movement in the 1970s and the New Apostolic Reformation in the 1980s, encompassing the gamut of what is generally called Charismatic Christianity.

Pentecostals and Charismatics emphasize experiencing the baptism of the Holy Spirit and the use of spiritual gifts (charismana). The former Latter Rain Movement also taught that the Lord was pouring out His Holy Spirit again, as at Pentecost, but that the gifts of the Spirit didn't necessarily include speaking in tongues as evidence that one was filled with the Holy Spirit. The Latter Rain's greater emphasis was that believers were meant to be empowered and equipped to be used in signs and miracles to prepare the world for the Second Coming of Christ. These beliefs and teachings now continue on within the NAR movement.

Unlike the Vineyard movement's recent establishment as an international denomination, New Apostolic Reformation does not yet have such classification. Neither for the most part are NAR churches a closely-knit organization. Rather, this wing of Christianity is loosely termed a *Worldwide Holy Ghost End-Time Revival Movement*—emphasizing miracles and manifestations as the means by which the kingdom of God will come to the world.

In addition, many independent Evangelical/Charismatic/NAR churches are now teaming up with the Catholic institution to embrace an ecumenical unification of the worldwide diverse Christian church. This should sound an alarm to those who study the Scriptures to find that believers should separate unto righteousness—not unify all religious doctrines or to glory in signs and wonders as a bond between believers.

NAR pastors and leaders are self-proclaimed and self-appointed apostles and prophets who govern their local churches, giving supposed *new divine revelations* for the body of Christ. Because of the great desire to experience God's outpouring, this "chosen" segment of the church will supposedly witness the visions, miracles, signs, and manifestations prompted by the Holy Spirit. The presumption is that God is now reestablishing the church system with governing apostles and prophets in order to lead His chosen people to their final victorious destiny of a burgeoning and dynamic end-time church that will have great effect in society. This seems admirable; however, NAR prophets and apostles teach unbiblical doctrines regarding the Gospel of salvation and of Jesus the Savior—which are explained in this chapter. Other Christians within the mainstream denominations who don't submit to the teaching of these authoritative apostles and prophets are viewed as the nominal church, being observers only, and sitting on the sidelines. According to NAR teaching, they will not receive any power to be used of God to see kingdom miracles come to pass, only because they have too little faith or are in doubt that such manifestations of the Spirit could happen.

But today, the entire body of Christ should discern what Paul said in Romans 15:19: **Through mighty signs and wonders, by the power of the Spirit of God…I have fully preached the gospel of Christ**. Therefore, we as Christians need to understand that genuine signs and wonders still accompany the Gospel preached today. Though when signs, wonders, and miracles are pursued separately, as priority over the Gospel message, the enemy infiltrates with signs and lying wonders, which 2 Thessalonians 2:9 speaks of. Knowing the difference is critical.

NAR leaders believe the apostleship position and its title is imparted by declaration and the *laying on of hands*. But nowhere in the New Testament do we find this directive. Acts 8:17; Acts 13:3; 1 Timothy 4:14; and Hebrews 6:2 are among the verses that speak of **the laying on of hands** to receive the Holy Spirit or to impart blessing—but never to impart apostleship. Rather, as 1 Corinthians 12:11 indicates, it is as the Spirit wills to give certain gifts for edification.

The disciples whom Jesus chose became the apostles that birthed the church of a new covenant. These twelve apostles had unique position of authority, as well as Paul, who was also later chosen by Jesus according to Acts, chapter 9. Paul was the last of the Messiah-ordained apostles. He was a unique apostle—a **chosen vessel**, as it says in Acts 9:15, but who considered himself the least of the apostles, as he states in 1 Corinthians 15:9.

We can biblically discern therefore that giving title and position of authority to present-day apostles who govern the church is not a New Testament edict. Ephesians 2:19–20 explains: **Now therefore**

ye are no more strangers and foreigners, but fellow-citizens with the saints, and of the household of God; and are built upon the foundation of the apostles and the prophets, Jesus Christ himself being the chief corner stone. The language is clear: the church was established upon a single foundation—Jesus, the apostles, and the prophets. Nowhere in the New Testament do we find a command to ordain new apostles within the ongoing church system. Nonetheless, appointed apostles of the NAR movement anticipate that most believers who are attuned to "the outpouring of the last days" should eventually submit to their presumed God-ordained leadership.

In a sense, there are still apostles of the Gospel within the church today: we call them missionaries or "messengers" sent out to preach the Gospel in another region. These, however, are not "governing apostles" but apostles in a witnessing and teaching genre. Even in this understanding, we must be cautious: within the church, a "missionary apostle" may not always preach the truth. In Revelation 2:2, Jesus commends the church of Ephesus for their discernment: He said, **And thou hast tried them which say they are apostles, and are not, and hast found them liars**. Today, those who claim apostleship status shall weigh a heavy hand of judgment from the Lord if they do not guard and defend the one true Gospel. Current-day preachers and teachers within the church are justified as a type of apostle only if they adhere to sound biblical doctrine—to humbly speak and to guide in the way of Gospel faithfulness. For the most part, NAR leaders have not discerned this; instead, they are focused on promoting men to governing apostleship position of authority over the flock. But subsequent apostle types within the church are not required to govern in the same way as Paul and the original twelve apostles did at the beginning of the Church Age (see Acts 1:23–26). There is no need to establish a new foundation of doctrine for the church. A governing apostle within the church today is therefore not a legitimate position ordained by God but is a promulgation of men.

The office of a prophet and the "prophetic anointing" is also misrepresented and abused by the New Apostolic Reformation. These ordained prophets merely prophesy of signs and wonders to come, but the position of a true prophet among the Israelites was mainly to warn the people of their sin: it was not a popular job to have. Deuteronomy 18 instructs that a false prophet should be put to death, but a true prophet of God will prophesy warnings to the people and will predict future events accurately every time. In predicting future events, NAR prophets have admitted to roughly 50 percent accuracy. The office of a prophet among believers today is primarily to call people to repentance—to speak God's Word (according to 1 Corinthians, chapters 12 and 14) and to warn the church of its apostasy. Jesus also warned that there would be many false prophets in the future who will bring unsound teaching and a different gospel.

NAR's inception and increasing popularity

C. Peter Wagner (1930–2016) was the organizer of the NAR Charismatic Renewal in America in the 1980s. In a 1999 ceremony by a group of leaders in the *New Apostolic Roundtable,* Peter Wagner was confirmed and commissioned as an end-time apostle. Wagner later announced that the year 2001 would be "*the beginning of the Second Apostolic Age*" and that the lost offices of New Testament prophets and apostles are now being restored to bring about proper church government before Christ returns.

Wagner states on page 134 of his book *Apostles Today*: "*When we submit to apostles, the Church government will be in place to receive the powerful outpouring of the Holy Spirit upon our cities, which will lead us to social transformation on a worldwide scale. Since the Church is once again under the leadership of living apostles and prophets, it can now complete its primary task of the Great Commission.*"

The difficulty with the theology of Wagner's statement is that the Great Commission from Jesus to preach His Gospel has been redefined by NAR leaders, with an addendum to also take dominion and sociopolitical control of the earth. This addition to the Great Commission is known as *dominionism theology* and is defined by the NAR as "The Seven Mountains Mandate"—reclaiming business, government, family, religion, media, education, and entertainment—all under the control of Christians. NAR apostles and prophets claim they have received divine strategies for advancing God's kingdom before the return of Jesus. This, however, is a deception: Jesus gave no such instruction for His church to establish His earthly kingdom before His arrival. The NAR's "revelation" is that God is now orchestrating this takeover, not from any scriptural insight but only because NAR prophets have prophesied it would happen. Teachers and promoters of "The Seven Mountains Mandate" are focused on equipping Christians with a "vision for the mission" by giving them the practical social tools to cooperate with each other as God's *change agents* in society.

New Apostolic Reformation leaders shun the term *dominionism* for fear that government leaders and the secular world in general might react negatively to a "radical Christian takeover." A level of ambiguity must be maintained so that Christian dominionism will be accomplished through efforts to educate, equip, and inspire believers—simultaneously combined with 24/7 prayer vigils so that the enemy's stronghold will be derailed. However, Jesus never told His followers to strategize a sociopolitical or moral takeover in addition to spreading the Gospel.

The NAR's teaching of Christian dominionism is dependent upon and fortified by the financial prosperity of believers and therefore leans heavily on the last part of Proverbs 13:22, which says: **The wealth of the sinner is laid up for the just**. Some within the NAR have deduced from this single verse that toward the end of the Church Age, the wealth of unbelievers will be transferred to Christians in order to set up God's kingdom. But this idea is nowhere mentioned in the New Testament, and its misguided theology is far removed from the Great Commission of Jesus.

On December 1, 2014, acclaimed apostle Peter Wagner posted a personal three-minute message on YouTube promoting his latest book *The Great Transfer of Wealth*. In the clip, Wagner briefly explained how and why this will happen, and then stated:

> *This is a book that will raise our expectations and increase our faith, and allow us in the body of Christ to be participants in God's plan to release huge amounts of wealth. God is going to provide*

> *over and above so that we can support every good cause and participate in reconstructing our whole nation, so that America once more will come back to God.*

After watching Peter Wagner's short message, I felt sorry for this deceived Christian brother who genuinely believed this to be the end-time power surge to establish God's kingdom on the earth. It actually makes no sense because this scenario is impossible. Why would people want to turn from their sin and seek God when wealthy Christians are in control? This concept is backward to the real Gospel, and neither does it make human logic sense knowing man's tendency toward sin. The wealthy who have power and control are usually despised by the poor and middle class within society. And if those in authority are also religious, they would be hated even more for their perceived narrow-minded, controlling, bigoted, and holier-than-thou pushy ways. The real Gospel cannot be effectively shared with biblically ignorant unbelievers who already view Evangelical Christians as religious nuts attempting to take over. In addition, Christians with political and financial power will have no effect in legislating moral laws in society without first humbly sharing the Gospel message. If we share with them a gospel of financial abundance for becoming born again, we have shared a double-standard gospel message!

The NAR's "*reclaiming the culture for Christ*" agenda may sound like a great plan. However, **Except the Lord build the house, they labor in vain that build it** (Psalm 127:1). If Peter Wagner took this verse into consideration, he must have then assumed that the Lord would **build the house** by first supplying the finances necessary to do so. This isn't a logical theory according to the New Testament because the strength of the church is sustained by the spiritual condition of God's people. People are drawn by the Spirit of the Lord and then planted in a local body of believers. The Holy Spirit will not draw people to a religion or a Christian organization because it has solid societal clout and a strong financial base. They cannot attain righteousness before God in this fashion because the unregenerate heart cannot be compelled toward the Gospel of salvation through friendship with Christian power and status.

Jesus said: **My doctrine is not mine, but his that sent me. If any man will do his will, he shall know of the doctrine** (John 7:16–17). When the real Gospel of God's will is understood, it will cut to the heart of man's rebellion against God, and morality will naturally follow. The control that money brings and a sociopolitical power given to today's disciples of Jesus is not a catalyst that causes repentance from iniquity for the rest of humanity. This backward plan to the Gospel has been concocted by well-meaning Christians who've been puffed up through the seduction of false prophecy to the church. A great transfer of wealth to Christians would produce little more than the ego of self-reliance and further reinforce the false *prosperity gospel.*

Negative talk, you say? Then consider Ezekiel 14:9–10, which can also apply to today's falsely appointed prophets:

> **And if the prophet be deceived when he hath spoken a thing, I the Lord have deceived that prophet, and I will stretch out my hand upon him, and will destroy him from the midst of my people Israel. And they shall bear the punishment of their iniquity: the punishment of the prophet shall be even as the punishment of him that seeks unto him**.

Yes, there are true ordained-of-God prophets within the church today, just as there were among the Israelites millennia ago. Realize too that the responsibility of a true prophet is the same today—that is, to prophesy the truth from the heart of God. Although, this passage in Ezekiel 14 tells us that the Lord Himself raises up the false prophets! Why would the Lord do this today? It is to divide the seekers of truth away from those who have itching ears for any kind of promising prophecy, such as Christian dominionism, prosperity theology, or the pursuit of miracles, signs, and wonders.

This above passage (Ezekiel 14:9–10) also informs us that even though the listener to a false prophet is naïve, they are still punished for believing the deception they heard. Therefore, it is absolutely imperative that we carefully study our Bible to discern and distinguish truth from error and the false teachings of those who claim to have God's anointing. **Beloved, believe not every spirit, but try the spirits whether they are of God** (1 John 4:1).

New Testament apostles built the early church by preaching the Gospel; they didn't try to bolster it with financial stability or in lobbying for moral men to govern the land. The first chapter of Romans gives us the example where Paul proves a justification by faith. In researching the prevailing homosexual acceptance in the Roman culture of that time (which Paul mentioned in verses 24 and 26–28), why didn't he instruct Christians in Rome to become politically active to overthrow the immoral government? It is because Jesus didn't call His disciples to lead in government! Instead, they were commanded to preach the Gospel. When men and women respond in repentance to the real Gospel, they will become moral in their actions, and even some will be inspired and directed by God to enter the world of government and politics. The Gospel of righteousness is therefore priority.

In the discernment of New Testament prophecy, an end-time Christian dominionism scenario totally contradicts Revelation 20:4—**And I saw the souls of them that were beheaded for the witness of Jesus, and for the word of God, and which had not worshipped the beast, neither his image, neither had received his mark**.

Christians have been beheaded in the past for their faith, but we know this verse is talking about the very end-time tribulation slaughter of the true followers of Jesus who will not worship the beast or receive his mark. Therefore, the end-time disciples of Jesus cannot dominate all facets of society, only because many of them will be exterminated. And since 1 Corinthians 1:18 reveals that the Gospel is an offense to most people, the NAR's focus on experiencing God through miracles, signs, and wonders is not seen as a threat to society. Everyone—believers and nonbelievers alike—wants to see miracles happen. But to the majority of the population, it is an offense to preach that one must acknowledge and renounce their sin. Since NAR churches prioritize signs and wonders, they will continue to be very successful and attractive, especially to young people who desire fulfillment and purpose in life by being used of God to do mighty acts.

In John 10:5, Jesus said of His own followers: **And a stranger will they not follow, but will flee from him: for they know not the voice of strangers.**

The "stranger" Jesus spoke of is simply a different voice—one who is not in acquaintance with the sound doctrine of His teaching. Humans don't have an instinctive sense to flee from a deceptive shepherd of the flock, unless through knowledge of the Scriptures they recognize the true Shepherd's voice. So Jesus gives us the analogy of the sheep and the shepherd. A pastor who does not follow the Gospel of Jesus is one who leads his flock astray unawares. We therefore must discern the Gospel of our Bible well enough to recognize when a wolf invades the flock. Revelation 19:10 reveals that when we are divinely led by the testimony of Jesus, we then become true witnesses of the Gospel to those with whom we are acquainted—family, work, school, social gatherings—influencing them for the kingdom of God. If instead we mesmerize them with a coming kingdom that is perpetuated and prepared by "strangers" of the Gospel, we are guilty of biblical eisegesis, and we become spiritually unfruitful.

Appointed apostles of the New Apostolic Reformation have ignorantly perverted the Gospel of the Bible in their eagerness to advance God's kingdom. Interestingly enough, in 2 Corinthians 11:12–13 (NIV), Paul says: **And I will keep on doing what I am doing in order to cut the ground from under those who want an opportunity to be considered equal with us in the things they boast about. For such men are false apostles, deceitful workmen, masquerading as apostles of Christ.**

Even in the beginning years of the early church, there were men with ambition to lead and teach their own religious agenda, yet they were not divinely called to do so and thereby created the deceitfulness of doctrinal error. This above passage shows us that false teaching of the Gospel comes from those who are arrogant enough to proclaim themselves "apostles of Christ" but who are not thoroughly versed in sound doctrine.

According to the accounts of Jesus's life and ministry in Matthew, Mark, Luke, and John, we see that He didn't have a healing crusade or a miracle crusade—but rather a repentance crusade. Jesus never allowed signs, wonders, and physical healing to be the focal point of His Gospel message. He told many who were healed to keep silent about it. What could be the reason? Partly, it was for placing emphasis on one's eternal soul rather than healing of their physical body. Yet, Jesus, being compassionate to the infirmities of humanity, healed them because He could!

Restraining the demonic through mystic practice

The New Apostolic Reformation employs the mystical practice of *"prayerwalks"* and *"prayer journeys"* to defeat and evacuate cultural and territorial evil spirits so that the Holy Spirit can have better influence. Instead of first sharing the Gospel message with people, it is deemed necessary to encircle a specific location or territory to drive out the demons. This also is without scriptural warrant. In the Bible, we see that prayer should be directed to God only. Verbally addressing and confronting evil spirits, demanding that they leave or be bound, is not a biblical directive. In fact, demonic spirits cannot be bound by our words as some have taught. If indeed they are bound, then who keeps letting them loose?

We read in Matthew 4:8–9 that Satan tempted Jesus by offering Him **the kingdoms of the world, and the glory of them…if you will fall down and worship me**, he said. Jesus didn't tell Satan that he had no such possession or authority to make such an offer; He obviously knew this was possible and just said: **Away from me, Satan!** When tempted by the enemy, we can do just as Jesus did—remind him that he has no power over us. But we cannot command demons to evacuate a location or cease from their deceptive hold over a particular person. Jesus didn't instruct us to "pray away the devil" before witnessing to the unsaved.

Even though Psalm 24:1 states: **The earth is the Lord's, and the fullness thereof**, we also read in John 16:11, 2 Corinthians 4:4, and Ephesians 2:2, that the devil and his legion have been given temporary control of the kingdoms of the earth. Though Satan and his evil cohorts are limited and subservient to higher authority, they cannot be overthrown in the realm which they occupy or before Jesus returns to earth. In Revelation 20:1–3, we read:

> **And I saw an angel came down from heaven, having the key of the bottomless pit and a great chain in his hand. And he laid hold on the dragon...Satan, and bound him a thousand years, and cast him into the bottomless pit, and shut him up, and set a seal upon him, that he should deceive the nations no more, till the thousand years should be fulfilled.**

This passage tells us specifically when Satan will be forced to relinquish his dominion and control of planet earth. It will not be accomplished through super saints who bind or limit satanic powers prior to the reign of King Jesus.

In Revelation 12:9–11, we see that Satan and his angels were **cast out into the earth** and that they are **the accuser of the brethren**. But of the saints it says: **And they overcame him by the blood of the Lamb, and by the word of their testimony**. Notice here that the saints will not overcome Satan and his angels by defying and rebuking them verbally but by their **testimony**—the testimony of their salvation.

In Ephesians 6:11–17, we are told how to defeat the enemy:

> **Put on the whole armor of God, that ye may be able to stand against the wiles of the devil. For we wrestle not against flesh and blood, but against principalities, against powers, against the rulers of the darkness of this world, against spiritual wickedness in high**

> **places. Wherefore take unto you the whole armor of God, that ye may be able to withstand in the evil day, and having done all, to stand.**

What is the whole armor of God? Verses 15–17 tells us it is **truth...righteousness...the preparation of the gospel of peace... taking the shield of faith, wherewith ye shall be able to quench all the fiery darts of the enemy. And take the helmet of salvation, and the sword of the Spirit, which is the word of God**.

Notice the structure of Paul's statement and the progression of thought. How do we wrestle against principalities and spiritual wickedness in high places? It is not by verbally wrestling against them but by our quiet confidence that comes from having the whole armor of God! Paul did not endorse confronting, rebuking, or binding demonic beings.

A related passage is 2 Corinthians 10:4–5: **For the weapons of our warfare are not carnal, but mighty through God to the pulling down of strong holds; casting down imaginations, and every high thing that exalteth itself against the knowledge of God, and bringing into captivity every thought to the obedience of Christ**.

The key phrase in this passage is **casting down imaginations**, meaning to have confidence of mind—to pull down, in our mind, any argument against the Gospel and to confidently reject any theology that would reproach or revile God's plan of salvation. It is bringing into captivity every thought, as stated. This passage has nothing to do with praying against a demonic grip on people. It is not the "strongholds of demonic power" that control people but rather the **strong holds** of **imaginations** that would argue against the orthodoxy of Holy Scripture. Demonic forces have control over people only for their fortified views in false beliefs or no belief at all. When the correct Gospel of salvation is shared with them, the Holy Spirit is present to bring truth to their mind. However, the Holy Spirit is not present when an anomalous or unscriptural method is used to banish the demonic.

The Gospel message is the only necessity to the confidence we have in Christ. Nowhere in these above passages are we given instruction or permission to speak directly to our enemies in the spirit realm. We should not verbally confront Satan or his demons directly, demanding that they leave an area or release their presumed stronghold on a group of people. It is a worthless effort because they cannot leave! They will only laugh at you! Demonic beings will not leave a certain culture or territory until the people within that culture or territory acknowledge their sin against God and repent of their unrighteousness. When they do so, they then have the potential (through further study and knowledge of God's Word) to gain the whole armor of God for themselves! They will then stand in confidence against the fiery darts of the enemy on their own. The witness of the Gospel message is therefore the only necessary requirement of believers.

In Matthew 9:37–38, Jesus said: **The harvest is truly plenteous, but the laborers are few; pray ye therefore the Lord of the harvest, that he will send forth laborers into his harvest**. We need only to be sensitive to the Holy Spirit and to pray for more laborers—that the Lord would open the eyes of the sinner to see the truth of the Gospel. Demonic strongholds are not mentioned here in Matthew 9. But as 2 Corinthians 10:4 says, **the pulling down of strong holds** of false beliefs in the minds of unsaved people is accomplished through witness of the Gospel message.

Jesus prophesied in Mark 16:17: **And these signs shall follow them that believe; In my name shall they cast out devils**. To accomplish this, we must be prepared with fasting and prayer as Jesus advised in Matthew 17:21 and Mark 9:29. Jesus does not refer to this as an easy casting out but with great preparation. In Mark 1:23–26, we read that Jesus spoke to an unclean spirit possessing a man. The spirit first addressed Jesus saying: **Let us alone; what have we do with thee, thou Jesus of Nazareth? Art thou come to destroy us? I know thee who thou art, the Holy One of God. And Jesus rebuked him, saying, Hold thy peace, and come out of him**. Therefore, a demon can be cast out from a single person, but because there is no scriptural indication that demons are hovering over whole communities, Jesus gave no command to first remove them from a territory or a particular culture. Demons don't have a mystical-type grip on people. Rather, they are only ignorant of the truth. When the Gospel is shared with them, and the truth is believed, it is then established in the mind and heart, and the demonic influence of ignorance and corrupt thinking vanish. Again the explanation of this truth is fully explained in Ephesians 6:11–17 and 2 Corinthians 10:4–5.

Skewed end-time theology

Pastor Bill Johnson of Bethel Church in Redding, California, is a frontrunner in the New Apostolic Reformation movement. Johnson is passionate to see miracles, healing, and victory come to the body of Christ—that it be a dynamic witness in society. His passion is admirable yet quite esoteric when finding that his agenda and enthusiasm is inspired through NAR prophets that "*signs and miracles will happen for the purpose of advancing the Kingdom of God.*" We must give pause and carefully investigate this confused and backward theology.

Pastor Bill Johnson wrote a book in 2006 titled *Dreaming With God: Secrets to Redesigning Your World through God's Creative Flow*. The book encourages Christians to seek to be used by God through listening and responding to specific prophetic strategies. On pages 89–90, he states: "*Prophetic ministry is not to be focused on the sins of the world. The prophetic in its purest form is designed to find the gold in people's lives, and call it to the surface. This approach changes the attitude of the world toward the Church, and makes it possible for us to be contributors to society, not just confronters of all that is evil.*"

Johnson's statement here seems encouraging but is pathetically bad hermeneutics. A true prophet within the body of Christ holds that position for the purpose of proclaiming sound Bible Gospel doctrine, spiritual motivation, and in some cases, to help guide the local body of believers in financial decisions. Yet the NAR supports Bill Johnson's above version of the prophetic ministry as mandate for strengthening the church. From a biblical perspective, his stated reasoning and need for prophecy within the church is derived from a distortion of Scripture. It sidesteps the NAR's already mangled interpretation of the Great Commission Jesus gave to the church. In Matthew 28:19–20, Jesus said: **Go ye therefore and teach all**

nations, baptizing them in the name of the Father and of the Son and of the Holy Ghost: Teaching them to observe all things whatsoever I have commanded you.

The NAR has misinterpreted the primary reason for this Great Commission from Jesus. Their vision and goal instead focuses on prophesying a "bolstering of gifts" within the church—finding "*the gold in people's lives,*" as Pastor Johnson puts it—as well as pursuit and prophecy of financial, social, and political dominion, which they believe Christians should have outside the church. When all of this is accomplished, and the majority of society is functioning in miraculous and successful living, Jesus can simply take over when He returns. This, however, is misguided end-time theology: both 1 Corinthians 6:9–10 and Galatians 5:21 tell us that the righteous will **inherit** the kingdom of God, not establish it. If, as Jesus said, **the kingdom of God is within you** (Luke 17:21), how then can Christians establish God's spiritual "inner kingdom" within themselves? They cannot! The NAR's theology of God's kingdom is a material and physical advantage—contrived in their own power. Since Jesus calls His kingdom a kingdom of inner spiritual righteousness, the two concepts cannot be theorized as the same.

Christian dominionism is also debunked by the plain and simple statement from Jesus in John 18:36 (NIV): **My kingdom is not of this world: if it were, my servants would fight to prevent my arrest by the Jews**. Isn't this insightful! Because most of Jesus's disciples understood His kingdom wasn't an earthly kingdom, they were passive about conquering the governing system. Even the wealth of all the nations can have no effect to establish the kingdom of God, simply for the fact that it's a spiritual kingdom. However, when Jesus returns, bringing a thousand years of peace to the earth, the redeemed will at that time inherit authority and rule over His physical kingdom. Before this event, the kingdom of God is not a visible kingdom: it is not economically or politically relevant.

Joel 2:12–13 reveals that the spiritual realm far supersedes the physical realm: **Turn ye to me with all your heart, and with fasting, and with weeping, and with mourning: and rend your heart, and not your garments, and turn unto the Lord your God**.

This passage informs us that the heart of man is invisible and spiritual, that **garments**—referring to physical things—are useless and ineffective to change the heart. The prophet Joel spoke these words long before the Messiah came to earth, and when the Messiah did come, what did He do? He didn't set up a physical kingdom to reign over! Joel 1:15 says: **Alas for the day! For the day of the Lord is at hand, and as a destruction from the Almighty shall it come**. The prophet Joel speaks of the coming demise of all earthly kingdoms and current economic stability or instability. In the day of the Lord—the time when Christ shall come again—the world's economy will be completely restructured to accommodate Jesus's own physical kingdom in worship and honor, which will change the social focus. The earth, its economy, and the spiritual condition of people will not thrive until the new single Head of Divine Authority takes His earthly throne, replacing the old demonically controlled system.

Unscriptural "signs of the kingdom"

Signs and wonders cannot establish God's kingdom. Our Bible does not proclaim a gospel of signs but a Gospel of righteousness—with signs following. There is a distinct difference.

In 2007, Bill Johnson published his next book *Face to Face with God: The Ultimate Quest to Experience His Presence*. He states on page 123: "*If signs are not following you, you had better follow them until they follow you. Remember, signs point to a greater reality. We are not to follow them for their own sake but because they lead us to the One who created them.*"

Pastor Johnson's conjoining quips concerning signs contradict each other: he wants us to earnestly "*follow them*" but then tells us "*not to follow them for their own sake*"—! Johnson's overriding thought, however, is that believers should anticipate and seek signs because they bring us closer to God. This cannot be true: rather, signs naturally follow the one who lives in righteousness. Following and seeking after signs is by no means a biblical method of seeking righteousness as Matthew 6:33 informs us.

The basic gist of Johnson's entire book *Face to Face with God* is to encourage all believers to seek the destiny of God's divine best for our lives through the pursuit of signs. He says on page 189: "*We owe Him miracles as a testimony that He is alive and that His face is turned toward us. I have told our church family, 'I'm not impressed with anyone's life that does not have character. But I'm not happy with that life until there is power.*"

What unnecessary pressure to put on all Christians who read Johnson's book or attend his church! In truth, God does not give equal ability to every Christian. There are differing spiritual gifts as Paul shows in 1 Corinthians 12:4–12: **Now there are diversities of gifts, but the same Spirit…but the manifestation of the Spirit is given to every man to profit withal**. Paul then tells that some of these manifestations of the Spirit have no visible sign, such as a word of wisdom, a word of knowledge, and discerning of spirits. In 1 Corinthians 12:29–30, he says: **Are all apostles? Are all prophets? Are all teachers? Are all workers of miracles? Have all the gifts of healing? Do all speak with tongues? Do all interpret?** The answer was…no! Therefore, it is a fallacy to seek only the gifts that lead to miracles and manifestations or to constrain the Spirit to fall on someone or to endow them with a particular gift. And yet the NAR movement is totally occupied with this endeavor.

Any local church can be influenced by unbiblical NAR strategies if their pastors agree to hold seminars and workshops on "Last-Day Kingdom Miracles" or "Prophetic Prayer Strategies" to fortify God's kingdom. These *New Age* mystical practices and techniques through which the Spirit can supposedly work actually define the New Apostolic Reformation movement as "Christian occultism." Being ignorant of their syncretism with paganism, NAR apostles and prophets have not discerned that their methods for seeking God are actually derived from ancient pagan beliefs, contrived ritual practice, and manipulated verbiage.

Esoteric divinity

Innately connected to the NAR's obsession with signs and wonders is the confused doctrine of the deity of Jesus. In Bill Johnson's book *Face to Face with God*, he denies the total divinity of Jesus, explaining on page 108: "*Jesus set aside His divinity, choosing instead to live as a man completely dependent on God.*"

Coming from a Pentecostal background, author of many Christian books and pastor of a large flock of believers, Bill Johnson declared here that Jesus ignored His divinity and preferred a human status only—that he was "*dependent on God*"—rejecting any declaration or manifestation of His own divinity. This is blasphemy and is opposed to multiple New Testament verses stating the opposite. Pastor Johnson then brings further confusion by contradicting himself later on page 199, saying: "*Jesus Christ was entirely God. He was not a created being. Yet He became a man and lived entirely within man's limitations.*"

Once again, Johnson's statements contradict each other. Our Bible tells us that Jesus did not set aside His divinity: rather, He demonstrated and proclaimed it! If Jesus "*lived entirely within man's limitations*" as Johnson stated, how could He walk on water, make blind eyes see, cleanse the leper, raise the dead, or feed the multitudes with such a minuscule amount of food? To the unbelieving cynic, who by chance might read *Face to Face with God*, the above declaration by Pastor Johnson may foster the idea that the miracles which Jesus performed were perhaps only magic tricks and illusions...or just the embellishments of the writers Matthew, Mark, Luke, and John:

- *Walking on water was Jesus's clever trickery of illusion.*
- *Supposed blind eyes were only closed eyes.*
- *The leper's skin was made smooth with healing ointment Jesus had discovered.*
- *Lazarus wasn't really dead but in a coma.*
- *Extra food was snuck in to feed the multitude.*

These doubtful and unbelieving statements about the miracles of Jesus are more than just false; they are blasphemous according to the salvation message of our Bible. If Jesus completely restricted Himself to the confines of human limitations and depended only on His heavenly Father for miracles to happen, then the message of salvation is lost! When Jesus is theorized to be only a man like the rest of us, His Gospel becomes a type of egalitarian doctrine, surmising that if Jesus could in a few short years accomplish such perfection and mastery of divine summon, surely we could also...because He was merely human like the rest of us! According to the New Testament, this cannot be the truth. Jesus most assuredly did not live entirely within man's limitations. But because Pastor Johnson specifically drives this point in his book *Face to Face with God*, he thus denies the deity of Jesus during His earthly ministry—teaching that He "*set aside his divinity.*" This theory is called *kenosis*: it is derived from the Greek word *kenoo*, which means "to empty." This word is used in the NASB version of Philippians 2:7: beginning at verse 6 (NASB), we read, **Christ Jesus, who, although He existed in the form of God, did not regard equality with God a thing to be grasped, but [emptied] Himself, taking the form of a bond-servant, and being made in the likeness of men**.

Philippians 2:7 is dangerously close to heresy in the NASB version because the wording implies that Jesus "emptied Himself of His divinity." The King James translation reads: **Christ Jesus...made himself of no reputation**, clarifying that He was merely "brought low" in human form.

Correctly interpreting the fullness of Philippians 2:5–8 determines that Jesus didn't give up any of His divine attributes since it does not list any of them specifically. Instead, this passage is referring to Jesus's humanity that moved Him with compassion and according to the will of His Father. Jesus left His majestic state in heaven and entered into the humble position of humanity. Therefore, Christ Jesus was fully God and fully man—"hypostatic union."

The *kenosis* theory of Jesus is heresy—teaching that He forfeited His omniscience, omnipresence, and omnipotence when taking on the form of humanity. Some say that Christ presumably did this voluntarily so He could function as a man in order to fulfill the work of redemption. This theory was first introduced in the 1850s by German Lutheran theologian Gottfried Thomasius. There may be an element of truth in this theory in the case of Jesus's omnipresence. Being human, He could not be omnipresent in a physiological sense. Although, in Matthew, chapter 8, Jesus knew that the servant of the centurion was healed at the moment they were speaking, even though the servant wasn't close by. Jesus manifested His divine attributes relating to His power and authority: He was spiritually omnipresent, even though He was physically restricted.

Jesus, our Brother?

In a 2009 sermon titled "The Kingdom of God Is at Hand," Pastor Bill Johnson stated: "*Jesus was born again. He was born through Mary the first time, and through the Resurrection the second time. He was born again! When Jesus was giving the Great Commission to his disciples, he was not God at that time. He was our elder brother*" ("Bill Johnson False Teacher," YouTube).

As explained earlier, the *elder-brother* concept of Jesus is dangerous doctrine. If Jesus was our spiritual *elder Brother* in a figurative sense, He then remains only a "figurative Savior" after rising from the dead. Or if Jesus was literally our spiritual *elder Brother*, this derives that the one who believes in Him is now literally divine as He is divine. Both theories are false. Our Bible nowhere indicates that Jesus was a "symbolic Savior"; this results in a vague and impersonal gospel message of *universal salvation* for all humanity. And thus, the prophecy of "the judgment" of which Jesus, John, and Paul talked about was only a kind of fairy-tale incitement for men to live morally. In either a literal or figurative interpretation of the *born-again/elder-brother* theory of Jesus, we find the entire disclosure to be heretical and blasphemous teaching according to Scripture.

Within his sermon "The Kingdom of God Is at Hand," Pastor Johnson gave no explanation of the interpretation of the Great Commission from Jesus. The New Testament precisely tells it was a commission to spread the Gospel—a Gospel based on the pivotal point that Jesus Himself is Lord. Yet Pastor Johnson says: "*He was not God at that time. He was our elder brother.*"

So...Jesus was neither *God* nor *Lord* when He gave the Great Commission to the disciples—but was only an *elder Brother*? This renders the Gospel itself as completely meaningless and is in great disrespect to the Son of God Himself! Jesus is not *our Brother*! He is the Second Person of the Trinity Godhead. He is to be highly esteemed, reverenced, and glorified far above any earthly or spiritual brother.

The *born-again/elder-brother* teaching of Jesus is great confusion and contradiction: it altogether derides and destroys the Gospel message. Likely, however, the average listener to such apostate doctrine hasn't thought through this false teaching far enough to realize its heresy. This is why we are told to listen with discerning ears and to test every doctrine. If we don't, we are slighted of a literal salvation message.

This *New Age Christianity* train of thought easily leads to the assumption that Jesus was the "firstfruit of the divinity of man"—either literally or figuratively. Likewise, when Bill Johnson stated in his sermon that Jesus "*was not God at that time,*" it presumably proved how Christian's have dominion and authority in the earth for the fact that Jesus was the first *born-again* man of deity—and we can now follow in the same manner when we become *born again with Him* in a spiritual sense. Again this teaching rejects the saving Gospel and defines the term "*born again*" as meaning something other than what Jesus described in John 3:3.

Whether the doctrine of the *born-again/elder-brother Jesus* is interpreted as metaphoric or literal makes no difference. Bill Johnson and many others within the NAR and Word of Faith movements highlight this point for the purpose of declaring the believers' confidence of equal authority with Jesus the Savior. This apostate and blasphemous doctrine is what many call *New Revelation Knowledge.* It however is *New Age* cultic false doctrine that has crept into the church and under the radar of many believers.

Greater miracles

The NAR's brand of eschatology declares that the church is now gaining back her confidence and is being restored to move in last-day manifestations and miracles of healing power. They believe it is the same **many signs and wonders wrought among the people** which Acts 5:12 speaks of. In reality, miraculous signs will indeed follow Christians when they have great faith in the real Jesus who said: **According to your faith be it unto you** (Matthew 9:29). However, the NAR movement sees themselves as last-day super-anointed Christians who will have faith enough to do even greater miracles than Jesus did. Is this possible? No. Jesus didn't say that greater miracles would happen after He departed. Read John 14:12 very carefully: Jesus said, **Verily, verily, I say unto you, He that believeth on me, the works that I do shall he do also; and greater works than these shall he do; because I go unto my Father**.

Though we generally read this verse as a prophecy from Jesus that His followers would do greater miracles than He did, it is actually just a proclamation that His followers would do "greater works"—which may or may not include miracles of healing. The two statements Jesus makes in this King James compound sentence are linked with the conjunctive word "because." This should give us a clue, even if the punctuation marks were removed. It was **because I go unto my Father** that Jesus's followers would remain behind to labor longer in spreading the Gospel message.

In Strong's Concordance, we find the word "greater" in this verse means "more," and the word "works" means "toil" or "labor." We therefore know that Jesus was informing His followers that they would "toil more" or "labor longer" in the same manner He had labored. Jesus had only three and a half years in His ministry to labor in what He described as "works," which was proclaiming the Gospel of righteousness, until He ascended to His Father. But Jesus's close disciples and we as His followers today would generally have a much longer span of time to labor for the sake of the Gospel. Hence, we see that Christians will not specifically do more amazing miracles than Jesus did but rather that most of us will simply "labor longer" in the same "works" of proclaiming the Gospel as Jesus had done.

The context surrounding John 14:12 is crucial to understand: in the very next verse (John 14:13), Jesus says, **And whatsoever ye shall ask in my name, that will I do, that the Father may be glorified in the Son**. Here, the word "whatsoever" in the Greek is *hostis*—a human reference such as "they who" or "any that." We also find that the word "ask" means to "call for" or "require," and the term "that will I do" has a wide application that could be interpreted as "to bring forth." Therefore, John 14:12 actually reads: **Whosoever you call for in my name, them shall I bring forth, that the Father may be glorified in the Son**. When we combine verses 12 and 13, we know that the "works" of laboring to spread the Gospel also requires God's help to bring to us those who shall be saved when we **ask in my name**, as Jesus said.

Because many have interpreted John 14:12–13 to say that believers will do "greater miracles" than Jesus did, some might see the above explanation of the text as a "*doubt and go without*" frame of mind versus a "*believe and receive*" frame of mind—a positive faith versus a negative disbelief in miracles. But it isn't. Read within the context: weigh and balance the exact words of Jesus and the apostles, and you will find reality, fact, and truth. Yes, there will be genuine miracles that accompany the Gospel proclaimed in these last days; but on a major scale, the Bible does not predict that multitudes will be physically healed or fully restored to perfect health just prior to the return of Jesus.

The revival question

The New Apostolic Reformation movement has declared: "*Revival is happening now!*" They believe this revival has come from a hunger to experience God, resulting in a revival of signs and wonders. However, this cannot be described as a spiritual revival: it is not a widespread response to the Gospel of salvation. A revival of manifestations and miracles cannot result in inner and personal spiritual regeneration. On rare occasion, people may repent from their sin after witnessing a genuine supernatural manifestation that glorifies God; but unless there is clear testimony of the biblical Gospel, a mere manifestation is not incitement for repentance from sin and to escape God's wrath in judgment. Though there will be genuine miracles, signs, and wonders from God in our day, our Bible says in five distinct places: **The just shall live by his faith**...and not by his or her own expectation of or experience of miracles and manifestations.

Neither should we evoke, condone, or rely on every dream or vision as genuine divine guidance from the Holy Spirit. All things must be tested according to the Scriptures.

Joining with Pastor Bill Johnson's teaching of the signs and wonders revival, other current NAR leaders—Chuck Pierce, Lou Engle, Rick Joyner, Patricia King, Mike Bickle, Lance Wallnau, Cindy Jacobs, Ché Ahn, Bill Hamon, Dutch Sheets, and many more—have declared that *"perpetual revival is now the norm: it will continue to increase, and should not cease."* But the New Testament does not indicate that a wide-scale genuine signs and wonders revival from the Spirit of God will occur in the last days. In fact, neither is there prophecy of a worldwide revival of repentance unto righteousness.

According to NAR teaching, an apostle-led and prophetically driven last-day church will culminate in the outpouring of manifestations for the unbelieving world to witness. Bethel Church in Redding, California, and other NAR churches around the world have joined hands with hundreds of smaller fellowships as well as megachurches like International House of Prayer in Kansas City; Hillsong, Sydney; and Hillsong, New York to teach and declare that the church must conquer the culture—that manifestations and miracles can and should be performed by every believer so that Christ can soon return.

In association with Bethel Redding Church is the Bethel School of Supernatural Ministry, where students pay tuition to learn how to prophesy and perform miracles. The school's in-depth curriculum of *Bible Interpretation and Application, Fundamental Theology and Church History, Outreach Evangelism, and Kingdom Theology and Identity* appear beneficial in equipping believers with the confidence and authority they must have to build God's kingdom upon the earth. Though because the Bible's doctrine of the Gospel is foundational and very simple, it cannot be enhanced with manifestations and miracles to show the way of salvation. Neither can the pursuit of "gifts" edify in the comprehension of biblical righteousness.

Those within the NAR movement have fallen under deception: they have been swept into a revival of sought-after "waves of experiential glory," "mystical encounters," and "endowment of Holy

Ghost power"—as exampled in the contrived "*fire tunnel*" ceremony. Well-meaning yet false-teaching pastors who perpetuate this frenzied mystic revival of signs and wonders have too far theorized, misread, and twisted Scripture to concoct a perverted and superstitious type of gospel that diverts away from and actually replaces and rejects the saving power of Jesus. Those who have investigated deeper into the NAR's off-based ceremonies and mystic practices have referred to them as "*witchcraft within the church.*" When discerning the NAR's false doctrine and observing their scripturally unwarranted activity, this author cannot disagree with that assessment.

Questioning NAR doctrine

A 2014 book titled *A New Apostolic Reformation?: A Biblical Response to a Worldwide Movement* by Doug Geivett and Holly Pivec is an objective and thoroughly investigative book that brings to light the unsound teaching of the New Apostolic Reformation. The book explains how and why NAR leadership have been misled by certain Bible passages and that those within this movement are genuinely sincere and inspired by what they believe God is doing in the earth today. Research by Geivett and Pivec explain how the NAR is unable to discern theological error, mainly because they continually review and prioritize Bible passages taken out of context that seem to support a prophecy of ever-increasing miracles of healing, deliverance, and power given to Christians in the end times.

Within the NAR movement, there are some who teach that "super Christians" are being prepared to gain immortality in their earthly physical bodies and will even participate in executing God's judgment on humanity. This eschatological scenario is not spoken of in Scripture. Unfortunately, the Latter Rain movement of the 1940s and '50s introduced many unsound doctrines within Pentecostal churches, which has spawned the current belief of last-days Christians becoming immortal. As explained on page 190 of *A New Apostolic Reformation?*, "*Some NAR participants will become immortal, according to one of NAR's most prominent leaders, Bill Hamon. NAR disciples who are already elderly will experience a reversed aging process, literally growing physically younger.*"

Scripture indicates nothing of the sort. Authors Geivett and Pivec note in their book that not all NAR apostles and prophets agree with Pastor Hamon's theology of reverse aging. Neither do they totally agree on a few other doctrinal and theological issues. Hence, how can this *Worldwide Holy Ghost End-Time Revival Movement* bring harmonious conformity and unity to the end-time church?

NAR apostles and prophets claim to receive "direct divine revelation" from the Holy Spirit, supposedly giving new and vital direction to the church. When the "direct divine revelation" misnomer is challenged by orthodox Christians, those within the NAR fire back, accusing them of having "*a spirit of religion.*" This proves the NAR's lack of scriptural discernment: the Gospel of salvation is not found in religion; it is found in the doctrine of the faith. Minimizing Bible doctrine by promoting mystic experience and direct personal divine guidance has thus produced evil fruit, as Jesus states in Matthew 7:17. We will know them by their fruits—the fruits of unrighteous and unbiblical teaching.

I've heard many Christians say they are "*inspired,*" "*amazed,*" and "*revolutionized*" by the teaching of these "*anointed pastors*" who speak of "*end-time divine revelations.*" This is a dangerous position. Psalm 118:8 says: **It is better to trust in the Lord than to put confidence in man**. This verse is a kind of blanket statement cautioning against putting total confidence in even a teacher of God's Word. If we follow them, we must know with certainty that they preach and teach biblical truth. Yet, how can we recognize false teaching unless a personal desire to study God's Word supersedes the contentment of allowing a presumed anointed pastor to teach us? Even in humbleness, one who teaches half-truths will in turn humbly deceive and destroy the congregation.

The New Apostolic Reformation launched the global satellite network GOD TV in 1995. Pastors who teach NAR doctrine and theology are also seen on most other Christian TV networks. Ever-increasing "manifestations of the Spirit" type of teaching has seduced many into the enthusiasm of a revival of power and authority for the body of Christ. But overall, this movement has not made any connection between the New Testament's stated "end-time apostasy" and the "arising false prophets" within the church. Because many deceptive miracles and signs are indeed occurring within these churches, the "glory of God" is primarily observed in manifestations only, and any doctrinal dysfunction or neglect is either overlooked or not perceived.

On the day when God will judge every human heart, He will have clear evidence of how to render His judgment. Those who sought signs, miracles, and mystical experiences instead of sound doctrinal truth will receive just reward. This is part of the specific warning from Jesus in Matthew 7:15–23. He said: **Wherefore by their fruits ye shall know them** (Matthew 7:20). What are these fruits Jesus spoke of? Is it good deeds? No! Even unbelievers do good deeds. Spiritual good fruits are produced through a belief in the truthful sound doctrine of the Gospel of salvation. In essence, the doctrinal truth of the Gospel itself is the good fruit.

Adulterous generation

Jesus said that those who seek after signs will not be given a genuine sign from God: they are **an evil and adulterous generation** (Matthew 12:39; Matthew 16:4; Mark 8:12; Luke 11:29). We can therefore discern that end-time sign seekers will experience only Satan's signs and lying wonders as 2 Thessalonians 2:9 states. Apostate believers remain apostate because they cannot recognize a deception so gigantic and pervasive. However, the genuine miracles of God are all around us—experienced even by the skeptical and the unregenerate, thus pulling them toward the Gospel of God's love. When they witness a miracle, the Christian should then encourage them in the Gospel message. Though if the emphasis is only on the miracle itself, the observer has no desire to seek righteousness and salvation—rather, they seek more miracles! The simple yet vital Gospel of Jesus thereby becomes obscured: it's back there somewhere in the religious theological shadows—not needing to be personally confronted or fussed over too much—because signs and miracles are where the action is!

Again according to 2 Thessalonians 2:11, God has allowed the demonic realm to bring deceptive manifestations—**strong delusion, that they should believe a lie**—to cause separation within the worldwide church. Those who seek God and His righteousness are polarized against those enticed with the excitement of anticipating miracles, signs, and wonders. And even some of God's righteous elect have been tricked and swept into this movement, unaware of the enemy's crafty diversion. Jesus warned us in Matthew 24:24, saying: **For there shall arise false Christs, and false prophets, and shall show great signs and wonders; insomuch that, if it were possible, they shall deceive the very elect**.

Just as the *born-again Jesus* teaching is a deceptive tactic against the Gospel of salvation, Satan also takes advantage to deceive us with amazing great signs and miracles and to propagandize a Christian conquering and domination of the culture with moral and financial clout—to distract and seduce even the very mature follower of Jesus. Unless Scripture is carefully studied to find the distinction, we may not perceive any deception because the nature of one's own deception is the ignorance of and blindness to the deception! That's why it's called deception!

The prophet Jeremiah relayed God's simple message that compares spiritual reality to physical deception: **And ye shall seek me, and find me, when ye shall search for me with all your heart** (Jeremiah 29:13). When we seek God with all our heart, we find Him in our heart! In a spiritual sense, we cannot personally find God when witnessing a sign, manifestation, or healing.

Separation unto righteousness

The sound doctrine of the Bible is simple, but when venturing outside the simple Gospel of Jesus by measuring our spiritual growth through our mystical experiences or our encounters with the miracles of healing, we have opened ourselves up to the demonic. God allows demonically induced miraculous and mystical experiences to happen for the purpose of distinguishing the heart's focus. Signs and lying wonders from the enemy are a deception—to take our eyes off the redemptive work of Jesus and instead to marvel at the experience. How can we distinguish the difference between the miracles of God and the miracles of the enemy, unless by scriptural knowledge we discern the source? One amazing experience leads to the anticipation of another, and rather than praying for a revival of righteousness, a wide swath of the Evangelical Church has now become obsessed with a revival of signs and wonders—leading us away from biblical righteousness toward satanic fraud.

Paul informs the church at Thessalonica of the coming anti-Christ deception within the church and even the whole world. Second Thessalonians 2:3 states: **Let no man deceive you by any means; for except there come a falling away first, and that man of sin be revealed, the son of perdition…** Here Paul is revealing the end-time spirit of deception that will culminate in the reign of the authoritarian anti-Christ man. The key term he uses is **falling away**: since the unregenerate cannot "fall away" from righteousness, the warning is for the followers of Christ—that they will be seduced away from the Gospel.

In 2 Thessalonians 2:7, Paul then says: **For the mystery of iniquity doth already work**, meaning that the enemy's secretive deceptions leading to sin had already begun within the body of Christ. Then in verses 8 to 12, he continues:

> **And then shall that Wicked be revealed, whom the Lord shall consume with the spirit of his mouth, and shall destroy with the brightness of his coming: even him (Jesus), whose coming is after the working of Satan with all power and signs and lying wonders, and with all deceivableness of unrighteousness in them that perish; because they received not the love of the truth, that they might be saved. And for this cause God shall send them strong delusion, that they will believe a lie: that they all**

> **might be damned who believe not the truth, but had pleasure in unrighteousness.**

The apostle Paul writes these poignant words to the saints at Thessalonica as a warning. It was meant to equip them in the knowledge of Satan's power and tactic. We see here that Jesus will not return until after Satan has done his deceptive work on the earth...and very specifically upon the ignorant Christian masses.

Most Christians cannot be deceived through a spirit of outright rebellion against God. So the enemy deceives them through the back door—a revival of lying signs, wonders, and manifestations, and a gospel of the *born-again Jesus* who paid for the sins of man by escaping the clutches of Gehenna. These false signs and false doctrines are the trickery of unperceived iniquity—a satanic footprint within the church—taking preeminence over the Gospel of righteousness. As 2 Thessalonians 2:10 states, the **deceivableness** comes from not having **the love of the truth**. The deceptive teaching of another gospel and the signs and lying wonders that are ignorantly proclaimed and performed by professing Christians—all to presumably build and strengthen the church—have instead succeeded in strengthening a counterfeit salvation and a counterfeit church.

Chapter 10

Supernatural versus Paranormal

It is essential that we understand the difference between the supernatural and the paranormal. In the earthly physical realm, the genuine supernatural power of God is never manifested to impress people or to glorify men. Every miracle Jesus performed was supernatural: they were miracles of physical healing, raising the dead, and feeding the multitude—they glorified God. Paranormal activity may impress the observer, but it's not from God because it does not glorify Him. Examples would include an object that moves, levitation, materializing matter, or any abnormal activity that diverts attention away from Jesus the Savior. In Matthew 14 and Mark 6, we read that Jesus walked on water. Was this a paranormal activity? No, it was supernatural because Jesus was God, and it glorified Himself.

The paranormal is very real. It catches the interest of Christians if they see it as a nonthreatening divinely given sign of God's glory. Once witnessed, we want to see more! Anticipated and sought-after manifestations have brought the appearance of a paranormal gold-dust "*glory cloud*" several times at Bill Johnson's Bethel Church in Redding, California. This sparkly cloud hovers above the congregation for a few moments and then disappears. The "*glory cloud,*" as it is called, is not from God; neither is it the glory of God. If it were, the congregation would be flat on their face before Him! This type of "manifestation" is either man-made or has indeed materialized through paranormal demonic activity for the purpose of tricking gullible believers—only because they ask for and are desirous to see signs and miracles from God.

In Exodus, chapter 7, we read that Pharaoh's magicians performed "enchantments" before Moses and Aaron. When reading the full text of what happened, we know that these enchantments were not merely magic tricks but were physiologically impossible and unnatural: they were paranormal. Since the magician's paranormal trickery opposed and mocked God's power, the supernatural power of God overpowered the paranormal manifestation when Aaron's rod swallowed up the magician's rod (Exodus 7:12). Likewise in 2 Thessalonians 2:9–10, when Paul said that **Satan with all power and signs and lying wonders, and with all deceivableness of unrighteousness** will sway them that perish, we should know that paranormal activity also falls into this category. The connection is this: those who promote and anticipate paranormal activity within Christianity, such as materializing gold dust or falling angel feathers referred to as "*divine*" or "*the glory*," have not discerned its satanic origin—a **deceivableness of unrighteousness**.

When enticed away from the Gospel or drawn to a Jesus not described in the Bible, the enemy moves in to further reinforce the deception. Those who anticipate increasing signs and wonders of supernatural healings or paranormal activity within Christianity become convinced that every such incident comes from God. But Satan knows that seeking miracles and manifestations does not spread the Gospel of salvation and so will create any distraction necessary. This is why we must test the spirits to discern the origin of any "sign" or even a supernatural occurrence of physical healing. Not all signs and miracles are from God; if the one initiating the miracle does not attest to and submit to the Jesus of the Bible, the miracle is counterfeit. Many Christians have been charmed by Satan's devices of supernatural and paranormal occurrences: they are drawn by the miraculous, rather than the Savior of their soul.

The supernatural reality of phenomenal counterfeit healing and dramatic paranormal activity was witnessed by Christian author and speaker Johanna Michaelsen when she lived near Mexico City in the early 1970s. Michaelsen told of her experiences in her 1982 book *The Beautiful Side of Evil.* During her time in Mexico, Johanna Michaelsen thought herself to be a Christian for being a follower of the mystic Jesus of psychic power. She began observing and assisting in "Christian psychic surgeries" performed by the mystic shaman Dona Pachita who healed people of physical defects, cancer, and terminal conditions. The healing power of which Pachita called upon was very real, yet it was not the power of Jesus, the Son of God. Michaelsen states that in most of these mystic surgical ceremonies, crude and rusty instruments were used on the patient, and in every instance, a crucifix was invoked, along with a nearby image of Jesus, and all was performed "in the name of Jesus." Michaelsen stated these surgeries were sometimes a bloody mess but that most recipients were either healed or experienced an improved condition. After having witnessed hundreds of ceremonies of miraculous healings, Johanna Michaelsen was enlightened to this demonic hold of a mystic counterfeit Jesus. She then ceased her participation in these ceremonies and began to embrace the real Jesus of the Bible.

Speaking at a 2016 conference on the subject of "Testing the Spirits," Johanna Michaelsen stated:

> *If a miracle, a sign, a wonder, a prophecy, a healing is performed by an occultist, or by means of a cult technique—whether it's internal like clairvoyance, ESP, or like the girl with a spirit of divination in Acts 16; or if it's external like the Ouija boards, crystal ball, tarot cards, palm reading, it is by definition not of God, regardless of how spectacular, holy, or angelic it may be. It is a demonic counterfeit—even if Jesus' Name is attached to it.*" (Johanna Michaelsen, "Testing the Spirits," YouTube, 36:42)

Johanna Michaelsen and her Michaelsen Ministries website have now taught exegetical truth from the Bible for many years—

rightly equipping Christians to discern and distinguish the satanic deception of counterfeit miracles and manifestations happening worldwide. Though miraculous healings are occurring, we must discern the source. Genuine healing—though likely temporary—also comes through contrived ceremonial and mantra techniques of occult mediums. Physical healing can also occur through a "declaration of healing" where a false Christ is taught and sought after. Again we must try the spirits: God allows "lying spirits" to seduce those who acquisition any type of healing mastery. (Compare Deuteronomy 13:1–3 and 1 Kings 22:19–23.)

Chapter 11

No Worldwide Revival?

Habakkuk 2:14 proclaims, **For the earth shall be filled with the knowledge of the glory of the Lord, as the waters cover the sea**. This verse is not speaking of revival in the world, but that the knowledge and **the glory of the Lord shall be revealed, and all flesh shall see it together**—during the millennial reign of Jesus, as Isaiah 40:5 declares. A "spiritual revival," as discerned from Scripture, is either a revival of repentance and devotion within the body of Christ and/or a revival of spiritual awakening and repentance among the general population. Last-day followers of the Lord Jesus will be victorious just as were believers in the early church. Even so, the Bible does not tell of a countless number of souls that will be harvested at the last moments of the age.

Revelation 7:9 says, **After this I beheld, and lo, a great multitude, which no man could number, of all nations, and kindreds, and tongues, stood before the throne, and before the Lamb, clothed with white robes, and palms in their hands**. Here, the apostle John is referring to all the redeemed throughout human history—not a multitude of the faithful who lived at the very end of the age. Jesus said, **But he that shall endure until the end, the same shall be saved** (Matthew 24:13). Nowhere did Jesus say that a great multitude would be redeemed just prior to his return.

Look closely at Joel 2:27–29. Verses 28 and 29 are amazing because they seem to allude to an end-time spiritual revival. But by neglecting verse 27, we easily jump to conclusions. The entire passage reads,

> **And ye shall know that I am in the midst of Israel, and that I am the Lord your God, and none else… And it shall come to pass afterward, that I will pour out my spirit upon all flesh…and also upon the servants and upon the handmaids in those days will I pour out my spirit.**

We must discern the full prophecy and train of thought here. In this age of the new covenant we live in, the Lord is pouring out His spirit on all peoples of the world—not only the Jews. We cannot theorize from this passage that most all flesh will be redeemed in an end-time spiritual revival. When it says **I will pour out my spirit upon all flesh** (verse 28), this means that other gentiles of all walks of life are now included and can receive salvation and the "gifts of the Spirit" if they will follow the Savior in righteousness—which before the Savior came was displayed only **in the midst of Israel** (verse 27). This passage is a prophecy of what will occur in the expanse of time after the cross of Christ—the time in which the spirit of God is made available to all people of the world.

Because the spirit of God is now being poured out on all peoples of the world, the enemy sees his time is short and so must distract and deceive as many devout believers as possible with mystical delusions and wondrous deceptive signs (2 Thessalonians 2:11). When drawn to a church for its dynamic new teaching of never-before-heard testimonies of prosperity, power, authority, miracles, and signs, we are actually being seduced by the enemy. Sadly, we have been reduced to simple Christians rather than discerning Christians. Biblical knowledge and a discernment of any and all false doctrine is essential to realize that much of the church is now entangled in the grips of a great digression, delusion, and deception as a result of the enemy's craftiness.

Certainly, any city or local church can experience a genuine revival in righteousness. However, many recent supposed outpourings of the Spirit have not had the earmark of unsaved people turning away from their unrighteousness. Instead, Christians already within the church have been inundated with Holy Ghost hype in "experiencing God" and in the quest for manifestations. But according to Acts 2:38, the Holy Ghost is received when we repent and are baptized. The apostle Peter didn't go on to say that Spirit-filled believers should also pursue many other manifestations or seek influence through economic success by direction of the Holy Spirit. Rather, the primary function of the Holy Spirit is to reveal the truth of the Savior and His Gospel as we see in John 16:13–14 and 1 Corinthians 2:13.

A prolonged period of worship and emotion within church walls is not a Holy Ghost revival. A Holy Ghost inspired revival of repentance begins within the believer and is spread into the community. Jesus commands us to share the Gospel of Salvation with those bound for eternal hell.

Acts 3:19 says, **Repent ye therefore, and be converted, that your sins may be blotted out, when the times of refreshing shall come from the presence of the Lord**. Many times of inner refreshing of the Spirit of God will come—but only if we remain repentant and persist in our conversion to the spiritually grounded Gospel. Old Testament passages such as Joel 2:27–29, Isaiah 40:5, and Habakkuk 2:14, which seem to point to an end-time worldwide revival, are in reality prophesying of a centuries-long progression in revelation truth of the new covenant Gospel and of the ultimate reign of Jesus.

In one sense, the Protestant Reformation, which began with Martin Luther five centuries ago, could be considered the beginning of a revival from the darkness of pagan Christianity. More people are genuinely *born again* today than at the end of the Dark Ages—a time when the Catholic church kept the scriptures from the common people. However, 1 Timothy 4:1 also informs us **that in the latter times some shall depart from the faith, giving heed to seducing spirits and doctrines of devils**. When thinking about this statement from the apostle Paul and by discerning the diminished and ineffective gospel being preached today within growing churches, we know this verse refers to many who are departing from the precise Gospel of Jesus rather than departing from church attendance. The end-time **falling away** spoken of in 2 Thessalonians 2:3 and Hebrews 6:6 are not referring to last-day Christians who will backslide and neglect God as we used to think. Though many have ceased their church attendance for one reason or another, we now discern through other passages that this is not the only meaning of these verses.

Now that a large portion of the church is well underway down the slippery slope of apostasy from doctrinal truth, we realize that the body of Christ is actually experiencing a progression of unsound doctrine being taught. Many Christians have deviated from sound Bible doctrine to a false type of religious gospel or a carnal gospel—all while remaining faithful to their church. The reason there is so little teaching in our churches about the end-time apostasy and the **falling away** the New Testament speaks of is because most clergymen are either ignorant of what it refers to or they don't see any apostasy happening in their own church, simply for the fact that the congregation is growing in number and therefore must be growing spiritually as well. Pastors neglectful of passages referring to deception are ignorantly focused on drawing in the younger generation through Christian entertainment and social programs, combined with an easier-to-swallow and less-offensive gospel message. It is all perpetuated and fortified by Satan the deceiver, who loves this preoccupation.

The Bible reveals that when the Antichrist man arises, he will bring peace and unity to the whole world. That's how he will deceive even some Christians in growing churches. The uninformed Christian who believes that "*keeping the faith*" involves only their faithful church attendance and a mere belief in Jesus will be easily deceived by the forthcoming religious system and the Antichrist man.

Daniel 9:27 states, **And he shall confirm the covenant with many for one week**. Obviously this one-week covenant (a seven-year covenant) is a seemingly friendly gesture. Second Thessalonians 2:4 states that he will **sit in the temple of God, showing himself that**

he is God. Misinformed and ignorant humanity and those trapped by false doctrines will be swayed by this Antichrist man, who will initially promote love and acceptance of all people as "children of God" no matter their belief.

In 2 Peter 3:16-17, Peter states that some issues the apostle Paul wrote about were hard to understand and that certain teachers of that time had distorted what he wrote to support their own doctrine. Because of this, he calls them **unlearned and unstable** and that it was **unto their own destruction**. He then says, **You therefore, beloved, seeing you know these things before, beware lest you also, being led away with the error of the wicked, fall from your own steadfastness** (NKJV). When fully understanding this passage, we know that the **error of the wicked** refers to those who distort Holy Scripture and that the listener is **led away** by them. Both are destroyed. Notice that the **"wicked"** spoken of in 2 Peter 3:17 are not said to be murderers, thieves, adulterers, and sorcerers, but those who distort Scripture! In fact, the word **wicked** used here in the King James Version is from the Greek word *athesmos*, meaning "lawless." It is the spiritually lawless who reject the laws of the kingdom of God.

Jeremiah 23:1 says, **Woe be unto the pastors that destroy and scatter the sheep of my pasture saith the Lord**. Today, a pastor can destroy God's people through the teaching of unsound doctrine. They may seem to have great love and compassion, but this is why they are so able to deceive. Therefore, though waves of revival may come within the church, they must be carefully discerned; they are not necessarily revivals from God. A scriptural "revival of righteousness" must of necessity come through sound doctrinal teaching—which many shepherds of the flock have today neglected.

Chapter 12

Gospel Derailment

Orthodox Christianity has always recognized *positive word* and *positive thought* theories of the nineteenth century's *New Thought* movement as cultic and incompatible with Scripture. Pastors perhaps ignorant that these *positivity* ideas have evolved from Eastern mystic theologies and practices nonetheless believe them to be beneficial for the church and have justified wrapping them in Christian terminology. Though there's nothing wrong with having a positive attitude and a mindset to always speak affirming and positive words, there is danger in applying any cultic methods to our spiritual growth and alongside the Gospel. We've been seduced to believe that our spoken positive words are essential for success and for the presumed fact that Jesus our Savior desires the very best for us. But by this pagan mixture with our Christian beliefs, we have bought into spiritual adultery with the doctrines of men. The outcome is a gospel heavily infused with modern psychology and metaphysics—invented to appeal to our human desire for happiness and fulfillment. What follows is a prime example.

Lakewood Church in Houston, Texas, pastored by motivational guru Joel Osteen, is currently the largest megachurch in the United States. In the weekly worldwide telecast, Pastor Osteen, guest speakers, and others on the Lakewood team bring great encouragement and inspiration for life by preaching the *positive confession doctrine.* Osteen states we will achieve our destiny and ultimately overcome our disappointments and strenuous circumstances by redirecting our thought process and by our words of optimism. The overriding thought behind most of Joel Osteen's messages: "*Reprogram your mind, and change will occur.*" This is a sensible statement almost nobody would disagree with. But careful discernment is essential. This mind-change formula has no bearing on the Gospel: we cannot mentally or through positive words reprogram our own mind in a spiritual sense. Rather, we must first be knowledgeable of the true saving Gospel, which reprograms our heart's focus through the Holy Spirit. Though Pastor Osteen's focus and method for change may sound logical and beneficial, his encouraging words fall short in doctrinal teaching. Osteen declares that *positive words* and a *positive attitude* is "*God's will for every believer*"—thus linking cultic superstitious theology with the Bible's message of salvation. This misnomer actually moves us away from sound biblical doctrine by giving the message that God's prioritizing will is for us to think positively and speak positive words in order to arrive at the personal destiny He has for us. Yet nowhere does the Bible give this strategy so as to accomplish God's purposes in our lives. It is a departure from the Gospel of salvation because it melds earthly success with spiritual success—which is impossible according to the many words of Jesus in Matthew, Mark, Luke, and John. God's divine destiny for us is eternal life; it is not the achievement of earthly success and earthly contentment.

Joel Osteen was greatly influenced by his father, Pastor John Osteen. When Joel assumed the pastorate position of his father's nondenominational Charismatic Lakewood Church, his preaching style was different, but the content of his sermons was initially similar to his father's more Bible-based gospel message. Within a short time, however, Joel Osteen redirected his focus to a friendlier, less offensive subject matter—proclaiming that because God directs our heart's desire, He is obligated to our success in life if we do our part by staying positive. Yet our personal earthly desires are far separated from God's spiritual desires for us. Though God puts a desire or a vision in our heart to strive toward, it will only be achieved successfully in His own timing and not by our ongoing positive attitude.

Pastor Osteen claims to speak the truth of God's Word. Unfortunately, he proclaims the mistruth of a different gospel with no eternal benefit—the gospel of health, wealth, and earthly success, which is nowhere found in the New Testament. Though Joel Osteen's inspirational messages are a powerful encouragement to his listening audience, they are strategically fused with unscriptural *New Thought* doctrines of *positive words* and *positive thought*, which cultist philosopher Phineas Quimby taught long ago.

According to Strong's Exhaustive Concordance of the Bible, nowhere do we find the words *positive*, *negative*, or *attitude* in the King James Bible. These English words originated about five hundred years ago: they are modern-day terminology and are nonexistent in the ancient Aramaic/Hebrew and Greek languages, which the Geneva Bible and the King James Bible were translated from.

Having confidence in Christ is what Paul encouraged in Philippians 3:4; he said: **For we are the circumcision, which worship God in the spirit, and rejoice in Christ Jesus, and have no confidence in the flesh**.

This is as close as Scripture comes to proclaiming a positive attitude in Christian living. And even within the same sentence, Paul said that we should **have no confidence in the flesh**! Paul wasn't addressing the issue of self-worth but rather that we must have a God confidence over and above trusting in our own effort or our own self-improvement to become righteous before God or to accomplish great things for Him.

Believing in the Gospel of the Bible is not a mere formality of acceptance; instead, we should cling to it because of our wretchedness. In Romans 7:24, Paul says: **O wretched man that I am! Who shall deliver me from the body of this death?**

Though using faith-filled words and having a positive attitude is beneficial in anyone's life, this does not change our personal need for the Gospel every day. We will always be sinners saved by His grace. The Bible shows us that we don't necessarily need a sense of self-worth or self-confidence to be used of God to accomplish greatness or to realize our potential, as Pastor Joel Osteen mistakenly states. In fact, the Old Testament gives many examples of men who were in doubt, apprehensive, and spoke unbelieving words—but God used them anyway to achieve His plan and purpose. Among the many apprehensive and doubtful men was Moses with his verbal wariness and insecurity (Exodus 3 and 4) and the prophet Elijah's fear of Queen Jezebel (1 Kings 19). These examples, and many more in Scripture, reveal that negative words, negative thoughts, and apprehensive behavior did not hinder God's agenda one bit.

It is true that our positive or negative words have effect in our own success or failure. But believe-ism optimism is not a directive in our Bible that brings about change. Rather, it is prayer that changes things—yet not always as we wish. Yes, we should have a positive attitude, give honor and respect to others, love God and forgive those who offend us, and be focused and bold in our Christian walk. But for the followers of Jesus who have these traits, the New Testament gives no such promise of overabundance, miracles of change, and earthly satisfaction. In fact, 2 Timothy 3:12 says: **And all that will live godly in Christ Jesus shall suffer persecution**.

The apostle Paul suffered persecution for preaching the cross of Christ. In Galatians 5:11, he states: **And I, brethren, if I yet preach circumcision, why do I yet suffer persecution? Then is the offence of the cross ceased**.

Here, Paul informs us that by doing works to gain salvation, the cross of Christ becomes unnecessary. The **offense of the cross**—the real Gospel—is therefore theologically rejected by carnal Christians who are told to focus on affirming words and positive thoughts to propel them toward God's will, earthly gain, and better conditions. But where does our Bible say this? Nowhere! In fact, the reverse! Our own contrived works of positive thinking and positive words absolutely overshadows and depletes the Gospel message of Jesus!

In this same manner and according to Galatians 5:11, Joel Osteen thereby preaches a gospel of circumcision of the mind and tongue—a works-based cutting away of every negative word and negative thought to obtain happiness, success, and a fulfilled Christian life. Yet in a spiritual sense, this is unprofitable and unnecessary.

Positivity itself leans heavily toward a mental satisfaction, while giving spiritual and eternal matters only a cursory handshake. According to our Bible, the only positive confession with any eternal value is the confession that "Jesus is Lord" over one's life. It is a verbal confession and a determined position of the heart. It is a powerful testimony not associated with success in business, in prestige, in authority, in self-confidence, or in mastery over life's financial problems.

Pastor Joel Osteen, among other Faith teachers, points to Proverbs 18:21 to support his theory of speaking things into existence with our positive words. The verse declares: **Death and life are in the power of the tongue: and they that love it shall eat the fruit thereof**.

Does this indicate we can create life or death...or create positive or negative circumstances by our verbal proclamation? If so, every believer has matching power with God the Creator! If you believe this is possible, then why are you ever sick? Proverbs 18:21 would thus stand on its own as the only Bible verse necessary for obtaining a good and perfect life! Rather, this verse is a warning for those who love to talk too much. It says they that **love it** (their words) shall reap the consequences—good or bad. A gossiper will speak **death** and will later **eat the fruit thereof** in their own life. Proverbs 18:21 is simply a warning to the gossiper: it does not mean that reality is created by the power of the tongue.

If positive words have such positive affect in our life, why does our Bible contain many negative proclamations and critical-sounding language? In fact, Jesus seems to be the worst offender! After telling us to seek first the kingdom of God in Matthew 6:33 (BSB), He immediately digresses, saying: **Therefore do not worry about tomorrow, for tomorrow will worry about itself. Today has enough trouble of its own**. After making encouraging statements, Jesus then descends into negativity—**Today has enough trouble of its own**! Jesus also said: **In the world you will have tribulation** (John 16:33). This also seems to be rather negative talk according to today's teachers of *positive confession*. Jesus must have been schizophrenic—speaking words of wisdom and hope, then suddenly negative words of gloomy hardship, practically in the same breath! Why did He feel the need to proclaim trouble, depravity, wickedness, malice, stress, and strife over our everyday lives by presumptuously and prophetically speaking it out loud here?

In Matthew 16:21–23, Jesus begins to speak very negatively to His disciples, telling them He must go to Jerusalem and suffer many things of the elders, chief priests, and scribes, and that He would be killed. But Peter, being the positive fellow that he was, rebuked Jesus for His horrific negative statements of tribulation and suffering to come. Then Jesus turned to Peter and said: **Get thee behind me, Satan: thou art an offence unto me**. According to the doctrine of today's Faith teachers, Jesus had thus rebuked all positive input and was intent on His path toward doom. What happened next? His own prophetic proclamation of scourging and death came true, and He was executed on the cross! What on earth was Jesus thinking? Why did He need to make such negative declarations? The ever-encouraging Joel Osteen says: "*The power of words—your words, affect your future. You've got to send your words out in the direction you want your life to go*" ("Joel Osteen Exposed," YouTube, 10:15).

Unfortunately for Jesus, He lived too long ago and didn't have the chance to attend Lakewood Church to hear Joel Osteen's positive messages of avoiding all negative talk. If only Jesus had realized how His verbal negativity created the reality of His own crucifixion! Right? Wrong! Jesus was prophesying of His own divine destiny, which then brought to all mankind the Gospel of truth and eternal life.

When doing a little research into the effect of cultic and pagan practices within Christianity—as we did earlier in the book—we find that Pastor Osteen preaches the unbiblical *law of attraction* theory of *New Thought* teaching. The Bible tells us to glorify God with our life—not exalt ourselves or to think of God as our personal wish granter as a result of our positivity. Though God doesn't want us to dwell on our trouble, it is not wrong to verbalize the fact of our trouble or lack: we are not speaking negative circumstances into reality by doing so. Our Bible does not teach this. Yet in light of the *positive confession* doctrine, Jesus's verbal declaration of His own demise would fall into this category of self-condemning negativity.

Jesus was also profoundly negative, judgmental, and cruel to the scribes and Pharisees, telling them they were fools, vipers, and hypocrites—right to their face! In Matthew 23:15 Jesus said: **Woe unto you, scribes and Pharisees, hypocrites! For ye compass sea and land to make one proselyte, and when he is made, ye make him twofold more the child of hell than yourselves**.

My goodness! Such abrasive and negative language spewed at these religious leaders who were only trying to do their very best! It seems this Savior of ours would have benefitted greatly from professional psychoanalytic counseling to help change His negative and degrading approach! Right?

In the same manner, weren't the apostle Paul's harsh judgmental words to the church at Galatia also uncalled for? In Galatians 3:1, he lashes out: **O foolish Galatians, who hath bewitched you, that ye should not obey the truth?** And again in verse 3, Paul says: **Are ye so foolish?** Using today's vernacular, Paul would have said, "*You stupid Galatians! Who messed with your mind that you no longer believe the truth? How dimwitted can you be?*"

Did Paul's critical and negative words cause harm? No! When taken to heart, it must have turned the Galatians around to see the error of their ways! Using negative-sounding terminology when making a right judgmental call is not sin. It is not unloving to convey the truth. It is not divisive to use strong words to point out biblical error. It is not an option to stand against evil: it is a divine command! Jesus, Paul, and many Old Testament prophets were justified in using strong language to shake the listener out of their prideful and unfruitful ways.

Yes, Pastor Joel Osteen is a loving, caring, compassionate, and encouraging pastor. But he is not focused on the Great Commission of the Gospel of righteousness. He is focused rather on self-love, earthly satisfaction, success, and contentment through positive speech and a positive mindset—a marvelous and deceptive departure from New Testament doctrine.

At Houston's Lakewood Church, an invitation to accept Jesus as the Lord and Savior is given at the end of each service. Pastor Osteen's instruction is to "*Just say this simple prayer: Lord Jesus, I repent of my sin; come into my heart; I make you my Lord and Savior.*"

Of course, there is nothing wrong with this prayer if it comes from the heart. Since, however, the content of Osteen's sermons does not focus on the real Gospel of the Bible, the seeker of a better life easily perceives this prayer as an afterthought or as a good suggestion to accept Jesus as Savior only for a supernatural assistance in obtaining a better life experience. Inevitably, this wrong focus keeps us in the sin of a self-absorbed lifestyle. Thus the significance of making Jesus one's Lord and Savior is not only misapplied but also misunderstood—repenting only of negative thoughts, negative words, and bad behavior—only to proffer a more happy and productive life.

Unregenerate man desires only to improve his circumstances while holding on to his sinful and selfish ways. Pastor Osteen inadvertently provides the avenue through which this can happen. Because the Lakewood congregation hears only a watered-down gospel message of positivity, linked with an easy one-time prayer to acquire God's favor, they are led down a broad road to spiritual destruction. The listener is not told to follow after Jesus in the pursuit of righteousness but rather to pursue self-confidence, self-acceptance, and self-love by the riddance of self-doubt and all negative influence. As 2 Timothy 4:3 warns, it is through tantalizing teaching that **itching ears** are played upon to discover how God desires our "best life now." Second Timothy 4:4 then says: **And they shall turn away their ears from the truth, and shall be turned unto fables**. When this passage is not understood as referring to the doctrine of the Gospel, the search for biblical truth is replaced with the search for happiness: we become convinced that our earthly happiness is God's greatest desire.

Joel Osteen admits when interviewed that he never talks about sin or hell within his sermons but lets the audience be convicted of their own wrongdoing. Yet how does avoiding this primary aspect of the Gospel in a church atmosphere lead people to the real Christ? We don't need to beat people up with the truth, but we can gently lead them to it by showing how Jesus spoke many times of sin and hell as an integral part of His Gospel message—which in turn reveals the reality and guilt of sin.

On Easter Sunday 2016, Joel Osteen preached a little differently. What began as a doctrinally sound sermon titled "The Power of the Blood," Osteen made insightful statements of the atoning blood of Christ as key to understanding the Gospel. He presented the correct comparison of new covenant faith against the old Mosaic covenant of sacrificing animals for sin. Though Osteen didn't mention the word *sin* as something to be acknowledged and repented of, his Easter message was theologically correct, until he rapidly digressed to endorse the apostate *prosperity gospel* of health and wealth provided by the atoning blood of the Savior. Stating the benefits of how Jesus's shed blood still speaks today, Osteen proclaimed:

> *They may have crucified His body, but they couldn't stop His blood from speaking. When we are sick, His blood says, by my stripes you are healed. When we need provision, His blood says, I became poor so that you could become well off. His blood is still crying out for freedom, redemption, salvation, and abundance.* ("The Power of the Blood," YouTube, 21:40)

Pastor Osteen made the mistake of linking the Gospel of salvation with a gospel of earthly abundance and friendship with the world system—a belief that earthly success, material gain, and perfect health was a component of our redemption and inheritance as believers. This cannot be possible. What does our Bible say? **Ye adulterers and adulteresses, know ye not that the friendship of the world is enmity with God?** (James 4:4). Reading this verse within its surrounding context, we see that James is warning believers of the sin of envying, lusting, and striving against those who have what they themselves don't have. James refers to spiritual adultery: one hand in the kingdom of God and the other in the entanglements of earthly satisfaction and manipulation for selfish gain. In contrast, Jesus preached something altogether different: in Mark 2:17, He said, **I came not to call the righteous, but sinners to repentance**. As such, the true followers of Jesus must turn from sin by pursuing

the kingdom of God and His righteousness (Matthew 6:33). They should then spread His Gospel (Matthew 28:19)—a good news gospel message of eternal life—not the good news of self-love, earthly satisfaction, and perfect health. Unfocused pastors of the flock have not discerned the Gospel message if they do not prick the conscience of the sinner by first calling them to repentance.

Insightful wisdom

Pastor Paul Washer, founder of HeartCry Missionary Society, describes false teachers and those who follow them, saying:

> *People are not innocent victims of false teachers. False teachers are God's judgment on people who really don't want God—but in the name of religion, plan on getting everything their carnal heart desires. That's why a Joel Osteen is raised up. The people who sit under him are not victims of him. He is the judgment of God upon them because they want exactly what he wants—and it's not God!* (Paul Washer, "How to Identify False Prophets," YouTube, 04:07)

Though Pastor Washer's words sound harsh, they are full of righteous anger against the false teachers of our day. Washer's amazing insight explains God's purpose in using false teachers to bring deception on the church as a means of separating the true disciples of Jesus from those focused on temporal things.

Pastor Joel Osteen's proclaimed "best life" is not a life of righteousness before God; rather, it revolves around earthly satisfaction, success, and fulfillment—with salvation of the soul as an afterthought. This is totally backward! What if all these earthly good things were taken away? Would we still serve Jesus if He only offered us Himself? What if Jesus offered us no promise of healing, no success, no worldly blessings, no miracles, signs, or wonders? What if we had to suffer pain and mockery instead of perfect health and friendship with all people? What if we were afflicted and tormented for following Jesus? What if we were poor instead of prosperous? What if the only good thing provided by the cross was His promise of eternal life? Would we still give Him our life? I submit that a majority of people would turn away. And yet the very early church experienced all of these hardships and lack but did not forsake their Savior: they did not turn aside.

In a certain sense, Pastor Osteen's uplifting messages of self-worth are indeed scriptural: every person has value in the eyes of God the Creator. But Osteen pushes this thought far from the spiritual realm by stating: "*The better you feel about yourself, the better you'll do. Most people are basically good people, and because we have good hearts, we must learn to love ourselves*" (Joel Osteen, "Stay Positive about Yourself," YouTube, 04:38).

The Bible makes no such declaration: to the contrary, the prophet Jeremiah said, **The heart is deceitful above all things, and desperately wicked: who can know it?** (Jeremiah 17:9).

After turning to Jesus as our personal Savior, there is no necessity of self-love. This concept is counterproductive to the real Gospel. Loving oneself is the psychology of Sigmund Freud—promoted as his remedy for man's mental ills. Though we have great worth in an eternal sense, there is no advantage in loving ourselves, whether spiritually regenerate or spiritually unregenerate. Sigmund Freud believed that by searching the inner mind, then verbalizing what angers us, we begin the peace process of inner healing, self-acceptance, and self-love. This is not a Christian teaching, however. To the follower of Christ, it will only lead to more frustration over our human inability to forgive others as well as frustration for not measuring up spiritually. Rather, we must despise our fallen nature and hold fast to the cross of Christ.

In Matthew 22:39, Jesus said: **Thou shalt love thy neighbor as thyself**. Does this mean we should strive to first love ourselves so that we can better love others? No! Jesus emphasizes caring for our neighbor just as we care for ourselves. Since our Bible nowhere states we should strive to love ourselves, a personal psychoanalysis is unnecessary. We cannot find peace and contentment by this method. Instead, Jesus gives us the simple solution:

> **Whosoever will come after me, let him deny himself, and take up his cross, and follow me. For whosoever will save his life shall lose it; but whosoever shall lose his life for my sake and the gospel's, the same shall save it. For what shall it profit a man if he shall gain the whole world, and lose his own soul?** (Mark 8:34–36)

In the culture of Jesus's time, a cross represented death. We must die to ourselves: we must give up searching for a contrived inner cure. We must forfeit our self-improvement—our psychoanalyzing—our love of self. We must see our need for spiritual righteousness in Christ and a total disgust for our depravity. We must come to the cross and repent of our sin. And yet, our righteousness in Christ provides for no earthly thing, no earthly satisfaction, or physical comfort. These are inconsequential to the spiritual realm. God's earthly blessing is only temporal; it has not come to us for our faith in Jesus. King Solomon wrote: **Keep thy heart with all diligence; for out of it are the issues of life** (Proverbs 4:23). In a spiritual sense, the "issues of life" are righteousness, peace, and joy in the Holy Ghost: these are the result of an unseen spiritual righteousness in Christ.

Christians cannot be divided in their passions: we must function in the world, but we cannot chase after the world's material system or its self-improvement system in preference over the Gospel. Jesus said: **Ye are not of this world, but I have chosen you out of the world, therefore the world hates you** (John 15:19). When participating in man's methods of self-improvement, self-love, and self-confidence, we have denied that Jesus has called us out of the world to be separate unto Himself. The only confidence necessary is a confident trust in Christ's atoning work.

The apostle John said: **Love not the world, neither the things in the world. If any man love the world, the love of the Father is not in him** (1 John 2:15). These words very much apply to our love for the wisdom of man, as well as a love for the material things of the world.

Chapter 13

False Prophet—False Gospel

An internationally known pastor having enormous influence within the Charismatic/Word of Faith movement was killed in a tragic accident in 2014 at age sixty. This man taught a false and heretical gospel message. Since those who closely followed his teaching are sure to lead many more astray in the future, it is therefore necessary to reveal from Scripture and without question the false doctrine he taught.

From Nassau, Bahamas, evangelist and motivational speaker Dr. Myles Munroe preached amazing sermons and inspiring insightful messages—many times with a degree of wisdom and truth. However, it was difficult to tell when he traversed from Bible truth to Bible error unless you knew the Scriptures very well and paid close attention. Dr. Myles Munroe's version of the gospel was mixed with doctrinal error to the point of proclaiming a far different gospel than what is found in the Bible.

In 1 Corinthians 5:12–13 (ESV), Paul said: **Is it not those inside the Church whom you are to judge? God judges those outside. Purge the evil person from among you**.

Who exactly was "inside the Church" that Paul told them to judge? In verses 10 and 11, he goes through a list of sins committed by so-called brethren, then warned the Corinthian church to have no fellowship with them. The only sin named in this passage that could slide under the radar as a possible unrecognized sin of Myles Munroe is "covetousness," meaning "eager for gain." It is the sinning and apostate brother who ascends to pastorate over the flock by way of proclaiming the gain of earthly prosperity through faith in Jesus. Covetousness cannot be harmonious with the Gospel of salvation because it promotes an eagerness for gain—a double standard in opposing doctrines, of which Dr. Myles Munroe was blind to, primarily for his endorsement of the believers' equality with Jesus the Savior.

When explaining his personal revelation of how the kingdom of God comes to earth, Myles Munroe stated: "*Prayer is man giving God earthly license for heavenly interference. God can only do what we permit him to do*" ("We Control God? Myles Munroe & Benny Hinn," Daystar, 2004, YouTube).

Dr. Munroe's explanation of his "*revelation*" is apostasy from the truth of Scripture. The Bible nowhere says that God moves only by our verbal proclamation or permission in prayer. God does not coax us into utterance so that He can move. This reduces the Creator God to one having limited power.

As do all other Word of Faith teachers, Myles Munroe references Genesis 1:26 for proof of his theory: **And God said, let us make man in our image, after our likeness: and let them have dominion over the fish of the sea, and over the fowl of the air, and over the cattle, and over all the earth, and over every creeping thing**. In the 2004 conversation with Benny Hinn, Munroe stated that according to this passage, "*God made Himself illegal on planet earth!*" This is a perversion of the verse and is nowhere close to its meaning. When we correctly discern the first few chapters of Genesis, we find that even though Adam was the pinnacle of God's creation and though he walked and communed with God for a time in the garden, he did not have equal authority with his Creator. Since the time Adam and Eve were created and throughout the remainder of the book of Genesis, it nowhere tells that God relinquished His authority in the earth simply because he gave Adam dominion over land and beast (Genesis

1:26 and 1:28). Reading just a little further, we see in Genesis 2:15 that **the Lord God took the man and put him into the garden of Eden to dress it and to keep it**.

By comparing these passages, we know that Adam had dominion only to tend the land and also had dominion over every other living thing. Hence, before he sinned, Adam did not have total authority in the spiritual realm, nor did he have the power to create.

A requisite book critique

Published in 2006, Myles Munroe's book titled *Kingdom Principles* gives some insightful truth on the kingdom of God, showing how Christians will have blessing, provision, and success in ministry as members of God's kingdom when they obey the kingdom laws such as the Ten Commandments. However, total authority over all of life's circumstances, as Munroe claimed, is impossible according to the Bible. It is extreme by orthodox standards, partly because it limits God's involvement if we don't pray or speak out what we believe He wants to do. Certainly, God moves in our lives when we pray in faith and for **Thy will be done** as Jesus taught us to pray. But by stating "*God can only do what we permit him to do,*" Myles Munroe makes the absolute conclusion that God is limited by us. His sovereignty over us is nonexistent and meaningless because we are in control of Him! When persuaded to believe this false doctrine preached by Myles Munroe and others within the Faith movement, we are then **denying the power thereof**, as Paul says in 2 Timothy 3:5.

In the beginning of Dr. Munroe's book *Kingdom Principles*, he states on page 16: "*The message of the Bible is about the establishment of a kingdom rulership on this planet from the heavenly realm.*"

On its own, Dr. Monroe's statement here sounds fairly reasonable: God's ultimate plan is to establish His kingdom on this planet. Munroe then states: "*It is about a divine project of governing earth from heaven through mankind.*"

We now see Dr. Munroe's theological position. But he was wrong. The main theme of our Bible is certainly not kingdom rulership by mankind prior to the return of Christ—but only that mankind must heed to God's sovereignty and His Gospel of righteousness. Nonetheless, this sets the tone for Munroe's entire book *Kingdom Principles*. In the following pages, he states that God's kingdom is already here on earth and that the concepts of kingdom living must be realized and applied by the believer for their own earthly dominion.

Halfway through the book, on page 120, Dr. Munroe says: "*God has given us authority over the earth. That means we're in charge. Whatever we say goes. This gives us a lot of freedom to do what we please with our domain.*"

By this point in Myles Munroe's book, we should discern that his theological, doctrinal, and spiritual vision has completely degenerated into opaque cataracts. While standing on shaky doctrinal ground earlier in his book, we now cannot keep our balance on top of a full magnitude 9 earthquake! According to Myles Munroe, God is on a long-term hiatus, and we are in charge. He can do nothing for us until we get His attention through our own spoken words of authority, thereby giving Him permission to move in the affairs of men and on our behalf. Yet how is this ridiculous idea even possible when seeing the many passages telling of God's power and authority in all of His creation? In reality, we don't even need proof from the Bible! Quite obviously, by the rationality of our human intellect, we should intrinsically know the obvious—that man is not in control of anything! But for the sake of stating the truth, let's read what would seem to be the zenith of all Bible passages stating God's absolute sovereignty over all things: **He that sitteth in the heavens shall laugh: the Lord shall have them in derision** (Psalm 2:4).

This simple declaration profoundly clarifies the matter of God's rule and control over all the earth. Reading the preceding sentences in Psalm 2, we see that God sits high above the earth, snickering at ruthless kings and devious men who plot against Him and His people. Psalm 2:5 then says: **Then shall he speak unto them in his wrath, and vex them in his sore displeasure**. Hence, we cannot manipulate God in heaven, nor can we command Him to move. God alone is in control of everything that happens on planet Earth.

We can make humble petitions and requests for better circumstances of change, but God will not bring change only because we speak it out loud.

Myles Munroe's false doctrine of man's authority in the earth concludes that the once majestic God was suddenly offended that Adam and Eve, the pinnacle and perfection of His creation, rejected Him by their sin and since that time has just been sitting on His throne, unable or unwilling to do anything for mankind unless those who seek Him speak out what they want done. Munroe's synopsis renders God a spoiled child who didn't get His way in the beginning, so He has secluded Himself with a pouty attitude. But when called upon and given permission, He springs into action! Therefore, God must surely be insecure and immature—but has a very big ego when acknowledged. Yet there are many passages telling of God's power, sovereignty, and even His jealousy! Exodus 20:5: **I am a jealous God**, plus nine other passages throughout the Bible that refer to God's jealousy. Does God's jealousy delineate His immaturity or lack of sovereignty and authority? Certainly not! In discerning the new covenant we live under today, we see that God is jealous just as He was in the old covenant era. The difference now is that His jealousy is revealed through Jesus the Savior. This is not an immature act on God's part in the slightest! It's an act of His power and sovereignty over mankind and of a jealous love toward mankind, which then determines the authority God has in all the earth!

But Myles Munroe was somehow compelled to tailor the biblical text to give believers more than just a confidence in their salvation—justifying also a supreme authority over every circumstance. He had unknowingly changed the Gospel of eternal salvation into a gospel of temporal satisfaction.

In his book *Kingdom Principles*, Dr. Munroe refers to Psalm 138:2, which says: **I will worship toward thy holy temple, and will praise thy name for thy lovingkindness and for thy truth: for thou hast magnified thy word above all thy name**.

By connecting this passage with Genesis 1:26, Munroe claimed that the meaning of **thy word** in Psalm 138:2 was a "*vow*" God made with Himself to give man authority and dominion in the earth—

which logically took priority over the importance of His name. But by careful examination of specific Hebrew words in this verse, we see another interpretation.

Here in Psalm 138:2, the meaning of the word "truth" is "establishment."

The meaning of "magnified" is "wax greater," "lift up," or "increase."

The meaning of "word" is "commandment" or "speech."

The meaning of "above" is "through" or "according after."

Putting it all together, Psalm 138:2 is interpreted: **I will worship toward thy holy temple, and I will praise your name for your love, and for establishing your commandments, which shall increase through thy name**.

Psalm 138:2 says nothing about a vow God made with Himself to promote man to the highest earthly authority. When King David wrote this psalm, there was no "Bible" he could reference as "thy word." Hence, the term "thy word" in Psalm 138:2 refers only to the Ten Commandments, which are more important in directing humanity toward eternal life—even more important than understanding the significance of His name.

God's power, authority, and dominion is stated in Psalm 115:3: **But our God is in the heavens: he hath done whatsoever he hath pleased**. In contrast, Myles Munroe's doctrine of "man's kingdom authority" is selfish, temporal, and nonbeneficial in an eternal sense: it is erroneous because it rejects God's sovereignty. His view of the creation of man is not God centered but man centered. It is puffed up with pride, self-entitled, and goes completely against how Jesus instructed us to pray, saying: **Thy kingdom come. Thy will be done in earth, as it is in heaven** (Matthew 6:10).

On page 120 of his book Munroe states that Christians are given "*a lot of freedom to do what we please with our domain.*" Is this what Jesus meant in Matthew 16:19 when He said: **And I will give unto thee the keys of the kingdom of heaven: and whatsoever thou shalt bind on earth shall be bound in heaven: and whatsoever thou shalt loose on earth shall be loosed in heaven**? No!

This verse makes perfect sense, knowing that obedience to the laws of the kingdom will unleash heaven's blessing for us, just as Myles Munroe says. But by his added proclamation that Christians have total authority in the earth to do as we please, we find Dr. Munroe's theology to be an extremely erroneous interpretation of this verse. Strong's Concordance reveals the word "keys" in Matthew 16:19 means to "lock," or "unlock": it is a verb of action—not a type of noun which we possess for a physical benefit. The "keys" are for unlocking the understanding of salvation and in the awareness of how the kingdom of God operates because of Jesus the Savior and through Jesus the Savior. These keys are not a formula for earthly success. Specifically, the keys of the kingdom of heaven are metaphoric and spiritual—it is the knowledge of the simple Gospel of righteousness. Today, any *born-again* believer who comprehends the saving power of Jesus and who desires to walk in righteousness possess these keys of the kingdom.

Let's now apply Dr. Munroe's version of "kingdom keys" to a specific area…

If we pray and believe for healing in our body, but after many months or years of praying nothing happens, does this mean we lack enough faith to possess kingdom keys for the purpose of healing? No! We should search the Bible for an explanation and consider what precedes Matthew 16:19. Look at verse 18: **Thou art Peter, and upon this rock I will build my church**. Jesus was speaking to Peter, who perceived through no human rationale that Jesus was the Christ, the Son of the Living God (verse 16). Peter's confession about Jesus is the basis for possessing the keys of the kingdom of heaven. We possess kingdom authority for our confidence of who the Savior is and the assurance of imputed righteousness in Him. It is that basic. The keys of the kingdom for "binding" and "loosing" are not for initiating action but for enacting and bringing to light the spiritual principles already ordained in heaven. Possessing these keys gives us the authority to do the will of God—to share the Gospel message. Matthew 16:19 makes the powerful connection between heaven and earth—two realms that are explicitly tied together. When entering the kingdom of God the proper way, we then automatically obtain the **keys of the kingdom**.

Though what about better conditions of daily life or prosperity and wealth? Did Jesus indicate that Peter could bind unfavorable conditions such as poverty or persecution simply because he had obtained the keys of the kingdom? Myles Munroe says yes! If so, what happened to Peter and the rest of the disciples after Jesus ascended into heaven? They really messed up, didn't they? They experienced few pleasant circumstances. None of them amassed any wealth, and there is no record of any of them having a totally wonderful life. In fact, according to the early church history writings of Eusebius and Hippolytus of Rome, most of the apostles, and many others, were martyred for preaching the Gospel and refusing to deny their faith:

- *Stephen (not one of the twelve disciples) was first to be stoned to death for preaching the gospel in AD 36.*
- *James Zebedee was beheaded in AD 44.*
- *Philip was stoned in AD 53.*
- *James Alpheus was stoned and clubbed to death when in his nineties in AD 63.*
- *Matthew Levi, author of the Gospel of Matthew, was martyred by being staked to the ground in AD 60.*
- *Jude, author of the book of Jude, was clubbed and crucified around AD 72.*
- *Simon Peter was crucified upside-down in AD 68.*
- *Thomas was speared to death in AD 70.*
- *John Mark, author of the Gospel of Mark, was dragged to death.*
- *Luke the Physician, author of the book of Luke, was hanged on an olive tree at age eighty-four.*
- *James, the brother of Jesus, author of the book of James, was thrown off the high temple wall by the Pharisees, then clubbed to death in AD 62.*
- *The apostle Paul was beheaded in Rome in AD 69.*
- *Andrew, Bartholomew, and Simon the Zealot were all eventually crucified as well.*

Jesus's disciples gained confidence when He was resurrected and appeared unto them for many days following. This confidence indicates they possessed the keys of the kingdom—the confidence to spread the good news of the Gospel. They did not obtain keys of authority to bind unfavorable conditions or to release financial abundance for themselves. The evidence that they didn't is in the simple statement from Jesus in Luke 17:20–21: **The kingdom of God cometh not with observation—for behold, the kingdom of God is within you**.

John 8:31–32 (NKJV) gives further insight: **Then said Jesus to those Jews which believed on him, If you continue in my word, then are you my disciples indeed; and you shall know the truth, and the truth shall make you free**.

Notice the simple connection Jesus makes here: if we believe and do what He says, we shall know the truth—the truth of freedom from unrighteousness. If Jesus's followers were set free from financial struggles or persecution for their religious beliefs, why then were they martyred? In John, chapter 8, Jesus does not instruct us to grab hold of any "keys of authority" over our difficult earthly situation. Rather, Jesus tells that we are set free from the doubt of God, heaven, and eternal life when we continue in His Word. Eternally speaking, this is all the confidence we need!

On pages 70–71 of his book *Kingdom Principles*, Myles Munroe stated that when Jesus said **Repent: for the kingdom of heaven is at hand** (Matthew 4:17), it wasn't so much about repenting of sin but was about repenting of an ignorance of the purpose of the kingdom of God. Munroe taught that understanding the authority and rulership we have as citizens of God's kingdom was the key to persuading the ignorant unbeliever to join and become a part of it. It is the benefit of having authority to claim prosperity, wealth, and perfect health as a kingdom citizen. This was Munroe's grave mistake—drawing believers and unbelieves to put trust in earthly benefits rather than confronting their sin, which Jesus died for.

Munroe states on page 71: "*The gospel message—the 'good news'—is more than the cross. The cross is the doorway that gets us back into the Kingdom. The Cross of Christ, therefore, is all about Kingdom restoration. It is about restoration of power and authority. It is about regaining rulership, not religion.*"

Pastor Munroe claims the primary reason for the Gospel message of repentance is to gain authority and rulership in the earth. But just as Myles Munroe twisted other verses, this also is a perversion of Matthew 4:17. Munroe states that when the keys of the kingdom are properly understood, we can begin using this kind of power when we're in compliance with the laws of the kingdom. Yet this is nothing more than a gospel of self-confidence, health, and material abundance, having nothing to do with genuine sorrow for sin.

In Mark 2:15–17, we read where Jesus was eating with publicans and sinners. When the scribes and Pharisees began to question the disciples as to why Jesus would do such a thing, Jesus heard it and said: **They that are whole have no need of the physician, but they that are sick: I came not to call the righteous, but sinners to repentance.**

Monroe avoided this verse—a passage showing that repentance is not for the purpose of gaining authority and rulership, but rather, it is sinners who need the physician: they should repent of their sin.

The evidence of Myles Munroe's false teaching is also contained within other passages that he neglected in his book and in his prosperity sermons: In Mark 6:12, it says of Jesus's disciples, **And they went out, and preached that men should repent.** No surrounding verses tell that repentance leads to earthly authority. Acts 17:30–31 tells the same: that God **commands all men everywhere to repent: because he hath appointed a day in which he will judge the world in righteousness.**

These verses, among others, reveal that righteousness will be given unto man if he repents from sin. He cannot become a part of God's kingdom unless he does so. But repentance from sin does not elevate us to earthly authority for being a kingdom citizen. Instead, Jesus taught only a change of mind about sin.

Read Luke 15:10: **There is joy in the presence of the angels of God over one sinner that repents.**

Jesus gives us the simple explanation: repentance is only from sin—not repentance from ignorance of kingdom authority. Do angels delight in the earthly success and material gain of humans—or in their supposed authority over adverse circumstances? No! Angels rejoice only for the sinner who genuinely repents form sin.

After Jesus arose from the grave and just before ascending into heaven, He appeared to His disciples, explaining many prophetic passages concerning Himself. He then said: **Thus it is written, and thus it behooved Christ to suffer, and to rise from the dead the third day: and that repentance and remission of sins should be preached in his name among all nations, beginning at Jerusalem** (Luke 24:46–47).

This statement from Jesus is yet another death blow to the gospel of health and wealth. Jesus says nothing here of gaining knowledge of kingdom authority for the purpose of perfect health and earthly gain. It is simply and only the doctrine of repentance and remission of sins as a result of the Gospel preached.

Myles Munroe's doctrine of God's kingdom is heretical and apostate. It hijacks the biblical instruction for salvation, declaring a presumed benefit of successful living over and above the issue of sin and alienation from God. It is counterproductive to the biblical doctrine of the Gospel Jesus preached. Dr. Monroe's gospel requires no sorrow for sin but only a conciliatory acceptance of the great sacrifice of God's only begotten Son…only to gain the asset and profit of earthly things. Who's doctrine should we believe? Dr. Myles Munroe or Jesus the Savior? We cannot believe both.

The Greek word for "repent" or "repentance" in every one of these above passages means not only "a change of mind" but also "compunction." *Webster's* dictionary defines *compunction'* as "*a sharp feeling of uneasiness brought on by a sense of guilt, remorse, and regret.*"

Finding these facts, we see that the Bible's Gospel of repentance is simply and solely about a remorse for sin and putting faith and trust in Jesus the Savior as Lord over our lives. At this point of conversion, we have entered the kingdom of God. But God cannot be fooled: in attempting to trick Him by verbalizing a sinner's prayer only to gain earthly authority, we are not genuinely converted unto righteousness nor have we entered the kingdom of God.

In Luke, chapter 8, after speaking to the crowd in a parable of the seed, Jesus then explains privately to His disciples in verses 10–11: **Unto you it is given to know the mysteries of the kingdom of God… Now the parable is this: The seed is the word of God**.

This is not complex. The seed is only the Gospel message of repentance from sin and a trust in Jesus the Savior. The seed is not an explanation of what the kingdom of God offers believers as some kind of mysterious or secret knowledge of power and authority over all things. Rather, the mysteries of the kingdom of God are revealed when the seed of the spiritual Gospel of righteousness is understood.

On pages 172 to 174 of Dr. Munroe's book *Kingdom Principles*, he explains the story from Mark 10:17–23 where Jesus tells a rich man how he could obtain eternal life by giving up his possessions and following after him. After quoting the passage, Munroe then stated:

> *Once we get into the Kingdom and start functioning properly, we inevitably become prosperous. Prosperity is a natural product of Kingdom living. But we must live by the standards of the Kingdom in order to prosper in the Kingdom. This rich young man had problems with Jesus' conditions because they ran counter to everything he had ever heard and believed about success and prosperity.*

Here, Myles Munroe had again flipped the script. Mark 10:17 actually says that the rich man asked only: **What shall I do that I may inherit eternal life?** The man was not asking Jesus how he could become even more prosperous: he simply wanted eternal life and wasn't sure he was going to get it even though he had kept all the commandments (verse 20). But Pastor Munroe continues down his path of scriptural perversion on page 173, saying:

> *Because of ignorance of Kingdom keys, this rich young man did not know how to become richer, so he chose to hold onto wealth that literally was*

> *killing him rather than enter into wealth that could give him life. Coming into the Kingdom of God neither makes you poor nor requires you to become poor. But you have to know the keys. This young man had grown up in a world where you get by taking. He could not understand the principle of a Kingdom where you get by giving. The way most of us in this world pursue success and wealth and try to get ahead is completely contrary to the principles and laws that God designed into creation.*

Munroe then conveys the idea that had the rich man grasped the full scope of being a part of God's kingdom, he would not only have gained eternal life but would also gain back all of his material wealth and more. He could have greatly profited through the application of kingdom principles applied in his life. This is great twisting of the text by adding nonexistent theological dogma. Munroe had neglected the focal point of Jesus's words through his perversion of the entire story—and especially overlooking Mark 10:21 where Jesus told the rich man he would have treasure in heaven, not on earth, if he gave up what he had. Thus, our heavenly treasure is not transferrable back to earth as Dr. Munroe taught. Our heavenly treasure stays in heaven, and God provides for our earthly needs from His own riches according to Philippians 4:19.

Myles Munroe's imaginary and deceptive version of kingdom keys also focuses on money management: as he stated in a sermon posted on YouTube, "*One of the most important kingdom keys is the principle of Management*" (Dr. Myles Munroe, "This Money Secret Will Shock You!" YouTube, 00:54). Munroe explains in this sermon how God expects us to be accountable and successful through careful money management. He goes on to say: "*God wants you to be an economist—to get the maximum out of the minimum*" (7:08). Munroe then strongly emphasized that a careful and diligent tithe calculation is necessary for God to answer our prayers for anything we desire. Yet if this kind of accountability were required by God to guide Christians to earthly success, Jesus had then misinformed Peter about the keys of the kingdom of heaven in Matthew 16:19!

When referring to Proverbs 10:22—**The blessing of the Lord, it maketh rich**—Dr. Munroe says: "*Once you get the keys of the kingdom and learn how they work, the blessing of God will bring you wealth without sorrow*" (*Kingdom Principles*, p. 174).

In truth, Proverbs 10:22 is not a promise of wealth for all who trust in the Lord. Now understanding that the keys of the kingdom do not provide us with wealth, we therefore know that Myles Munroe's interpretation of Proverbs 10:22 has "*prosperity theology*" written all over it! Just a few verses later, Solomon wrote in contrast to Myles Munroe's teaching, saying: **Riches profit not in the day of wrath: but righteousness delivers from death** (Proverbs 11:4 NKJV).

The second part of Psalm 62:10 also warns: **If riches increase, set not your heart upon them**. Think of the many angles of this simple verse. For instance, **if riches increase** at least implies that the blessing of material riches does not come by our own manipulation but more rightly through God's divine purpose. And to the one who engineers their own wealth, whether by investment strategy or by the method of *give to get*, it is nearly impossible to not set your heart upon material gain and riches. Unless the heart's focus is directed heavenward, we either consciously or unconsciously chase after riches once they begin to increase.

Dr. Munroe's doctrinal delusion

In 1998, Myles Munroe preached a series of sermons from his home church in the Bahamas titled "Kingdom Principles"—from which his book *Kingdom Principles* was birthed. He correctly explained how Jesus preached the kingdom of God rather than preaching a religion, but Munroe then perverted this truth by saying: "*Jesus said the message is the Kingdom. Jesus never preached on prosperity; he never preached on deliverance; he never preached on healing; he never preached on blessings. Jesus preached on the Kingdom because the Kingdom positions you to have access to all those things! So, you don't get them once in awhile—it's a lifestyle*" (Dr. Myles Munroe, "The Kingdom Principles of Keys Part 3," YouTube, 47:05).

If Munroe's theology of prosperity, healing, and earthly blessing comes by pursuing the kingdom, then the apostle Paul was a bit confused when he said in Romans 14:17: **The kingdom of God is not meat and drink; but righteousness, and peace and joy in the Holy Ghost**.

According to the Gospel of Jesus, Paul was not confused in the slightest. Possessing the keys of the kingdom of God is not the realization of power and authority to gain material wealth, deliverance from tribulation, physical healing, or ease of life. It is not observed in outward circumstance but is the inner righteousness that cannot be seen. If Myles Munroe's theology were true, then wealth and perfectly favorable conditions of daily life would be a visible sign for all people in God's kingdom who verbally declare it. But we can't deduce this from our Bible. Comfort and prosperity cannot bring righteousness, peace, and joy. Dr. Myles Munroe was indeed a false prophet! His gospel message was not founded upon the Rock but upon unstable "keys of self-sufficiency." In Matthew 7:26, Jesus refers to those like Myles Munroe as **a foolish man, which built his house upon the sand**.

Acute apostasy

Again from his home church in Nassau, Bahamas, Pastor Munroe preached a sermon in 2006 titled "The Gospel of the Kingdom." At the beginning of his sermon, Munroe stated: "*The gospel of the kingdom is the good news about a kingdom. Therefore, our message, our good news is not about Calvary. Jesus Christ is not the gospel. The kingdom is the gospel*" (Dr. Myles Munroe, "The Gospel Good News of the Kingdom," YouTube, 00:05).

If "*Jesus Christ is not the gospel,*" as Munroe stated, then according to the New Testament, no one has entered the kingdom of God even though they've repented of sin and believed in Jesus Christ as their Savior! Myles Munroe's teaching is profoundly blasphemous false doctrine!

Later in his sermon, Dr. Munroe states:

> *Do you know why the people on your job really ain't Christian right now? 'Cause you are preaching to them Jesus Christ! See, that's not what you're supposed to preach! You preach the kingdom of God to the folks on the job. Tell them that you can get your citizenship back. There is a kingdom that belonged to you before you were even born. You were born to be a part of the government rulership that has dominion of the earth! Your condition is not supposed to control you. You're supposed to control them. Your circumstances are not supposed to run your life: you're not supposed to be dominated by your circumstances and your emotions and your problems. You're supposed to be on top of this thing! Folks want to hear that! People ain't worried about no blood on no cross. They want to know how they gonna fix their problems! Circumstances are not supposed to run your life. You are supposed to run your circumstances!* (26:16)

This is acute doctrinal apostasy. Paul told the church at Corinth: **But we preach Christ crucified** (1 Corinthians 1:23). If one preaches "attaining kingdom authority" as priority over Christ crucified, they preach another gospel! When desiring to become a kingdom citizen only for the sake of dominion over all things, we have not truly repented from sin. Munroe's theology of the kingdom of God is precisely *not* the gospel! Believing in a Jesus who gives you a conquering earthly authority will not give you eternal life. You have trusted in the wrong Jesus—a Jesus invented by deceived, depraved, and apostate minds.

If you come to Christ for any reason other than genuine sorrow for sin and to flee the wrath of God, you come for the wrong reason.

Simple scriptural discernment

Pastor Myles Munroe had theorized a complicated and difficult to comprehend doctrine. But the words of Jesus are simple and straightforward. Again Matthew 6:33 says: **But seek ye first the kingdom of God, and his righteousness; and all these things shall be added unto you**. Luke 12:22–32 is closely linked: Jesus comforts us by the assurance of God's provision in our lives. In verse 31, He tells us to seek the kingdom of God instead of worrying about how we will survive. Jesus did not tell us to seek kingdom authority but kingdom righteousness. Continuing in Luke 12:32, He says: **Fear not little flock; for it is your Father's good pleasure to give you the kingdom**. When reading the full context of thought from verses 22 to 32, we see that on this side of eternity, being a part of God's kingdom does not include or guarantee riches or perfectly favorable conditions—but only provision. Want more proof? Read the very next verse—Luke 12:33 (NIV): Jesus says, **Sell your possessions and give to the poor. Provide purses for yourselves that will not wear out, a treasure in heaven that will not be exhausted**.

Right here is another simple verse totally debunking the *prosperity doctrine*. Jesus states there is no merit or eternal glory in earthly treasure.

One of the many insights we learn from the devil's temptation of Jesus in the wilderness (Matthew 4) is how Jesus could have used his voice of authority to cause change. In verse 3, Satan said to him: **If thou be the Son of God, command that these stones be made bread**.

The devil knew that Jesus had power to speak to the stones that they become bread! Even though Jesus was hungry after having fasted forty days, He replies to Satan: **It is written, Man shall not live by bread alone, but by every word that proceedeth out of the mouth of God**.

Did you catch something here in Jesus's reply to the devil? He didn't speak aloud any command to cause that change but rejected such reckless behavior! He had honored His Father's spiritual words of life proclaimed in the Scriptures. How dare Christians usurp an authority over God by selfishly declaring prosperity, material blessings—or even a command for physical healing. By verbally claiming or commanding a specified outcome, we reject God's sovereignty over us! The Son of God didn't overrule His Father's authority. How dare we!

The selfish and carnally minded Christian who believes in a gospel of increasing comfort and prosperity will be led into a void of spiritual complacency. It is not always God's will for our circumstances to be favorable. In fact, Jesus Himself stated just the opposite for those who follow him. When we walk in Christ, there is confidence in the Scriptures, peace in every circumstance, and victory over sin, which overshadows material gain and comfort or lack thereof. Our victory is in the power and presence of the Spirit: it is the "authority of confidence"—not the "confidence of authority." When twisting the terminology, we have thereby invented a man-centered gospel.

The authority a Christian possesses is "conviction of mind," not an authority to cause change.

Myles Munroe's theology of God's kingdom lends to the belief that anything is possible by calling it into reality. Yes, our Bible tells us that God uses people to do His deeds. However, if this translates into a total authority over every situation, then why can't Christians stop wars or heal all diseases by the divine authority they possess? Though if war and disease are God's will, then it is also God's will for mankind to suffer. If mankind suffers, God must not be listening to the fervent prayers of believers with kingdom authority. Instead, He listens only to the prayers for material blessing and favorable circumstances in the life of the believer! This merry-go-round of illogic deduces that Christians have control primarily over personal circumstances but not world circumstances. So where is the compassion for the poor and the destitute in this doctrine? There is none! Where is the compassion for people alienated from God by their sin in this doctrine? There is none! It's a self-centered gospel! God cares only about improving the circumstances of His chosen people but cares little for the rest of suffering and sinful humanity? How so? Luke 19:10 absolutely dispels this idea: Jesus said that He came to **seek and to save that which was lost**.

The late Pastor Myles Munroe's gospel theology of kingdom keys venerated idolatry: his theory of the kingdom of God was for the service of man rather than glorifying God. He was one of the many false prophets who Jesus warned of as a precursory sign of His return.

Chapter 14

Babylonian Mixture

Though this chapter is devoted to the false doctrines of Catholicism and other religious institutions, we as followers of Jesus can still join forces with them for the betterment of humanity. We are called only to stand firm in our belief and to avoid any mixture of false doctrines and paganism with our faith in Christ Jesus. This mixture, by biblical definition, is the mistake of ecumenism—the promotion of unity and cooperation between all religions.

Orthodox Catholicism embraces only partial Bible truth, adding pagan tradition and lifelong works for salvation, which labors against the simple Gospel of the Bible. Yet both Catholic and Protestant creeds are now being shaped by liberalism and ecumenism. In addition, independent churches and whole denominations joining the ecumenical efforts of the World Council of Churches (WCC) is now fulfilling Bible prophecy of a mediocre gospel taught within the last-days church. The WCC organization participates in humanitarian efforts, with the stated goal of "*Christian unity in justice and peace in the world as an expression of faith in the Triune God.*" Because of the unifying nature of the WCC agenda, the doctrine of the gospel must be justifiably compromised for the acceptance of religious diversity, social diversity, and support of political morality.

To date, the Catholic Church has not joined ranks with the World Council of Churches, but the attempt to unite Catholics with Protestant Evangelical Christians is now well under way. What's wrong with an "ecumenical church" agenda from a biblical perspective? Let's find out...

Blind acceptance of heretical doctrines

From the 1940s to the 1970s, healing evangelist Kathryn Kuhlman preached little on Bible doctrine but much on experiencing the Holy Spirit. In Kuhlman's interdenominational healing services and in her weekly TV program *I Believe in Miracles*, she often stated her conviction of the "oneness-union" that Protestants and Catholics share through the glory of the Holy Spirit. Yet part of what defines Protestant Christianity is the disagreement over heretical Catholic doctrine. Though inspirational in her Holy Spirit teaching, Kathryn Kuhlman's brand of experiential Christianity unwittingly aided in changing the church's attitude toward a softer inoffensive gospel message. Through the propagation of ecumenism within the twentieth-century church, we are far down this road of no return in the twenty-first century.

Since the term *Catholic* means "unity," it is no surprise that in 1986, Pope John Paul II initiated a plan for the *unification of all denominations and religions*. Pope Francis has now made further inroads and has even told Catholics to reject Catholicism—in the sense of seeing themselves as exclusive—and to instead reach out and embrace people of all religions as part of the family of God.

In January 2014, Charismatic/Word of Faith pastor Kenneth Copeland invited Bishop Anthony Palmer of the Anglican Episcopal Church to speak at the annual *Ministers Conference* held in Texas, in which a few thousand Evangelical, Charismatic, and Pentecostal pastors were in attendance.

Bishop Tony Palmer was a member of the *Roman Catholic Ecumenical Delegation for Christian Unity and Reconciliation.* Bishop Palmer, though not a Catholic, urged the unification of Catholics and Charismatic Christians, explaining that "*the Protestant*

Reformation is over" by way of a 1999 signed document between the Roman Catholic Church and the Protestant Lutheran Church. The document was later also signed by representatives of the Worldwide Methodist Church. Bishop Palmer stated:

> *The protest made by Martin Luther five centuries ago—that one was saved by faith in Christ alone, and not through good works—has now disappeared. This statement has been modified in this agreement document with the Lutheran Church to now say: "We are saved by grace through faith alone—unto good works."* ("Bishop Tony Palmer and Pope Francis—The Miracle of Unity Has Begun," YouTube, 23:14)

Though Catholics and Protestants both agreed through the 1999 document that believers are "*saved by grace through faith alone,*" the definition of "grace" is theologically dissimilar in Catholic and Protestant institutions. Catholicism sees grace as an ethereal substance earned by sacraments and administered by priests. This renders salvation as not from the Lord but from an institution. The Protestant view of grace is God's mercy of the covenant: it is undeserved and unmerited favor. When ignorant of these opposing terminologies and interpretation of grace, the ecumenical movement seems beneficial for the spiritual unification of all religious people.

Regardless of dispute over the interpretation of grace and of the Gospel, the agenda to unify all believers is deceptive in other ways as well. Bishop Palmer stated: "*It's the glory that glues us together, not the doctrines*" (22:22). But Palmer couldn't have been more biblically ignorant in making this statement. Scripturally speaking, there can be no unity in the glory of the Holy Spirit if there is no agreement over the doctrine of the Gospel. Since the doctrines of New Testament faith are foundational for salvation, Protestant denominations cannot possibly unite with Catholicism unless the Catholic institution first rescinds their own religious laws. They must renounce their doctrine of the priesthood having authority above Jesus; they must reject all association with pagan rituals; they must denounce the doctrine of Mary being another mediator between man and God, and they must annul the requirement of penance for sin.

Jesus said: **But when the comforter is come, whom I will send unto you from the Father, even the Spirit of truth, which proceedeth from the Father, he shall testify of me** (John 15:26). It is the testimony of Jesus that glues Christians together in the faith. The "glory of the Spirit" cannot stand on its own, separate from the doctrine of Jesus's well-defined Gospel of salvation.

At this 2014 *Ministers Conference*, Bishop Tony Palmer stated:

> *Perhaps we are all Catholics again. But we are reformed...we are Catholics in the universal sense. We're not protesting the doctrine of salvation by the Catholic Church anymore: we now preach the same gospel. I am coming in the spirit of Elijah...by the turning the heart of the fathers to the children, and the heart of the children to their fathers; to make ready a people prepared for the Lord. Thus, the prophesy from Malachi 4:6 is now being fulfilled.* (26:05)

(By implication, Palmer was deeming the Catholic Church as "*the fathers*" and Protestants as "*the children.*" In reality, Malachi 4:5–6 prophesies of the soon return of the spirit and power of Elijah in the person of John the Baptist, who called the Jews back to repentance and restoration.)

Bishop Palmer then played a video message from Pope Francis addressing Pastor Copeland in which the pope urged unity of Charismatic/Evangelicals with the Catholic Church and with a request to set aside doctrinal differences. Kenneth Copeland responded back to the pope, agreed with this plan, and also promised Bishop Palmer he would visit the Vatican soon—which he did later that year, bringing with him a delegation of Evangelical leaders. Heretical Catholicism and a popular branch of the Evangelical Protestant Church had shaken hands. Yet in Revelation 17:4–6, the apostle John perfectly describes the institution called the Roman Catholic Church—**Mystery, Babylon the Great**—which has committed **abominations**. In Revelation 17:8, John goes on to say: **And they that dwell on the earth shall wonder, whose names were not written in the book of life from the foundation of the world, when they behold the beast that was, and is not, and yet is**.

In this verse, the word "wonder" (*thaumazo*) means "admire." Over the last many centuries, those who admire and follow after **the beast** (the papacy of Rome) do not have their names written in **the book of life** because they have idolized men of high position who pervert the Gospel of Jesus. Now embraced by the Evangelical Charismatic Church, the Ecumenical Movement, supported by many religious institutions, is perpetuating a one-world religion. This stratagem is debunked and denounced by Jesus in Luke 12:51–53, warning His followers not to unite with all who believe in God—but to separate from them who teach heretical doctrines and false teaching of His Gospel.

Papal heresy

Aside the biblical discernment that the position of the Catholic priest and papacy replace the authority of Jesus Christ over His church, the pope's stated interpretations of other theological issues also mock God's sovereignty and power. On May 22, 2013, an article in the *Huffington Post* quoted the newly elected Pope Francis when he spoke before the Pontifical Academy of Sciences: Pope Francis stated:

> *When we read about the creation in Genesis, we run the risk of imagining that God was a magician with a magic wand able to do everything. That is not so. God is not a divine being or magician, but the Creator who brought everything to life. Evolution in nature is not inconsistent with the notion of creation because evolution requires the creation of beings that evolve.*

On October 28, 2014, *USA Today* published an article with the same statements from the pope, showing his support of the Darwinian theory of evolution as an acceptable explanation to the beginning of life on earth. Pope Francis's assumption brings to the table the idea that perhaps God was not powerful enough to have created everything just as the Genesis account describes. It also shows the pope's doubt of the Bible's truth and authenticity in general.

In these same articles, which also appeared in the November 3, 2014, edition of *Inquisitr.com*, it was also revealed that Pope Francis, when recently presiding in Mass, stated: "*All who do good are redeemed—even atheists.*"

This statement contradicts Scripture. Psalm 14:1 says: **The fool hath said in his heart, there is no God**. Though Pope Francis claims to be Spirit filled and believes that Jesus is the Savior, he has at the same time rejected the Gospel of Jesus by stating the above. If Jesus is the Savior, that means He came to save the unbelieving atheist from his atheism. But if the atheist ignores the Gospel and continues his rejection of God, he remains a "fool" and is not redeemed, even though he may do good works.

The **falling away** Paul speaks of in 2 Thessalonians 2:3 goes far beyond the *prosperity gospel* and the *born-again Jesus* teaching. We see that a dissolving of doctrinal divisions between Evangelical Christians and Catholics is also an apostate departure from sound doctrine within the Protestant Church. Second Thessalonians 2:4 then says: **The son of perdition; who opposeth and exalteth himself above all that is called God, or that is worshipped; that he as God sitteth in the temple of God, showing himself that he is God**.

This speaks of the last-day anti-Christ man who will exalt himself. Although speculative at this time, it is not so unimaginable that a pope could one day assume this position. In Catholicism, the pope is already proclaimed as "*God upon the earth.*"

Those within the Evangelical Church desiring to unite with the bishop of Rome in acceptance of all who appear to love God, no matter their doctrine, are scripturally characterized as condemned for their mixture with pagan religions. God was angered and removed Himself from the Israelites when they became corrupted with foreign gods and pagan practices. Why would it be any different today? When followers of Jesus align themselves with those who teach unsound doctrine, they have voyaged out on their own, and God leaves them to their own devices, just as He did the Israelites. This is why those within the Evangelical Church who move forward in uniting with Catholicism cannot see the error of their ways: the Holy Spirit of God has left them alone because they have befriended those who practice paganism and follow the doctrines of men. They have begun to **wonder after the beast**, as Revelation 13:3 says.

Billy Graham's impact on the world

In the twentieth century, the late evangelist Billy Graham preached the basic and simple Gospel of the Bible in his many crusades around the world. In addition, Reverend Graham had a huge impact on improving race relations and Christian ideals of desegregation in the Southern United States in the 1950s. Graham said:

> *I believe that the answer to our great moral problems, our social problems, lies in the Gospel of Christ and in the transformation that He can bring. We need legislation, yes. But legislation cannot improve the morals of America alone, or social problems alone. It must come from something deeper, because our problem is basically spiritual.* ("Billy Graham's Friendship with Martin Luther King Jr.," YouTube, 12:50)

Applying the Gospel of salvation to the problem of race relations was a great insight of Billy Graham. Though some Christians criticized Graham's friendship with Dr. Martin Luther King Jr. over his political methods for change, Graham's spiritual focal points stood strong. We can now look back and see that this was what could have been the end of the bigoted "superior White church" mentality in America. No doubt this was a good and radical attempt by Graham to better integrate Black and White congregations and to quell White supremacy attitudes. For the most part, however, this did not happen within racially diverse communities. Today there are still relatively few fully integrated congregations.

As time passed, all Christians who relied on Billy Graham's insightful wisdom and unifying efforts were eventually led down the road of deception in Graham's subsequent doctrine of a *universal Christ*. His past endeavor to unify all believers in Christian fellowship transitioned into a focus on unifying all religions instead.

In a May 1997 interview with Crystal Cathedral pastor Robert Schuller, Billy Graham stated that all people who have an awareness of God will be saved, even if they are unaware of the Gospel of the Bible. He stated to Pastor Schuller:

> *I think that everybody that loves Christ, or knows Christ, whether they're conscious of it or not, they are members of the Body of Christ...whether they come from the Muslim world, or the Buddhist world, or the Christian world, or the non-believing world, they are members of the Body of Christ because they've been called by God. They turn to the only light that they have, and I think they are saved, and that they're going to be with us in heaven."* ("Billy Graham Denies Christ—Interviewed by Robert Schuller on *Hour of Power*," YouTube)

Here, contrary to what the Bible reveals, Billy Graham inadvertently denied that Jesus is the only way to God the Father. His support of *universal salvation* was proclaimed in the key phrase he used: "*whether they're conscious of it or not,*" indicating that because of God's love and the cross, the sins of all people are forgiven—whether they know it or not. Though some might rather interpret Graham's statement to mean that God can and will forgive all people—whether they know it or not—think what his statement meant to Muslims, Buddhists, and nonbelievers watching this interview. The good news from the great evangelist Billy Graham was that nearly everyone who believes in some kind of deity will make it to heaven! Graham's statement made no biblical or doctrinal sense because the Muslims, Buddhists, and nonbelievers he referred to do not know or love Christ: they have completely rejected His divinity and the Gospel's path to eternal life.

Our Bible tells that God will punish iniquity. Therefore, having only a "God consciousness" or "Christ consciousness" does not save us from God's wrath. Jesus said: **I am the way, the truth and the life: no man cometh unto the Father but by me** (John 14:6). Hence, "coming unto the Father" indicates an action and is far more than just an awareness of a Supreme Being or an admiration of the man named Jesus.

In researching Billy Graham's life, we find that after having a *born-again* conversion at age sixteen, he enrolled in Florida Bible Institute a few years later. This liberal arts college incorporated an ecumenical agenda of examining and accepting all denominational beliefs about Jesus and the cross, which later likely prompted his effort to unify all denominations and all religions. In the beginning of Billy Graham's public ministry, however, and his 1949 Los Angeles Crusade, he preached against Communism, Muhammadism, and Catholicism as being the world's greatest threat to the Evangelical Church. Just a few years later, by 1952, he was embracing a wider audience, including Catholics, to gain a more diverse influence. His ambition seemed admirable in making the Gospel more inclusive to other religious groups. However, the Bible tells us that the Gospel of salvation is not an inclusive gospel of all beliefs but is very exclusive to all other religions.

Unbelievers, Catholics, Mormons, Jehovah's Witnesses, and people in other cult groups did indeed hear the correct Gospel message when attending a Billy Graham Crusade. Though in his crusades, any person coming forward to receive Christ filled out a "decision card" to tell the association what church denomination they came from or preferred. Those who replied "*Catholic*" were then referred back to a local Catholic bishop in their hometown: they were sent back to serve an institution that does not teach sound Bible doctrine. However, to Graham, it made sense to now befriend orthodox Roman Catholics in spite of their heretical views and contrary definition of grace—most likely because of his indoctrination of accepting all religious themes at the liberal Florida Bible Institute he had attended long ago.

In his later years of ministry, Billy Graham further cultivated a relationship with Catholics and never confronted their unsound doctrine or expressed disagreement with it. In his autobiography *Just As I Am*, published in 1999, he states that in his trips to Rome, he had many in-depth discussions with the pope and Vatican theologians. In 2003, radio and television host Larry King interviewed eighty-four-year-old Billy Graham on *Larry King Live*. When King asked Graham if the theological differences between Catholicism and Protestantism had ever created a rift, Graham replied: "*The Pope and I agree on almost every theological issue, and the issues we disagree on are unimportant*" ("Billy Graham Exposed by Dave Hunt," YouTube, 01:59).

In light of the doctrines of Catholicism being opposed to the biblical doctrine of salvation, Graham's reply to Larry King was disappointing, to say the least. He either justified or didn't recognize any theological difference between Catholicism and Protestantism.

Billy Graham was sold out to the deception of the Ecumenical Movement and, in his later years, became more vocal in supporting it. In his autobiography, he tells that the method of unifying with other religions was justifiable, stating that because of his crusades, "*many people genuinely came to Christ.*" While this may be true, the gospel that Graham preached was thus compromised to now include Catholic doctrine by simply not warning of its heresy. Though Billy Graham preached the real Gospel in decades past, he stated on page 303 of his *Just As I Am* autobiography: "*Our message was clear, and if someone with a radically different theological view somehow decided to join with us in a crusade that proclaimed Christ as the way of salvation, he or she was the one who was compromising personal convictions, not we.*"

This mentality reveals that preaching the Bible's precise Gospel was not crucial enough to Graham to exclude those wanting to join with the association who could potentially bring in heretical theology—thus compromising the effectiveness of the real Gospel.

God wants unity in His church but not at the expense of truth. Second Corinthians 6:14 states: **For what fellowship hath righteousness with unrighteousness?** Verses 16–18 then states: **And what agreement hath the temple of God with idols? Wherefore come out from among them, and be ye separate saith the Lord, and touch not the unclean thing; and I will receive you, and will be a Father unto you, and ye shall be my sons and daughters, saith the Lord Almighty**.

According to this passage, a difference in doctrine does separate and should separate the true disciples of Jesus out of the worldwide religious church. God's agenda is not to unify all churchgoers. Again Revelation 18:4 and 2 Corinthians 6:17 state just the opposite: God desires faithful disciples of Jesus to **"come out from"** and **"be separate"** from the religious apostate.

I cannot even speculate whether Billy Graham will receive a "crown of honor" in heaven. In his evangelistic crusades, he preached the real Gospel, which brought many people to salvation. Yet later in his life, his public compromises to the Gospel seem to reveal that his heart was torn between his love for the Gospel and his love and friendship with all mankind, which brought him great respect and admiration. However, in Luke 6:26, Jesus said: ***Woe unto you, when all men shall speak well of you! For so did their fathers to the false prophets****.*

Chapter 15

Universalism and a Little Leaven

In this chapter, we discuss the false doctrine of the *Universal atonement* of Jesus the Savior—a doctrine that more than a few Christians now ignorantly accept as Bible truth. Though when reading many Bible passages explaining the Gospel of salvation, we easily discern that the theology of *Universalism* is heretical teaching that alienates the believer from the truth.

Universalism's definition of the gospel is this:

> *Jesus did not pay the price for our sin on the Cross; rather he abolished sin altogether. The sin of all humanity, past, present, and future, simply disappeared from the sight of God. Therefore, sin no longer offends God because He naturally forgives us of it. Acknowledgment of sin, and repentance from it is pointless: we need only to accept God's forgiveness by realizing that the Savior provided an inevitable and unavoidable reconciliation with the Father. Ignorance of God's forgiveness, or not accepting it, causes us to remain in an ambiguous undesirable mental anguish and lifestyle. But those who accept*

> *God's forgiveness are freed from the judgment and guilt of sin—without repenting of it.*

This *Universal* interpretation of the Gospel assumes that "*payment for sin*" and "*forgiveness of sin*" are synonymous terms. This is impossible for the fact that the word "payment" is a noun, and the word "forgiveness" is a verb. Interpreting the Gospel in this manner completely removes the need for repentance and a regenerate heart.

First, let's read a few Old Testament passages: 2 Chronicles 7:14 states: **If my people which are called by my name, shall humble themselves, and pray, and seek my face, and turn from their wicked ways; then will I hear from heaven, and will forgive their sin, and will heal their land.**

Proverbs 28:13 (ESV) states: **Whoever conceals his transgressions will not prosper, but he who confesses and forsakes them will obtain mercy.**

We also read that the Israelites were required to sacrifice animals as an atonement for sin: **For the life of the flesh is in the blood: and I have given it to you upon the altar to make an atonement for the soul** (Leviticus 17:11 NKJV).

Prior to the cross of Christ, as these passages indicate, God required man to turn from his sin and also commanded the continual sacrifice of animals in order to be forgiven of their sin. Today, by way of Jesus's one-time atonement, His shed blood replaced the blood of animals as the payment for sin. Yet if Jesus's payment also caused an automatic forgiveness of sin, God had then made an audacious mistake by sending His Son into the world two thousand years too soon! If the theological conjecture of *Universalism* is true, Jesus should have paid for the sin of all mankind on the final day of human history. Since, however, this event happened long ago, we thus have a discrepancy regarding God's unequal treatment of His chosen people who lived before the cross: they had to sacrifice their animals as well as repent of their sin in order to be forgiven. But according to the doctrine of *Universalism*, all who live after the cross are off the hook for everything! They have no responsibility whatsoever—not even to repent of sin. This ridiculous doctrine renders the entire New Testament as meaningless gibberish over a nonissue!

When understanding the seriousness of the New Testament, we know that the sin of all mankind was *not* automatically abolished through the cross of Christ. Bible exegete gives no such interpretation of salvation. Pastors who tell their congregation "*God loves you just as you are*" have presented no Gospel message at all. Their preaching agenda may not be the doctrine of outright *Universalism*, but nonetheless, the Gospel of salvation is not preached, and the listener remains ignorant until Bible truth is found.

Universal Christianity provides no understanding of our own responsibility to turn from sin and what it means to walk the "narrow path" of salvation. New baby Christians giving ear to this *Universal Christ* doctrine are lulled into having only a warm and fuzzy adoration of God's loving-kindness—giving no concern to the biblical definition of the Gospel of righteousness through repentance. But in Matthew 10:28, Jesus tells that God will justifiably cast any into hell who do not do His will: **But rather fear him which is able to destroy both soul and body in hell**. Teachers of *Universalism* avoid this and many other such verses of warning.

As the writer of this book has witnessed, even a mature follower of Jesus can be seduced by the subtle deception of *Universalism*. Many cannot see its apostate and heretical base in doctrine, either for a lack of knowledge regarding the definitive Gospel and/or for their love and admiration of those who proclaim a *Universal Christ*. Its abstract theology regarding sin is completely foreign to the Bible's definition, understanding, and application of the Ten Commandments. Those who promote this blundering doctrine must certainly know it to be speculative at best. In truth, it is fictitious and satanic false doctrine according to our Bible, but it now appears more widespread and in varying forms within religious themes. Discerning Christians should realize the great contradiction of a *Universalism* theology in hundreds of Bible passages. Hebrews 9:28 is just one of multiple verses that refute it: **So Christ was once offered to bear the sins of many;**

and unto them that look for him shall he appear the second time without sin unto salvation.

If *Universal salvation* were Bible truth, this verse would read, "*So Christ was once offered to bear the sins of all; and unto all shall he appear the second time without sin unto salvation.*" In other words, when Christ returns, those who did not believe in Him as the Savior will realize their mistake, and Jesus grants salvation to them because of the Father's great love and forgiveness for all humanity: all sin is wiped away, including the sin of unbelief. Yet if unbelief is forgiven, God's righteousness is scorned and mocked! In Matthew 12:32, Jesus addressed the issue of the "unpardonable sin"—the sin of unbelief: **But whosoever speaketh against the Holy Ghost shall not be forgiven, neither in this world, neither in the world to come**.

Our Bible tells us to discern God's will—to repent of our sin, abide in the Lord Jesus Christ, and to keep His commandments. Philippians 2:12 says: **Work out your own salvation with fear and trembling**. Since according to many other New Testament passages we cannot perform enough works to obtain eternal life, we know that we are saved not only by God's grace but also by aligning our daily walk in submission to the instruction of Scripture—**Examine yourselves, whether ye be in the faith; prove your own selves**, as Paul says in 2 Corinthians 13:5. It is not a strict obedience to the Ten Commandments but of self-examination of the heart's focus on the sound doctrine of the Gospel. A *Universal*-type belief removes any such examination of salvation assurance or specific doctrine. Instead, it's an easy no-fuss theology, rationalizing that God understands our human frailty, and we need not worry about anything: only accept God's love and forgiveness. This fallacy cannot be the truth. Jesus specifically condemned this kind of belief, telling us we will lose eternal life if we do not repent.

In Galatians, chapter 5, after stating the unimportance of circumcision—which some thought was still necessary—Paul explained it was no longer an issue and in fact was to be rejected as having any significance in light of the new covenant. In Galatians 5:7–8, Paul then says: **Ye did run well; who did hinder you that ye should not obey the truth? This persuasion cometh not of him that called**

you. This passage can also directly apply to current-day Christians who've accepted a *Universal Christ* teaching. Then in verse 9, Paul says: **A little leaven, leavens the whole lump**. Why did Paul say this here? Because in context, he was indicating that even one small error in doctrine can taint the most well-intended salvation message. We should know our Bible well enough to discern the truth; if not, we will be **tossed to and fro, and carried about with every wind of doctrine by the sleight of men and cunning craftiness, whereby they lie in wait to deceive** (Ephesians 4:14).

The deception of an off-centered gospel is also related to hypocrisy. In Luke 12:1, Jesus said: **Beware ye of the leaven of the Pharisees, which is hypocrisy**. The Pharisees were good religious men, but they were hypocrites for not discerning their own leaven of indolence and lack of sincere love for God. We can easily fall under the same delusion today; therefore, it is our personal responsibility to **prove all things** (1 Thessalonians 5:21); **test the spirits** (1 John 4:1); and **examine yourself whether ye be in the faith** (2 Corinthians 13:5).

A deceived shepherd, armed perhaps with the "leaven of ego," subtly deceives his flock. Jesus warned of this concept when He referred to the Pharisees' spiritual blindness in Matthew 15:14—they were **the blind leading the blind**, he said. The Pharisees couldn't see their own leaven of religious hypocrisy. Just the same, neither do many of today's pastors intend to be **workers of iniquity** (Matthew 7:23) because they don't know they are deceived! A false-teaching pastor will use man's wisdom and insight (leaven), in addition to accrediting Bible verses taken mostly out of context to support their inspiring message. But in 1 Timothy 4:16, Paul admonishes Pastor Timothy: **Take heed to thyself, and unto the doctrine; continue in them: for in doing this thou shalt both save thyself, and them that hear thee**. This verse is very clear: giving heed to **the doctrine** is what saves us! The reason we should be wise to discern unsound doctrine is to separate from them that teach it. We can and should love all people; however, Paul tells us in Ephesians 5:11 to **have no fellowship with the unfruitful works of darkness, but rather reprove them**, meaning "convince" or "tell a fault." When we see one making scriptural error regarding the Gospel of salvation, we are to convict and convince them of biblical truth. If they will not listen, we should have no spiritual fellowship with them. Perhaps because *Universalism* theology seems to lovingly encompass and accommodate the diversity of all people, its rejection of the Gospel of salvation is largely undetectable to many sincere Christians. But when studying the Scriptures to find the truth of the Gospel, we discover that *Universalism's* doctrine of salvation altogether mocks God's holiness. An increased tolerance for differing opinions of the Gospel's definition is the great apostasy of the latter Church Age.

A classic example of Gospel misrepresentation is the *Universal* teaching of Rob Bell, former pastor of Mars Hill Bible Church in Grandville, Michigan. In his 2011 book *Love Wins*, Rob Bell states that most all humanity will ultimately be wooed by God's love either in this life or the life to come—and that there is no literal hell of torment awaiting people. Mr. Bell's theology does not coincide with the many times Jesus warned of hell and His vivid description of its activity, physical pain, and suffering. Jesus spoke in parables to illustrate the kingdom of God, but He also told of a literal description of heaven: **In my Father's house are many mansions: if it were not so, I would have told you** (John 14:2). Hence, His descriptions of hell are most certainly literal as well.

The "hell" of Rob Bell's imagination is purgative and temporary. He describes it not as a literal place of physical torment but a state of mental anguish for not realizing God's forgiveness that was provided by the cross. By spreading this *Universal* gospel message, Bell has drifted far from God's well-defined instruction for salvation: he has perverted portions of Scripture and has neglected or explained away passages that are too offensive. Some Evangelical pastors still give him their support and are tolerant of his views: they don't want to reject him altogether because, after all, he seems to have love and compassion for all people.

Many other high-profile apostates like Rob Bell are proponents of *Universal Christianity*; they are guilty of trivializing the Gospel of salvation. As one collective voice, they tell us, "*God is love—so just bask in that love and enjoy eternity.*"

What does our Bible say about eternity? Many passages tell us it begins with "judgment." Psalm 9:7–8 says: **But the Lord shall endure forever: he hath prepared his throne for judgment. And he shall judge the world in righteousness, he shall minister judgment to the people in uprightness**. And Hebrews 9:27 says: **And as it is appointed unto man once to die, but after this the judgment**.

From these few passages and others such as Matthew 12:36 and Revelation 20:12–13, we see that **the judgment** is the destination of every person. What is the reason for this judgment unless there are degrees of reward or degrees of punishment? Seeing this scriptural warning, how can we ignore this prophesied judgment—or see it as merely figurative? Our Bible states it as a reality. Therefore, the simple yet precisely stated Gospel of the Bible is also reality. According to the Gospel of Jesus, we must **repent and believe**. Repent of what? Sin! But…if sin is only metaphoric or just a sort of mental anguish or ignorance of an automatic atonement by Jesus, then we don't need to confront our sin, feel guilty for it, or repent of it! Under the "no doctrine" theology of a *Universal gospel*, life is free and easy, and sin is just a bad word that applies only to the hideously evil. There is no condemnation for violating the very archaic Ten Commandments, and we need only to accept God's forgiveness and love Him in return… because He loved us first.

This is the *Universal* redemptive analysis of the Emergent Church gospel—the false gospel of a merging together church of diverse yet universalistic beliefs.

Misguided passion of Universalist teachers

Theologians and teachers of *Universalism* are passionate in their beliefs. Yet when we study what our Bible has to say about the Gospel of Jesus, we find that the *Universal gospel* is a teaching soft peddled—a lukewarm attitude against the sin of man's rebellion against God and the neglect of His Word. The teacher of *Universalism* passionately believes that God in heaven is desperate and determined to gather all humanity unto Himself for the purpose of eternal fellowship. If this is so, we must of necessity scratch many passages from our Bible: in particular, Revelation 21:7–8 and Revelation 22:14–15. Take time to read these verses. They and countless others mean absolutely nothing if *Universalism* is the truth: they are obvious mistakes within a very flawed book we call the Bible.

In a DVD titled "*The True Gospel*," *Universalist*, theologian Malcolm Smith gives his definition of the gospel. Smith emphatically states:

> *The gospel is not telling you to do something, but it is the good news that through Jesus, God has forgiven you already, and reconciled you already! He has delivered you already! Faith is not some work that I do to get forgiven: it is simple gratitude. Repentance is changing your mind about who Jesus Christ is, and that if he be the Son of God, and if he be "one" forever with our humanity, and if he rose from the dead, then He is Lord of all. I am then delivered and saved. I've repented; I've changed my mind about Jesus Christ; I've changed my mind about me, about the Father, and I abandon myself in reckless trust to such a God as this. This is the gospel!* ("True Gospel—Malcolm Smith," YouTube)

When Malcolm Smith says "*the gospel is not telling you to do something—it is simple gratitude,*" we should know he is teaching false doctrine. If we correctly interpret the Gospel of the Bible, we see that faith is not "gratitude for salvation." The fundamental instruction regarding the Gospel is to respond to it—to do something about it. It is a "*response for change,*" not a "*feeling of gratitude.*" Gratitude and thankfulness for salvation comes as a result of responding to the Gospel of faith. When Jesus used the word "repent" in Mark 1:15, it is interpreted as "*to think differently about sin.*" Only being grateful that Jesus paid for our sin on the cross does not give us peace with God, nor does it result in salvation. We must also turn from our unrighteousness. **For all have sinned and fall short of the glory of God** (Romans 3:23 NIV). The *Universal gospel* stops right there and assumes that because **all have sinned**—a perceived past-tense phrase—we need not fuss over sin any longer because Jesus took care of the problem two thousand years ago. So addressing our sin—past, present, and future—is unnecessary! Again this twisted doctrine—being no doctrine at all—is a mockery of the entire New Testament.

In a 2015 radio interview conducted by host Mark Simpson of Jesus Exclusive Savior ministry, Christian *Universalist* theologian Dr. C. Baxter Kruger was asked to give his thoughts on *Universal faith*. Dr. Kruger began with his basic theme, stating: "*Faith is the discovery that He has already related Himself to me, and to us. It's an eye-opening event. Repentance is a radical reorientation of the way we think*" ("C. Baxter Kruger—Faith, Repentance, Universalism," YouTube, 03:22).

The subtleness of deception in these statements from Malcolm Smith and Baxter Kruger shows that the vital key to biblical salvation has been completely lost in their warped interpretation of Scripture. Because of Jesus's work of atonement, God has indeed "*related Himself*" to man, just as these theologians say. However, God is not reconciled to man until he **comes to the light** as Jesus said in John 3:20–21: **For every one that doeth evil hateth the light, neither cometh to the light, lest his deeds should be reproved**.

This statement by Jesus totally crushes the idea that repentance is only a realization that God has reconciled us unto Himself without any confession of our sin…or sorrow for it. How are the evil deeds of man ever "reproved" or of any consequence if all we do is realize that God has "*related Himself to us*" through the death of His Son on the cross? If this were true, then every statement from Jesus concerning sin and the Gospel could be deleted from Matthew, Mark, Luke, and John! What we are left with is only a feel-good, lukewarm Christianity because of God's easy to accept *Universal* plan of reconciliation.

Many people declare a belief in Jesus, but unless conviction of guilt is realized, and sin is renounced, the cruel and torturous death of Jesus means nothing personally. When swayed by a *Universal* view of Calvary's cross, we are still pending a decision: we are in limbo between a decision for eternal life and a decision against it. Jesus said we will therefore lose eternal life because we made no effort to choose: **So then because thou art lukewarm, and neither cold nor hot, I will spew thee out of my mouth** (Revelation 3:16).

Even though *Universal Christianity* theology has come from "Christian brethren," it is, theologically speaking, a lukewarm religion. Because these brethren reject the idea of repenting of sin as the fundamental facet of the Gospel, they have thus deceived the body of Christ. They have neglected New Testament verses like 1 John 1:9: **If we confess our sins, he is faithful to forgive us our sins, and to cleanse us from all unrighteousness**. Here, the apostle John says we must **confess our sins**: we must acknowledge them. Through a *Universalism* belief, however, one could see "sin" and "ignorance" as synonymous, thus interpreting 1 John 1:9 to say that God forgives us *if* we confess our ignorance of not knowing that the Savior has already bought our salvation. But the very next verse, 1 John 1:10, absolutely clarifies the matter: **If we say we have not sinned, we make him a liar, and his word is not in us**. This proves that "sin" and "ignorance" are not synonymous. Multiple New Testament passages tell us that "transgression" is "the act of sin": it is "unrighteousness," and we must repent of it. When we turn from our sin and trust in the Lord Jesus, we are then washed in His blood and are renewed in our mind unto righteous intent—and even that our names are recorded in the Book of Life. But we will not receive eternal life until we **endure to the end**, as Jesus said in Matthew 24:13. *Universalism* theology stops short of this, declaring that there's nothing we must further endure after merely realizing God's presumed automatic forgiveness.

A fascinating comparison of two passages reveals the behind-the-scenes monumental complexity of man's salvation:

Psalm 8:3 tells that God created the heavens with **the work of thy fingers**. And Isaiah 52:10 says: **The Lord hath made bare his holy arm in the eyes of all the nations; and all the ends of the earth shall see the salvation of our God**. This Old Testament verse was a prophecy of the coming Gospel of salvation through Jesus the Savior. The salvation of humankind was not an easy accomplishment for God: it was by the strength of **His holy arm** (Isaiah 52:10), whereas creating the universe took only **the work of thy fingers** (Psalm 8:3). It took all of God's capacity to sacrifice the physical body of His only begotten Son to gain a relationship with those who would repent and believe. The doctrine of *Universalism* trivializes all of this.

Chapter 16

Atmosphere of Trickery

Quite sadly, it would appear that the influence of Christian television upon believers has largely caused their spiritual blindness. Though decades ago much of Christian programing began with doctrinally sound Bible preaching and exhortation, it has now severely diminished to a mere watered-down gospel message, drawing the viewer toward a sort of hybrid church that all are welcome to join. Merely recite a sinner's prayer, and you're in! Your ticket to heaven has been purchased! In reality, a heartfelt sorrow for sin is only the beginning of a long journey on a narrow path that must be traveled for a lifetime.

Much deterrent dialog within seminars, sermons, and talk shows featured on Christian TV networks—CBN, TBN, Daystar, Inspiration Network, GOD TV, BVOVN, the Church Channel, Hillsong Channel, Revelation TV, and others—are leading way in the spiritual apostasy among believers. Detouring from the Gospel encompasses many facets—not only teaching a deceptive false Christ but also focusing on moral and political issues as priority of our time. Nearly all programing on these Christian TV networks need to be ecumenical in nature to have wide-ranging influence and financial success. Compromising and widening the Gospel of salvation to include diversity of beliefs is therefore necessary. As a result, in the last few decades, televised church services have in turn influenced local churches to acquire a "seeker-friendly" way of presenting the Gospel. It is the "Gospel of accommodation," as coined by the late Christian author David Wilkerson, founding pastor of Times Square Church in New York City. The Gospel's offensive message toward sinners has been adjusted to appease and attract those not desiring to confront their unrighteousness before God. Today, many churches bend over backward to suit the needs of the people—giving them comfort and entertainment and to see their social needs are met. An empty watered-down gospel message of "*God loves you*" and "*God is for you*" is presented by liberal-minded pastors so as not to offend anyone. However, our Bible tells us that God cannot be "for us" unless we take seriously the Gospel command to confront our sin. God loves us, but He cannot abide with unrepentant sinful man for eternity. So God sacrificially provided the way of escaping our guilt of sin. When the biblical way of escape is compromised and weakened through an inoffensive gospel, we easily fall through the cracks and remain unjustified. But the Gospel of Jesus cannot be compromised. Our neglect of its doctrine or lax interpretation of it cannot set the standard for Bible truth. This is a bitter pill to swallow for some who think God must surely be more loving and lenient than that. In truth, the Gospel of salvation is only through the Lord Jesus—nothing else. It has nothing to do with religious works and duties, methods for church growth, or even a compassionate tolerance for diverse lifestyles within the kingdom of God. Jesus describes all of this as a **wide gate…and broad way that leads to destruction** (Matthew 7:13). There is no such thing as *believe-what-you-want Christianity.* In a misguided attempt to grow and have positive effect in society, a large portion of the church has drifted far from the orthodoxy of Holy Scripture and instead advocates acceptance of diversity and "feel-good Christianity."

The great nineteenth-century English preacher Charles H. Spurgeon once said: "*We shall not adjust our Bible to the age, but before we have done with it, by God's grace, we shall adjust the age to the Bible*" (Charles Spurgeon quotes, Google search).

If Spurgeon thought this statement was relevant for his time—a time when the church was leaning toward more liberal and pragmatic theology—how much more so today!

In the January 30, 2003, edition of the Australian *Sydney Morning Herald* newspaper, an article titled "The Lord's Profits" focused on megachurch Pastor Brian Houston and his successful Hillsong Church congregation. When interviewed by the journalist writing the article, Pastor Houston was asked: "*Why is Hillsong is so popular and prosperous?*" Houston replied: "*We are scratching people where they are itching.*" Pastor Houston's answer was typical of the growing seeker-friendly movement—playing upon itching ears bent toward the declaration of earthly Christian benefits.

Though Brian Houston has recently stepped down as lead pastor, Hillsong Church and its new leadership, Phil and Lucinda Dooley, continue down the same slippery slope of apostasy—preaching a watered-down gospel, linked with compromising concepts of positive prosperity and narcissistic tenet. The prophecy from 2 Timothy 4:3 is being fulfilled before our eyes—**For the time will come when they will not endure sound doctrine; but after their own lusts shall they heap to themselves teachers, having itching ears**.

Primarily in many larger megachurches, the preaching of biblical sound doctrine is either replaced or overshadowed by promotion of the Christian good life, combined with manipulative and repetitive ear-tickling and eye-popping rock-concert style worship and entertainment—all to conjure an emotional response. There is a great disconnect within many churches from the apostle Peter's declaration of the Gospel of repentance in Acts, chapter 2. If wayward Christians don't wake up to the reality of how far they have drifted from the biblical definition of "righteousness in Christ," then the harloting bride, whom Jesus once knew and loved, will find herself cut off, rendering her marriage to the Bridegroom impossible.

Jesus speaks of the end of the age in a parable of the ten virgins in Matthew 25: He said in verse 2, **Five of them were wise, and five were foolish** at the time of the Bridegroom's coming. This would indicate that a mere half of all last-day Christians will have the fruit of the Spirit in their lives, and the rest will not be doing the Master's will when He returns. The five foolish virgins refer to the believers who did not discern and pursue spiritual and doctrinal truth, as revealed in Matthew 25:3 (NIV): **The foolish ones took their lamps but did not take any oil with them**. Even though they benefitted from their Christian fellowship and God's common grace, they had not sought the Gospel of Jesus the Savior. In Matthew 25:12, Jesus ultimately tells this vast group: **I know you not**. Jesus's parable of the ten virgins reveals not only the waywardness of Christians caught up in the entanglements of life's pursuits and pleasures, but it also refers to devout yet ignorant and gullible Christians who were taught a counterfeit Jesus and a counterfeit gospel.

End-time prophecy experts Hal Lindsey and the late Grant Jeffrey (seen on Christian television in recent years) have mesmerized people with proof of Bible predictions of world events coming to pass in Israel and the Middle East nations. Though these men were experts in their field, they had not researched the Bible's prophecy of apostasy and spiritual deception within the end-time church. Avoiding this primary component of church eschatology causes believers to overlook the precise doctrine through which they are justified to be received by Christ. Relying on a geographical-type prophecy or militant aggression against Israel and the upheaval of nations as proof that the Second Coming of Christ is near provides no eternal security if we are preoccupied with a different gospel.

Tares of iniquity

God does not desire or require a unity of all religious people; rather, He is calling today's disciples of Jesus to **come out from among them** (2 Corinthians 6:17). Reading within the context, we discover "them" to be any who oppose God's Word or who preach a different gospel opposing God's salvation plan. We see a similar warning in Revelation 18:4: **Come out of her, my people, that ye be not partakers of her sins, and that ye receive not of her plagues**.

Christians can indeed unite with unbelievers for the betterment of humanity—showing compassion to the distraught, the poor, and the hurting. But to unite all faiths for the purpose of a one-world church is counter to Revelation 18:4. In this verse and also in Revelation 17:5, the apostle John spoke of "her" as an institution of heresy, leading multitudes astray—**Mystery, Babylon the Great, the Mother of Harlots and Abominations of the Earth**.

As has been proven, a large segment of the worldwide Evangelical Church has apostasized from the Bible they once believed in—heading down diverse theological roads to certain destruction. We now discern this to be the apostasy of the last-days lukewarm church, of which the New Testament speaks. Though most megachurches continue to grow larger and larger, this is no evidence of an end-time spiritual awakening. And though not every large Protestant congregation has apostasized from the Gospel, the evidence of those that have apostasized is that they preach a false-Christ, works-based, sin-dodging, non-offensive gospel. The current movement toward merging all denominations and religions compromises the Gospel of Jesus with all other dangerous doctrines. Therefore, and according to Scripture, Christians who do not discern that they should **come out of her** (the apostate, compromising, and ecumenical type church) will be forcefully removed as Jesus states in Matthew 13:41: **The Son of man shall send forth his angels, and they shall gather out of his kingdom all things that offend, and them which do iniquity**. This insightful passage in Matthew 13 begins in verse 24 where Jesus speaks in a parable of the kingdom of heaven being like a man sowing good seed. The enemy then came and sowed tares on the same ground—meaning within the fellowship of the church. In verse 25, Jesus tells why this goes unnoticed: **But while men slept, his enemy came and sowed tares among the wheat, and went his way**. This indicates that false doctrine is sown alongside truthful doctrine within the church, but because godly men slept in a spiritual sense, they weren't aware of it: they were not awake and vigilant to sound doctrine.

In Matthew 13:29–30, the reapers are told to let the tares grow with the wheat, **lest while ye gather up the tares, ye root up the**

wheat with them. Let both grow together until the harvest: and in the time of harvest I will say to the reapers, gather ye together first the tares, and bind them in bundles to burn them: but gather the wheat into my barn.

In Matthew 13:37–43, Jesus then explains the parable so they could understand:

> **He that soweth the good seed is the Son of man; the field is the world; the good seed are the children of the kingdom; but the tares are the children of the wicked; the enemy that sowed them is the devil; the harvest is the end of the world; and the reapers are the angels. As therefore the tares are gathered and burned in the fire, so shall it be in the end of this world. The Son of man shall send forth his angels, and they shall gather out of his kingdom all things that offend, and them which do iniquity; and shall cast them into a furnace of fire: there shall be wailing and gnashing of teeth. Then shall the righteous shine forth as the sun in the kingdom of their Father. Who hath ears to hear, let him hear.**

Here, it is obvious Jesus is not referring to believers versus unbelievers but those within His kingdom—the church. All within the kingdom are believers in Jesus, but because some are guilty of spreading and accepting a "doctrine of tares"—**them which do iniquity** (verse 41)—a separation of souls is the judgment at the end of the age. **First the tares** (verse 30) are gathered together in their like-minded apostasy: they are the false teachers and seduced believers. They are in contrast to the **righteous** who will **shine forth as the sun** (verse 43). These two groups are today becoming increasingly distinguishable and separate from each other, making easy the forthcoming judgment.

In Matthew 24:42, 25:13; Mark 13:33, 35–37, and 14:38, Jesus told us to "watch." In Matthew 25:13, He said: **Watch therefore, for ye know neither the day nor the hour wherein the Son of man cometh**. Mark 13:35–37 records the same, and then He adds: **Lest coming suddenly he find you sleeping. And what I say unto you I say unto all, Watch**. In Mark 14:38, Jesus says**: Watch ye and pray, lest ye enter into temptation.**

When Jesus said "watch," He meant: keep awake spiritually—be vigilant to the sound doctrine of the Gospel. In 1 Corinthians 16:13, Paul also said: **Watch ye, stand fast in the faith**.

The connection between Matthew 7:21–23; Matthew 13:24–43; and Matthew 24:37–41 is evident and obvious: unrighteous Christians will depart into punishment because they did not "watch"—they were not careful to discern the truth: they were deceived to turn away from sound doctrinal teaching because of the false prophets. But they that do the will of God shall escape His wrath and gain eternal life. First Thessalonians 5:9 states: **For God hath not appointed us to wrath, but to obtain salvation by our Lord Jesus Christ**. And Jesus said in Revelation 3:21: **To him that overcometh will I grant to sit with me in my throne, even as I also overcame**. Believers in Jesus will "overcome" only through a steadfast belief in a very specific Gospel. Because the judgment of the church is necessary, God has allowed Satan to control carnal pastors who do not genuinely seek after and preach sound doctrine. Thus, believers are personally accountable and must be alert to follow the Gospel of the Bible. Are we searching for and believing in the truth? Or are we listening to the enemy's deception of a different gospel—a worthless gospel of tares?

The diversion of moral politics

Once again, according to Isaiah 55:8–9, God is far greater and wiser than we—having ways incompatible to our human thought process. And yet the God of heaven has made the plan of salvation simple for us to understand—reforming the soul and spirit of man heavenward. But within Evangelical Christianity, moral politics seems to have replaced the Gospel message—especially at election time in America. Though Christians should defend God's standards, the avenue of politics and government is not a scriptural method for moral reform. And ironically, Christians are not united in their moral views and thereby do not vote the same but are divided in allegiance to their favored political party. This political nepotism of many believers reveals an ignorance and negligence of the Gospel they claim to believe in. Here's why...

Morality and justice in government is upheld biblically as we see in Proverbs 29:2: **When the righteous are in authority, the people rejoice: but when the wicked beareth rule, the people mourn**. In our American democracy, even though our leaders ascend to power through the voting process rather than by lineage, moral leadership is not guaranteed. Realize also that the sin and immorality of individuals can never be personally dealt with even when a "moral candidate" is elected or when moral laws are passed. The unregenerate are still blind to their iniquity even though religious conservative factions attempt to change laws not aligning with biblical standards.

Christians are not biblically justified to reduce the Gospel to moral issues only. Evangelicals relying on their conservative party to transform societal norms to align with pro-life and heterosexual ideals of Scripture are guilty of Gospel negligence, just as are Christians who support the agendas of the liberal left for its human rights and anti-racism position. Both parties have a particular moral focus which the Bible supports, and yet both parties ignore the moral focus of the opposing party! This is blindsided enough, but in addition, personal spiritual fruit of a Christ-centered lifestyle cannot be a by-product of either agendum. In fact, the fruit of the Spirit—**love, joy, peace, gentleness, meekness, temperance**, as stated in Galatians 5:22–23—is greatly diminished if anger and intolerance against others, including Christians with opposing political views, takes root. From a New Testament perspective, Christians hoping for and campaigning for legislated morality have entirely missed the point of their Christian witness. Though believers are free to be actively employed in government as a witness for Christ and to uphold biblical standards, Jesus told us only to testify of the salvation Gospel. A heart that responds to this Gospel will be changed by a keen awareness of God's moral laws, resulting in actions of personal change. Those not responding to the Gospel remain unregenerate and give little or no attention to God's standards of holiness. This unregenerate majority pull the political strings on election day, only because Christians are divided and cannot agree on which party is more corrupt. In truth, it's an irrelevant battle and debate for the fact that the strategies of the morally astute sects within both parties come from the perspective of moral fairness and moral justice rather than a witness of and devotion to the Gospel of salvation. Though most Evangelicals prefer the platform of the Republican Party because it better aligns with God's moral laws, this does not prove that God has a favorite political party. If He does, then why are Democrats elected about half the time overall? Why can't God swing a conservative victory every time? In reality, He could if He wanted to! But He doesn't! This proves that God is not in the business of moral reform only but instead is focused on saving souls. Hence, God is far above the Evangelical box many believers have put Him in.

Knowledge and discernment of historical facts is essential.

In the early twentieth century, preaching and lobbying against the evils of alcoholism, fornication, gambling, and racketeering was considered mandate in the Gospel-believing Christian community. Decades later, the "religious right" Moral Majority/Christian Coalition movements led by Jerry Falwell and Pat Robertson mobilized fundamentalist Christians to once again be advocates for biblical standards and moral reform through the political process. Christian activism had by that time shifted its focus toward opposing the more seemingly urgent issues of abortion rights and gay rights laws—which also brought racial discrimination matters into the mix. The attention given to these particular issues caused a massive rift in the Christian community. Some good-hearted believers applauded gay rights and pro-abortion laws as morally fair. But many other Christians opposed them because they neglected God's moral standards. The upheaval caused increased Christian advocacy on both political sides—solidifying partisan bickering even to this day. As the political divide widens, so does the church remain divided over specific problems of justice, ethics, and morality. Blind allegiance to one political party results in equally urgent moral matters of the opposing party being viewed as inconsequential. Many in the service of government, believing they are morally upright in one genre, are in turn morally bankrupt in another. Those elected to the liberal left use their political clout to maintain the laws considered by those on the conservative right as opposed to biblical laws. Yet the swindling, racist, misogynistic political figures of the conservative right are just as guilty of immoral behavior.

Though Republicans and Democrats of past and present have always been at odds over policy and the level of government regulation, the "Christian morals" contribution has deepened the chasm of divide. Politics has become a nasty, divisive, finger-pointing business. Statements attacking the integrity of a candidate or the stated "*evil and destructive policies*" of a particular party have postured a pitting against one another. Pastors who from their own pulpit lash out against the "*satanically inspired voting patterns of ignorant Christians*" are themselves spiritually unfocused and unloving; they are ignorant of many historical facts and are unyielding to scriptural warnings against such divisive language and accusations. In 2 Timothy 2:24, Paul warns: **And the servant of the Lord must not strive; but be gentle unto all men**. Politically moral-minded believers must give heed to this admonishment, only because the source of the decades-long disagreement and conflict between noble party principles is easily discovered to have stemmed primarily from fundamentalist "Christian morals" intervention.

Most Evangelical Christians seem not to be aware that up until 1880, abortion was not illegal in America but was widely practiced under common law: the moral decision of aborting an unborn child was made privately and with no laws against such assault on human life. The matter began to gain attention in 1857 when the all-male American Medical Association pressed for abortion restrictions, seemingly as a rebellion against women becoming active in the medical field. Not until 1869, at about the same time that abortion became politicized, did the church begin to condemn it. Before that time, even the Catholic Church accepted and recognized the ethics of a woman's physical experience as "common law control" of her own body. Also, because religious White male patriotism demanded that maternity be enforced only among White Protestant upper-class women—to ensure White race purity and dominance—abortion became illegal in every state in 1880 and remained so until 1973. During this period, women were at medical risk if they wanted to terminate their pregnancy. From another viewpoint, however, this likely increased the number of unwanted babies coming to full-term and ultimately benefiting society. Amazingly, Christians still argue over which scenario better pleases God.

In 1971, two years prior to the *Roe v. Wade* Supreme Court decision legalizing abortion, the Southern Baptist Convention passed a resolution calling to make abortion legal and more accessible. When the Supreme Court decision was handed down in 1973, many Evangelicals of the time applauded the ruling because it marked an appropriate distinction between personal morality and public policy. But Christians with a different view were outraged that government law had now overruled biblical law. Then in 1976, a religious backlash against the US government gained full steam after the IRS rescinded the tax-exempt status of Bob Jones University for its racially discriminatory policies. This Christian institution, and others with the same race-bias policies, now had a similar moral conundrum, just as the newly passed abortion rights law had become to Christians accused of being liberal minded. Opposition against any government involvement in personal beliefs and practices galvanized conservative Christians to fight for humane and moral justice, while setting Christians with a more liberal view on the defensive edge.

The religious right had hijacked the Republican Party, causing many conservative Evangelicals to become public activists for the Right to Life anti-abortion campaign beginning in the early 1980s. Ironically, this activism was fused with a hypocritical racist mentality from the Moral Majority and Christian Coalition factions at the forefront of supporting Black education restrictions and directly associated with ghetto-preserving "redlining" policies. The result was a justified reaction from Black Christian Democrats who then entered the political fray, largely because White Republican Evangelicals gave no consideration for the evils of racial inequality—insomuch that it was not perceived as a moral issue needing to be addressed. Thus, the anti-abortion Christian became pitted against the anti-racism Christian. The hypocrisy of choosing political sides over a single moral issue removes any witness for Christ and His Gospel to the observing unregenerate population. All they can see is the bickering over who's right and who's wrong.

Though Christian involvement in politics helps to focus on moral awareness in society, the feuding over which moral issue should take priority keeps the Gospel of salvation back there somewhere in the shadows of insignificance. Many elected leaders on both sides of the political aisle are corrupt, deceitful, or hypocritically blind to counterpart sins. Therefore, the followers of Jesus are greatly misguided and distracted when trusting in government for answers to America's moral decline.

An entire book has been dedicated to this subject—*The Myth of a Christian Nation* by Christian theologian and pastor Greg Boyd.

The legitimate concern over racial inequality comes from a biblical perspective: there, of course, is no such "superior race." For many years, we have used the words *race* and *racism* inaccurately according to the Bible. The only scriptural type of "race" is the race of mankind. In a certain sense, labeling people as Black or White or any other color promotes the separation of humanity by skin shade. We find ourselves thoroughly entrenched in this inaccurate *race* terminology, keeping discrimination alive and causing alienation and distrust of one another. Nevertheless, if we don't use race terms like *White supremacy* or *Black inequities* to enlighten issues of prejudice and ignorance, the moral problem of race discrimination may become lost in obscurity.

Just as God is grieved and most assuredly is rolling His eyes over man's skin-shade discrimination, He is also grieved over any unborn aborted child simply because He is the Creator of all life. God is also grieved over Christian bigotry and aversion against homosexuals.

Why? Because according to John 3:16, God loved all humanity so much that He sent His only begotten Son to redeem all who would believe. We must be compassionate toward all who are lost just as we once were. In John 4:35, Jesus said that the **fields**, compromised of all sinners, are ripe and ready **to harvest**. Today, while Christians argue and debate over personal political views and particular moral policies, the fields of lost humanity are still waiting to be harvested. The conflict over which moral problem predominates became a Christian against Christian battle, only because unfocused believers prioritized moral politics in government over and above the integrity of the Gospel message.

Now that *Roe v. Wade* has been overturned on the federal level, Evangelicals and Catholics celebrate, but Women's Rights activists—some of whom are Christian—now take the stage in protest. Whose life is more precious or important to preserve and protect? Is it the mother or the unborn child? Most White Evangelicals and Democrats for Life of America (DFLA) side with the unborn child, and nearly everyone else, including many Black Protestant Christians, side with the mother because both the Women's Rights and Black Rights movements were grounded on the same footing. This is why many Black Protestant congregations don't want to be known as "Evangelical," even though they proclaim the true Gospel. It's a pathetically sad commentary.

Is the moral sin of aborting an unborn life more condemning than the moral sin of racism? No! Rivalry over which sin is more detestable is futile because Matthew 5:21–22 and 1 John 3:15 tell us that murder and hatred are the very same sin! As such, neither the Christian Republican nor the Christian Democrat can claim correct prioritization from a biblical perspective. The liberal left is just as biblically justified to fight for racial justice and comradery as is the conservative right justified to fight for the life of the unborn child. What is the solution? There is none because Christians have taken political sides! The majority of American Christians have been forced into this position because the previous generation deemed that God mandated His chosen people to be a beacon of morality rather than sharers of the Gospel. So we are now forced to choose:

should women have full control over their own physical affairs just as men have always had? If so, the sanctity of all life is at risk! Should Blacks become totally vindicated and integrated in secular society and within the body of Christ as well? If so, the ignorant and racist mindset of White Protestant superiority rebels! It's a no-win situation because sinful, bigoted, apostate Christians have traveled the wrong road of politics. What spiritual fruit have we reaped by going down this road of apostasy? Zero!

No matter who is elected president, no matter who is elected senator or congressman, no matter how the Supreme Court rules, Christians will always be divided and oppose each other because Satan has orchestrated it that way. He has killed us, robbed us, and destroyed us because of our slackness to the Gospel and a moral-politic nepotism.

A religious/political agenda prompted the scribes and Pharisees to try and trick Jesus by bringing to Him a woman caught in the act of adultery. The law by which they based their accusation (Leviticus 20:10) demanded that both the man and the woman be put to death for their sin. But they brought only the woman, and Jesus exposed their hypocrisy by refusing to condemn her; He then said to them: **He that is without sin among you, let him first cast a stone at her** (John 8:7). The passage then tells that only the woman and Jesus were left alone, causing her own self-conviction and the guilt of her sinfulness to be personally forgiven by the Savior and not by condemnation of the law—the very same political and moral conflict we face in America today. Though government authority is necessary according to the Bible, Jesus and the apostles never advised believers to infiltrate government so as to force morality. But since politics and religion have now merged thanks to differing opinion and input from Christians, anger and division reign supreme between political parties as well as within the church.

According to the book of Acts, when the Gospel of Jesus was fully grasped by the extremely bigoted Jewish people, the attitudes of those who believed on the Savior slowly reversed. Acts 10:34 states how Peter saw the truth of equality of all mankind in the eyes of

God—even the Gentiles: he declared, **Of a truth I perceive that God is no respecter of persons**. Since God has no favorites, neither should Christians: they must have equal respect and empathy for all nationalities. From a Christian perspective, the fight for equal Black opportunities and many Women's Rights issues have come from the biblical position of valuing all human life—justifying moral fairness and equal treatment of all people. Yet this focus has now gone to an extreme because many mixed-nationality and African American Protestant congregations also defend and accept the LGBTQ community as deserving equal recognition in society because they've also been discriminated against. This is not only a biblical oversight but unnecessary for the fact that "gays" (LGBTQ) are already protected under our amended constitutional laws just as any ethnic group is, simply because they are members of the human race. God's moral laws now come into play over this issue. Many Christians standing behind the liberal left position appear to turn a blind eye to newly legislated same-sex marriage laws which condone homosexual behavior as normal—thus interpreting it as a biblically acceptable lifestyle. This indoctrinates many believers with the idea that God made some people internally different, just as He made them externally different in skin color—thus rationalizing an acceptance of the gay person's "choice." However, skin color is not a choice. But by scriptural ignorance, sexual preference has become a "choice" according to the liberal thinking Christian, even though statements in the Bible oppose this idea: **From the beginning of the creation God made them male and female** (Jesus the Savior, Mark 10:6). Using only this Bible verse against the sin of homosexuality is not enough; we must bring other passages into consideration:

Leviticus 18:22; Romans 1:26–28; and 1 Corinthians 6:9–10 clearly warn against any physically unnatural or perverted sexual behavior as sin. These passages condemn homosexuality, and yet this sin is excused within some congregations, likely for the legitimate philanthropic value of the gay person's contribution to the community and, of course, because God loves all people.

Yes, God loves all people, so He sent His Son to die for all sins, including homosexuality. Those living in a homosexual lifestyle may claim they were born with that tendency. And they are correct! There is no scriptural argument against this analysis: humanity is born with a built-in magnet to a myriad of all kinds of sin, as perfectly explained in Psalm 51:5 and Romans 5:12. According to multiple New Testament passages, if we habitually continue in the act of any sin, we haven't yet had a mind-regenerating *born-again* conversion to the Gospel of Jesus. It's not a matter of opinion or feelings but of scriptural truth. Jesus said in Matthew 18:3 that we must be "converted" to be part of the kingdom of God and to break the bondage of sin. Mankind's sinful tendencies and desires can be transformed by the life-changing good news of the Gospel of righteousness.

Conservative right-wing Christians are also just as guilty of scriptural error for opposing gay people seeking employment or who want to become politically involved. Objecting their vocational pursuits only for their gay lifestyle is hypocrisy. Why aren't adulterers and atheists also opposed in the same way? Why do we condemn homosexuality as a worse sin? The Bible tells us that everyone is a sinner! We as believers shouldn't approve any lifestyle of sin, but we must respect and love all people even though they sin. How else will they know the love and forgiveness of Christ? Lashing out against "gay involvement" in society is not a Christlike attitude. The only sin Jesus condemned was the hypocrisy of the religious Pharisees—of which many Christians are guilty of for their disdain of gay people. And just the same, our scorning, segregated, and bias attitudes have teamed up with contention, strife, and division persisting within the body of Christ over moral political issues. This directly opposes Paul's exhortation and explanation of the fruit of the Spirit in Galatians 5:22–23. Because the Gospel should take priority, Christians must be warned of their divided ways against it and of their overly zealous indignation opposing one another. All malice and quarreling over the primacy of racial issues, same-sex issues, and abortion issues have exposed our carnal tendencies ever since politics and religion merged in the 1970s.

Paradoxically, at this very same time in America, a man of great moral character was elected to the presidency. This man of integrity didn't allow his devout Christian convictions to infringe upon the laws of the land he presided over. His name was Jimmy Carter—a Democrat, who was later mocked and criticized by conservative Evangelicals as a weak and ineffective president who had no moral backbone. Yet no Christian president before or since has come close to upholding the biblical "separation of church and state" ideology as Jimmy Carter had demonstrated.

Though voting for a morally upright candidate seems a mandate to most Christians, the changing of societal norms through the avenue of politics is not compatible with the Gospel Jesus preached. The New Testament gives no command to Christians to strategize morality in government or to rally around a hero of Civil Rights as priority over the salvation message. Though these efforts shed light on our moral decline and in and of themselves are a good and noble effort, in the long run, they are ineffective and useless unless the hearts of people are transformed by the love of Christ. Though Christians should defend the Bible's moral standards, we must not grieve the Holy Spirit: we must be wise and informed of what we speak, showing extreme love and compassion. If we don't, we are easily perceived as bigoted and extremist religious fanatics.

The racist and misogynistic attitudes of our ugly American past boiled to the surface in the Women's Liberation, Civil Rights, and Gay Rights movements. These movements, in addition to the volatile quandary over abortion, remain at the heart of our polarizing divide, especially in the Christian world. It has all become Satan's playground, and many of us continue to actively participate in fueling the fires. When will it end? Only when the Lord Jesus returns to bang many heads together. Revelation 21:4 states: **And God shall wipe away all tears from their eyes**. In a certain sense, it would seem this passage is more than metaphoric. Why will the redeemed followers of Jesus be weeping at the beginning of eternity? It is for our lack of compassion, love, and respect for our fellow man—railing against each other, even within the body of Christ—thus requiring the pain of a head-banging ceremony.

Is this a too far-fetched interpretation of Revelation 21:4? Perhaps. But you must admit it would apply to our blindsided lack of love for the unsaved and the entire body of Christ as well. But God is merciful to the repentant: Jesus said, **Be ye therefore merciful, as your Father also is merciful. Judge not, and ye shall not be judged; condemn not, and ye shall not be condemned: forgive, and ye shall be forgiven** (Luke 6:36–37). In Romans 12:18, the apostle Paul also exhorts: **If it be possible, as much as lieth in you, live peaceably with all men**. And the last commandment Jesus gave His disciples before going to the cross was **that ye love one another** (John 13:34).

Many of us haven't taken any of these exhortations seriously. Rather than spreading the Gospel to the unsaved around us, we have overtly sought to enlighten the world of its ethical and moral mistakes and to scold and detest our brothers and sisters in Christ who don't agree with our own opinionated political views. Surely we will incur judgment for such grievous scriptural oversight and apostasy.

Chapter 17

Knowledge of Deception

Today, many Christians remain steeped in religion and false doctrines. Though when our eyes are opened to the simple Gospel of salvation, we will also discern the simple and deceptive teachings that oppose it. As time passes, there is evidence of a distinct division between those intent on following a Holy God revealed in the Bible versus those who follow only a loving God who accredits blessings of abundance and success. It is the latter who have not earnestly studied their Bible, and thus, sadly, rely on a Jesus who doesn't exist. In the presumption of prayers being answered, the deception deepens, and the enemy has us hooked on the euphoria of God's material blessings, supplied by obedience to the tithing law of the old Mosaic covenant and the superstitious mystic power of our spoken words. Indeed, the judgment seat of Christ will be harsh for many.

Gnosticism

In recent years, Christians have been seduced to "experience God" via many avenues. This primarily is called *Gnosticism*—an esoteric knowledge of the divine in sought-after experiential manifestations and in the "power of spoken words," to name a few. Also, the

Gnostic practice of *contemplative prayer and contemplative worship*—a mystical Hindu-type repetitious mantra—is occurring within the Protestant Church. It is the subtly introduced concept of prayerfully repeating words or a scriptural phrase over and over in an effort to focus on God. This *contemplative/Gnostic* mantra is now in our worship music, especially within Charismatic, NAR, and nondenominational churches. Yet it is not a method by which we are told to worship God. Because of emphasis on verbal repetition—a pagan practice—it places one's focus on becoming closer to God through that method only. These practices are part of what describes *Gnosticism*—combining orthodox Christian doctrine with mystical or philosophical doctrines of Eastern pagan culture.

Through *gnosis*—the path to God realization—we supposedly gain divine knowledge and a deeper spiritual experience aside from the doctrines of Holy Scripture—achieving direct contact with the Divine. But finding communion with God through this technique is a misnomer and is even satanic in nature according to Scripture. In Deuteronomy 12:30–32, we read that Moses warned God's people, saying: **Take heed to thyself that thou be not snared by following them** (referring to other gods, and the methods to worship them by)…**saying, how did these nations serve their gods? Even so will I do likewise. Thou shalt not do so unto the Lord…thou shalt not add thereto, nor diminish from it.**

When seeing this warning in our Bible, we should realize that engaging in *contemplative/Gnostic* practices to become closer to the Lord and to experience His presence is unacceptable. *Contemplative prayer* and *contemplative worship* is a Christianized version of Hindu and Islamic mantra-type experiential worship. Though it may seem innocent or beneficial, in reality, we are not worshipping the God of the Bible. Instead, we have become corrupted from the simplicity that is in Christ by focusing on **another spirit**, as 2 Corinthians 11:4 warns of. We cannot syncretize our faith in Christ with paganism or East-Asian shamanistic practices. Jesus said: **But when you pray, use not vain repetitions, as the heathen: for they think that they shall be heard for their much speaking** (Matthew 6:7).

The *"Gnostic Christian"* (an oxymoronic term) seeks a path to enlightenment, peace, and divine connection—pressing toward the discovery of the mysteries of God and unity with the cosmos. Nowhere does the Bible tell us to pursue such an experience or spiritual venture. Jesus told us to seek the kingdom of God through a righteous relationship with God the Father; He didn't tell us to strive for harmonious unity with all that surrounds us. Neither did Jesus instruct us to seek a mystical mind-clearing experience such as today's yoga-type meditation.

Long ago, *Gnostic* practices became popular among beguiled Christians who believed they could acquire salvation and divine knowledge through *contemplative meditation*. These mainly were Catholic monks known as the Desert Fathers living in North Africa and the Middle East during the Early Middle Ages. In the centuries that followed, many Catholic mystics such as Hildegard of Bingen and Teresa of Avila influenced people to seek divine experience through unbiblical methods of *contemplative prayer and meditation*. Sixteenth-century Roman Catholic priest Saint John of the Cross was also known for his deep spiritual experiences with God. He taught beginners to use imagination and fantasy in their quest to communicate with God. He later taught them to practice periods of meditation and to keep an empty mind so that holy images and words would form. This exercise is not Christian in nature: emptying one's mind is also a practice of Hindu/Eastern experiential meditation. Biblical meditation is filling our mind with God's Word. Romans 12:2 says: **Be not conformed to this world: but be ye transformed by the renewing of your mind, that ye may prove what is that good, and acceptable, and perfect will of God**.

Today, because of *Gnostic* and *New Age Christianity* influence, Romans 12:2 has been interpreted to say, "*Be transformed by your imagination; empty your mind to discover God's great mysteries, and find unity with Him.*"

Because Word of Faith and NAR teaching encompasses the *positive confession* theology, verbalization and declaration of anything is presumed to become reality: the words themselves, whether positive or negative, become factual and will come to pass. Likewise, when seduced to add *Gnostic* doctrines to our faith in Christ, the *positive confession* doctrine aligns perfectly with *contemplative prayer and worship*. It is tactfully presented as *New Revelation* from the Holy Spirit—that our repetitious positive words of faith and our verbal repetition of Scripture will produce the same reality, resulting in unity with the Holy Spirit. In truth, however, the fullness of the "*power in words*" theology is a mind-bending deception from the enemy: it is scriptural distortion and Christianized superstition. Scripture tells us to share the Gospel with those around us, which is the only "power" and "seed" of the spoken word. The Savior declares this as our only calling. Instead, many Christians are now persuaded to turn inward by merely vocalizing their personal desired reality or their spiritual desired reality. Unbeknownst to many, this unbiblical teaching has come through deceptive snares of meditational cultic mysticism and *New Thought/positive confession* theology.

Additionally, Christians giving ear to the teaching of celebrity pastors, Christian or non-Christian authors, and well-known personalities who appear to be enlightened with a plan of world peace and the revelation of God's "invisible cosmic key" to unlock the understanding of humanity's divinity will, in the end, be disappointed. The Bible prophesies this age will end in hatred, violence, and devastation, then a thousand years of peace and restoration begins when Christ returns to reign with His remnant faithful bride.

This is Bible truth. We should therefore strive to find and to know the real Jesus of the Bible and the narrow way of salvation, separate from the doctrines of men and *Gnostic* mysticism. Those who seek friendship with a Jesus who paved the way for man's divinity or a Jesus who provides for earthly satisfaction and success will be easily seduced by the coming religious "man of sin." Speaking of him in Daniel 8:25, it says: **And by peace he shall destroy many**. This man will come in peace, promising safety and provision for all. But, in a deceptive peace, he shall destroy in a spiritual sense within religious conformity.

A personal spirit guide

Testimonies of angelic visitations seem to be on the increase. But Scripture does not tell us to seek divine guidance in this manner, and neither should we take seriously any solicited or unsolicited direction given by what appears to be angelic. Being visited by what appears to be an angel is no guarantee that it's an angel from God. As stated earlier, in 1 John 4:1, the apostle John instructed us to **try the spirits whether they are of God**. This testing of the spirits is for discerning unsound doctrine and any message from a visual apparition: it must be compared with the Word of God. A demonic being can also appear as angelic, proclaiming lies and deception. This is how Joseph Smith received his "enlightenment," which resulted in the Mormonism cult. In 2 Corinthians 11:14, Paul states: **And no marvel; for Satan himself is transformed into an angel of light**.

Scripture does not tell us that closeness to God comes by seeking apparitions or mystical signs and wonders. In an eagerness to learn how to acquire divine intervention and divine guidance, believers are easily led to the acceptance of craftily Christianized Eastern mystic practices of mind control (visualization) in occultic techniques of *guided imagery* for arousing a personal spirit guide. However, any method whereby we can call upon and visualize a spirit guide, an angel, or even what appears to be the real Jesus Himself is denounced in Scripture as witchcraft. In the pursuit of a divine sign or confirmation, many have opened themselves up to demonic intervention.

In the Old Testament, we find warnings against contact with wizards, familiar spirits, and the like. Leviticus 19:31 says: **Regard not them that have familiar spirits, neither seek after wizards, to be defiled by them**. And Deuteronomy 18:10–12 says: **There shall not be found among you one...that useth divination, or an observer of times, or an enchanter, or a witch...or a consulter with familiar spirits, or a wizard, or a necromancer. For all that do these things are an abomination unto the Lord**.

Though these warnings are obvious areas to avoid, the deception of **another Jesus...another spirit...or another gospel** in 2 Corinthians 11:4 also come from the same demonic realm. When deceived into "experiencing God's presence" through any unbiblical "new methods," we are guilty of divination and have given heed to another spirit—a seducing spirit. Again this is witchcraft. In Galatians 5:21, we see that witchcraft is listed among the works of the flesh. Yet today, Christianized methods of witchcraft have become an acceptable method for seeking and experiencing God—especially in churches that seek after signs and manifestations and who promote *contemplative prayer*, and *contemplative worship*. Such practices are embraced as a result of scriptural neglect, supposed direct revelation, and false teaching by church leadership. We must discern the warning from the prophet Jeremiah: **The prophets prophesy lies in my name…they prophesy unto you a false vision and divination, and a thing of naught, and the deceit of their heart** (Jeremiah 14:14).

Believers who are not educated to Christianized occultic techniques or deceptive apparitions will naturally trust in and follow anything mystical. They are seducible just as are the unregenerate.

The emergent church

Those who promote the Emergent Church movement (the merging-together church) teach the "*Light within all, through all, and around all*" theology. Christians are easily swept into this occult realm by many high-profile pastors and speakers perceived as loving, compassionate, and insightful to success—giving inspiration for living the happy, contented, and fulfilled Christian life. Yet this "*Light within all*" is not a Christian doctrine but is *New Age spirituality* seduction. Its deceptive teaching is a global phenomenon that presumably will one day change the cellular structure of the human race. When eventually believed by nearly everyone, we will have world peace. It is the alternative to Armageddon. Or at least this is what many would hope for. However, this solution to the dilemma of mankind's downfall is not the solution our Bible gives. And Jesus Himself prophesied of the violent, destructive, and hateful end of the age. In reality, the intolerance of the narrow-minded follower of the real Jesus will be the reason for the coming end-time persecution against the true church. They will be seen as ignorant, bigoted, and intolerant—the cancerous cells within the fabric of society who reject any self-realization of "*God within*."

Multifaceted ideologies of the *New Age Christianity* movement are partly to blame for the waywardness of the church today. But those who discern Bible truth will easily recognize this *New Age* deception as

- *earthly justice and achievement over eternal heavenly treasure,*
- *experience over biblical reason and exegesis,*
- *spirituality over doctrinal absolutes,*
- *feelings over scriptural truth.*

If your church has begun to follow these patterns, you are a part of the *Apostate Church*—the *New Age Emergent Church*—the organization of believers who have successfully merged secularism and religion through compromise of Gospel faithfulness. Loving and sincere pastors have unsuspectingly given ear to **seducing spirits and doctrines of devils** (1 Timothy 4:1) with insightful aid to the faltering and divided church. Yet these efforts doctrinally oppose the exclusivity of the Gospel Jesus proclaimed.

Within Christianity, the Emergent Church, with its postmodern ideas of *"truth interpreted by experience"*—or *"truth is as one perceives it"*—is largely to blame for the biblical illiteracy of many Christians today. Because of this schism and severance from the simple Gospel of salvation, many believers are now beguiled with skepticism about Bible truth—persuaded that God is only a God of love and that if there really is any such thing as absolute truth, surely God will overlook our indecisiveness over it or neglect of it.

Emergent Church leaders are quick to announce the good and fruitful outcome of all beliefs and faiths coming together. It is these, however, who have not seen with spiritual eyes the many passages warning that not all beliefs are pleasing to God. Every doctrine cannot be correct: unity and fellowship of the faith is not sustained by accepting just any belief. The following passages prove it:

- Romans 16:17–18
- Galatians 1:8–9

- Ephesians 4:14
- Philippians 3:16
- 1 Timothy 1:3–4
- 1 Timothy 1:18–20
- 2 Timothy 2:16–18
- Titus 1:10–11
- Hebrews 13:9
- 2 Peter 2:1
- 2 Peter 3:17

New Age illumination

Theologically diverse non-Christian *New Age* philosophies that gained popularity back in the 1960s have now also deceived many Christians. The teachings of those who sought spiritual guidance through the "*enlightenment*" that the "Essence of God" has always been within us has now become mingled with religious doctrine of the church. In the non-Christian *New Age* movement, the term "born again" was and is still understood as "*the cosmic illumination of the inner self as deity*." This concept has evolved and is now adapted into the theological doctrines of some Christian groups. As such, popular *New Age Christianity* theology declares that the enlightenment of accepting Christ is merely a shift in the perception of self. It is moving away from self-ego to the realization of "*Christ within*": you save yourself by abandoning self-pride—recognizing that you are a vital part of God Himself—for the betterment of humanity and ultimately to gain peace of soul and spirit.

However, when carefully analyzing such reckless theology from a biblical perspective, we easily determine this not to be the dwarfing of ego but rather the ultimate ego trip—replacing our puny and insignificant human ego with the indwelling of literal deity—an absurd and biblically incongruous concept.

When the immature Christian is persuaded to follow this teaching, they have entered a stage of apostasy—stepping away from the Gospel of salvation that God offers into the cajolery of an automatic oneness with God via false teaching. The Bible declares no such doctrine of either literal or figurative deity for mankind. Thus, *New Age Christianity* theology is non-Christian teaching—a type of cult religion.

Emergent Church and New Age Christianity teachers such as Brian McLaren, Leonard Sweet, Frank Schaeffer, Pastor Rick Warren, and many others would surely disagree with this book you are reading because it proclaims a particular interpretation of the Bible and of the Gospel. They will tell you, "The nonsense of the Evangelical premise of the saved/lost paradigm has severely crippled the church."

In truth, it's not the saved/lost paradigm that has crippled the church but the twisting of and even rejection of the salvation Gospel message. If the Bible is not perceived as a very precise and dogmatic book—to be interpreted only one way—then the Christian faith has surely become dysfunctional and ineffective.

The New Age connection with Christianity

Again Word of Faith theology predominantly teaches that the divine nature of God indwells the believer. It is the same theory as the non-Christian *New Age* teaching of "God within all"—but with a caveat of Holy Ghost infusion: you must be *born again* unto righteousness. Unbeknownst to many sincere Christians, it is occultic teaching. The divine nature of humans, even in a metaphoric sense, is apostate and unsound doctrine according to Scripture. The New Testament tells us that the Holy Spirit indwells us, but it does not tell that we have become "as God" when we accept Jesus as our Savior.

The philosophy that the Essence of God is within all people and in all things is now being acknowledged and taught within the church. This *quantum physics* theory, spiritualized by *New Age Christians*, is termed "*Quantum Spirituality.*" It seemingly reveals that subatomic particles of our makeup are the Energy of God and the Source of God. This supposed *enlightened teaching* has not only permeated throughout secular society but is also within Christian books, Christian movies, and on Christian television. Those who promote this game-changing *spiritual oneness* are the teachers of a false

Christ. They proclaim that Jesus came to show us the way of unity, happiness, and success through the realization that the *Source of God* is already within us: we must simply realize it, claim it, live by it, and begin to love one another. We then somehow morph into pseudo-equality with the Creator Himself, who is naturally the Source of love, light, and energy. This subtle *New Spirituality* propaganda has had great influence on the church today. When we become aware of this broad scale of changing ideas, we know that much of the church is also in a transition of terminology being used—which in turn ushers in a transfer from biblical Christianity to *New Age* religious unity.

Self-help books of mind power

In 1937, secular self-help author Napoleon Hill published his book *Think and Grow Rich*. This book of inspiration and application for achieving success in all areas of life has been hailed as reality-based by millions of people around the world. Mr. Hill's book promotes the idea that our positive and affirming words and thoughts have great effect in our development and success. In a human sense, Napoleon Hill's methods do work and are therefore interpreted as truth. However, as Christians, seeing this as the primary way through which God brings about our personal success is not discerning of God's sovereignty over us, nor is Napoleon Hill's book scripturally based by any means. The theories and advice in Mr. Hill's book side-step a submission to God's primary Gospel plan. *Think and Grow Rich* reveals methods of success through tapping into areas of dangerous and satanic *spirit-mind control.* Positive thoughts and affirming words are good, but many Bible passages warn of acquisitioning any kind of outside spirit. When given over to control of a source other than God for advancement and success, we place ourselves under delusion—which again is in great contrast to how Jesus taught us to pray in Matthew 6:10: **Thy kingdom come, thy will be done**—not *my will be done*. When applying Matthew 6:10 to our daily lives, we realize that we cannot speak or think success and prosperity into reality only by our positive mind-control agenda. We cannot assume it is God's obvious will for us to have whatever success or material abundance we desire. It is only if God gives the ability and wisdom to achieve it. Determination is one thing; being submissive to God's will is another. If we have unselfish motives, we can ask God for wisdom and knowledge to move forward in our desire to help struggling and suffering people and to give financially toward the advancement of the Gospel. Positive ambition and affirming words such as "*I can achieve*" and "*I will achieve,*" without prayerfully submitting to God's will and sovereignty over our lives, is a misguided effort and an unperceived spiritual diversion by the tempter and deceiver of our souls. It is no surprise that Word of Faith pastor Dr. Myles Munroe ignorantly endorsed *Think and Grow Rich* in his motivational "Keys to Personal Success and Prosperity" messages.

The secular "keys of success" were then deliberately coupled with the spiritual "keys of the kingdom of God" when Christian author Norman Vincent Peale wrote *The Power of Positive Thinking* in 1952. Many other Christian psychological and self-help books, too numerous to list, have been written in the years since. This genre of self-help religio-psychiatry began a new revolution within Christendom: the followers of Jesus are now encouraged to add the mind-altering positivity theology to the Gospel message.

In 2006, media personality Oprah Winfrey endorsed and promoted a book titled *The Secret* by Rhonda Byrne. This self-help book touts the *law of attraction* theory, which supposedly determines the complete order of the universe and of our personal lives. Rhonda Byrne's book concludes that our thoughts and words, whether positive or negative, will produce positive circumstances or negative circumstances accordingly.

The Secret makes no reference to turning from sin as the initial stage of reconciliation with God and is therefore non-Christian in its approach. Yet Rhonda Byrne's book was championed as "*theologically Christian*" by Oprah Winfrey, a professed *New Age Christian.*

On the back cover of *The Secret* and on page 164, we find the statement: "*You are God in a physical body.*" Notice that the word "*God*" is capitalized. We are God! This teaching is blasphemous and severely compromises Bible doctrine. *The Secret* also endorses guided imagery in visualization as a means of personal spirit guidance.

Just as the books *Think and Grow Rich* and *The Power of Positive Thinking* both convey the method for positive change and success, *The Secret* has a similar theme: "*When you speak and believe that you can, then you will; but when you speak and believe that you can't, then you won't.*" It is the "*like attracts like*" theory, having no ties whatsoever to Bible doctrine. But the positive mind-control methods within these and other similar books surmise that humans have the ability to change their own circumstances through thought power and positive words. Even though there is an element of truth to this positive way of life, we must be cautious to discern this mental advantage we have in light of our Christian faith. Obviously, we can't have a negative attitude about life—being doubtful or fearful—and still expect to accomplish any positive input for the kingdom of God. But we can be an inspiring witness through our positive words of encouragement in the Gospel of salvation. This is biblically understood as the verbal witness for Christ. However, mere positive vocal expressions of encouragement or declarations of success are in another category altogether. If we believe this method to be the cause of change, we have theoretically determined that there is no higher power than us. In light of scriptural truth, it is rather through prayer and faith that God is working within us for His positive, productive, and good purposes in our lives.

Christian books of pretense

Do you as a Christian think you're immune to today's *Emergent/ New Age Christianity* influence? Think again! The enemy has pulled out all the stops because he sees that his time is short. It should be no surprise to learn that much preaching and teaching on the Internet and on Christian television is doctrinally unsound. In Matthew 10:16, Jesus said: **Behold, I send you forth as sheep in the midst of wolves: be ye therefore wise as serpents**. Followers of Jesus must be wise and discerning because many Christian books, whether instructional, devotional, or novel-like, are riddled with *New Age*, occultic, or *Universalism* theology: they are apostate and doctrinally unsound. Briefly, here are just a few examples…

Celebration of Discipline

Celebration of Discipline: The Path to Spiritual Growth, by Richard Foster, is an instructional book designed to give central spiritual practices of the Christian faith. Mr. Foster's book embarks on a journey of inward disciplines of meditation, prayer, fasting, and study. This, of course, is a vital part of the spiritually disciplined life of a believer. However, Richard Foster's book also promotes the *New Age* mystic practice of *guided imagery*—a technique of generating and evoking mental images for inspiration and guidance. In *New Age* terminology, this is called "*channeling*." Devotion to New Testament orthodox Christianity is thereby linked with pagan occultic practice in Foster's book.

On page 26 of *Celebration of Discipline*, 1978 first-edition printing, Foster states: "*You can conjure the real Jesus, who will come at your command, and stand before you.*"

According to the author, this method of conjuring a mental image of Jesus is helpful and even necessary in the Christian walk. But this easily transforms into a very real mental image of Jesus and thereby is satanic in nature according to our Bible. Channeling any spirit, even Jesus, is sorcery and divination of a demonic nature: it is forbidden in Scripture. The real Jesus will not appear to us by our own manipulation or divination of *guided imagery*: Jesus the Savior cannot be summoned to appear through a mental ritual. Instead, we have summoned a spirit guide from the demonic realm who is all too delighted to be a Jesus impersonator. It's a marvelous deception.

The practice of "meditating in visualization" for the purpose of spiritual growth is nowhere hinted in our Bible. Our spirit is not our imagination: our imagination is as distinctively different from our spirit, just as Eastern mysticism is far different from biblical Christianity.

Isaiah 2:6 gives clear warning against Eastern religious practices: **Therefore thou hast forsaken thy people the house of Jacob, because they be replenished from the east, and soothsayers like the Philistines, and they please themselves in the children of strangers**.

Here we find that false religion comes **from the east**—and that God will leave us to our own devices if we entertain such teaching and practice. The mental exercise of *guided imagery* is no different from the graven images the Israelites were guilty of worshipping: they sought the consolation of other mediums, causing God's anger against them. If during our Christian walk we delve into the realm of *spiritism*, *guided imagery*, and the like, we have not only entered dangerous waters of the spirit world, we have forsaken God's ways, and His hand is removed from us. Any personal guidance produced by the method of *channeling* is, in reality, from the demonic realm. It is witchcraft. Again, Leviticus 19:31 and Deuteronomy 18:10 warn us against involvement with "familiar spirits" and "witchcraft." We also read in 1 Chronicles 10:13–14 that God slew King Saul for consulting mediums in preference over inquiring of the Lord.

Celebration of Discipline also gives many examples of Catholic mystic practices such as the technique of *contemplative prayer*. As mentioned earlier, this is focusing on a single word or Bible verse, repeating it over and over…then waiting quietly to hear what God might say to you. This type of meditational prayer has no scriptural support whatsoever; rather, we must gain wisdom and guidance by reading our Bible. If the answer you seek is not addressed through biblical knowledge and wisdom, you have free will to decide for yourself. Today, God's will and purpose for our lives is only to believe in the Gospel of Jesus and to share it with others. We need not agonize over seeking divine guidance over who to marry, which car to buy, where to live, or what vocational path to take. Proverbs 3:6 encourages us, saying: **In all thy ways acknowledge him, and he shall direct thy paths**. This is simple to understand: we should include the Lord into our daily decisions; when we do this, He directs our every move. We must not seek a mystical sign or a personal spirit guide to help make a decision. (Also read Lamentations 2:3 and Jeremiah 11:10–14.)

When we engage in *contemplative worship and prayer, spiritism*, and *guided imagery*, we have stepped outside of God's biblical instruction, and His hand of restraint covering us from the evil one is removed. The door is then open to any demonic spirit who quickly enters into our quiet time of seeking guidance or inspiration—giving a deceptive or unnecessary answer. Instead, Christians should be in continual meditation in God's Word: according to Hebrews 1:1–2, this is how God speaks to us today.

Philippians 4:6 (NIV) says: **Do not be anxious about anything, but in everything, by prayer and petition, with thanksgiving, present your requests to God**.

Psalm 63:6–7 also says: **I remember thee upon my bed, and meditate on thee in the night watches. Because thou hast been my help, therefore in the shadow of thy wings will I rejoice**.

This passage tells us that meditation is only on the Lord; it is not quiet time spent in anxious anticipation of a special or personal word from God or in seeking a "spirit guide" to receive a word of direction. Rather, it is resting in the assurance of being **in the shadow of thy wings**.

In Psalm 27:14, David says to simply wait—**Wait on the Lord: be of good courage, and he shall strengthen thine heart: wait, I say, on the Lord**.

The Purpose Driven Life

Ecumenical Pastor Rick Warren of Saddleback Church in Lake Forest, California, authored a 2002 book titled *The Purpose Driven Life*. The title of Pastor Warren's book grabs the attention of most Christians because they want their lives to count for something in God's economy. Though Warren's book uses Christian lingo and is inspirational in how God uses our lives for His purposes and to influence others, it gives the reader no knowledge of how to biblically initiate a relationship with God: it is devoid of proclaiming repentance from sin as the starting point of the Christian walk. Instead, *The Purpose Driven Life* walks the reader through Pastor Warren's "*40-Day Journey*" of discovering God's plan for personal destiny. Though there are good and truthful insights in the book, Warren's focus on developing a "unity with God" for the purpose of finding one's destiny is actually self-seeking and is profoundly detached from the Gospel of the Bible. Seeking friendship with Jesus to find purpose in one's life is not the biblical way to become *born again*: we are not qualified for salvation by only buddying up with Jesus. Our Bible tells us that when repentance from sin is first prioritized, a right relationship with God then begins, and the journey of finding our personal destiny will then come naturally over time. But we must stay focused on the Gospel and the reason Jesus came into the world. The Father did not send His Son to help us climb the ladder of achievement, success, and serendipity, either within or without the church.

Rick Warren also published a DVD series based on his *Purpose Driven Life* book. At the end of the series, he invites the listener to repeat a prayer, saying:

> *Dear God, I want to know your purpose for my life. I don't want to base the rest of my life on wrong things. Today I want to take the first step in preparing for eternity by getting to know you. Jesus Christ, I don't understand at all, but as much as I know how, I want to open up my life to you. I ask you to come into my life and make yourself real to me. Use this series in my life to help me know what you made me for. Thank you, amen.* (Rick Warren, "The Purpose Driven Life," YouTube)

This kind of prayer is completely lacking any thought of repentance from sin. It recognizes the need for God, but it's a self-seeking way of asking Jesus to help you on a "Christian journey" without first having a true *born-again* change of heart.

After reciting this prayer, Pastor Warren then stated: "*If you just prayed that prayer, you've become a part of the family of God!*"

No, Pastor Warren! Turning from sin is first required to be in the family of God!

Rick Warren is a clear example of a current-day compromising false teacher. His many ecumenical and *Universal*-based books for Christians, including *The Purpose Driven Life* and *The Purpose Driven Church* lead people down a path of deception—believing that their salvation comes through finding purpose and destiny, resulting in a society of growing, dynamic, and successful people.

A subtleness of deception on pages 87–88 of *The Purpose Driven Life* shows how to become "*a best friend of God*": Pastor Warren states, "*Friendship with God is built by sharing all your life experiences with him. Because God is with you all the time, no place is any closer to God than the place where you are right now. The Bible says, 'He rules everything, is everywhere, and is in everything.'*"

Here, Pastor Warren also explains Ephesians 4:6 from the NCV (New Century Version Bible), which says: **There is one God and Father of everything. He rules everything and is everywhere, and is in everything**. This verse in the NCV Bible would at least imply that the very Source of God is intrinsically within all things and all people. However, the King James Bible says something far different: **One God and Father of all, who is above all, and through all, and in you all**. Blatant *New Age* false doctrines have been inserted into newer versions of Holy Scripture, and Rick Warren has chosen his favorite modern version of the Bible to fit his hypothesis.

Ephesians 4:6 must be read within its full surrounding context. In the King James Version, the interpretation of verse 6 is derived from verses 4 and 5: Paul is specifically addressing those who are in **one body, and one Spirit, even as you are called in one hope of your calling. One Lord, one faith, one baptism**. It is therefore only those who have responded to the call of righteousness in Christ Jesus: they have received the Spirit, which Paul then says is **in you all** in verse 6. The Essence of God Himself is not within all humans, thereby causing a natural "*friendship with God,*" as Pastor Warren declares.

Jesus Calling

Jesus Calling is a 365-day Christian devotional written by Sarah Young. The book is comprised of loving and encouraging "messages from Jesus." However, the reader may not notice the subtle mystical *New Age Christianity* phrases in many of these daily messages.

In the introduction to her book, Sarah Young reveals that the method of writing the devotional was derived from meditating on Scripture, then waiting quietly with pen in hand to write down what

Jesus would say to her. She also states that her inspiration for writing *Jesus Calling* came from reading the book *God Calling*, published in 1935. Young described this book as "*a devotional book written by two anonymous 'listeners.'*" These "*listeners*" (channelers) used techniques of quietly listening and writing down what they believe God said to them. In reality, the authors of *God Calling* heard and wrote down messages from the spirit realm of darkness to bring only a *Universal* message of love, hope, and peace, with no Gospel message of repentance from sin or of faith in Jesus the Savior.

On page 12 of her introduction to *Jesus Calling*, Sarah Young wrote: "*I knew that God communicated with me through the Bible, but I yearned for more. Increasingly, I wanted to hear what God had to say to me personally on a given day. I decided to listen to God with pen in hand, writing down whatever I believed He was saying.*"

Here in her own words, the *Jesus Calling* author admits that Holy Scripture was insufficient and that she wanted to hear more. However, the Bible gives no directive for quieting one's self, then listening for Jesus to speak additional words to us. There are times when the Holy Spirit may indeed give us personal guidance to help make important decisions regarding spiritual matters, but when anticipating a constant directive through *contemplative* meditation or in replacing the canon of Holy Scripture, we become wide open to spiritual delusion.

Jesus Himself was supposedly "channeled" by Sarah Young, who then wrote down in the *first-person* singular form what she heard. Jesus is therefore perceived to actually be speaking to the reader of the book. Since Sarah Young asserts to have written down everything Jesus said to her, the reader must conclude that her journal is as authoritative as the Bible. Though perhaps much of *Jesus Calling* could potentially be the words of Jesus to us, it is very presumptuous and even doctrinally unsound to claim that Jesus will guide us or come close to us before we admit our guilt and sorrow for sin—which Sarah Young altogether fails to mention in this devotional.

New Age Christianity terminology is used throughout *Jesus Calling*. Sarah Young's portrayal of a loving and compassionate Jesus, with no indignation against sin, attracts the biblically ignorant reader.

Jesus is seemingly desperate for companionship. But in light of Bible truth of the self-sufficiency of the Godhead, we know that Jesus the Savior does not need us. We need Him.

The *Jesus Calling* daily devotional for July 8 begins with Jesus saying: "*When you seek my face, put aside thoughts of everything else. I am above all, as well as in all.*"

Yes, Jesus is "*above all,*" but His Essence is not "*in all*" as the Emergent Church and *New Age Christianity* teaches.

Carefully ponder a few contrasting passages: Psalm 39:5, **Verily every man at his best state is altogether vanity,** and Isaiah 40:22, **It is he that sitteth upon the circle of the earth, and the inhabitants thereof are as grasshoppers; that stretcheth out the heavens as a curtain**.

These verses indicate that God is far distinguished and separate from His creation: He is not inherently united with man or the "Substance within man." In fact, we can derive from these above verses (and many others) that man is full of vanity if he believes himself to be "the Substance of God."

Within the daily devotional for August 24, Jesus says: "*I am all around you, hovering over you even as you seek My face.*" Then toward the end of the devotional for this particular day, Jesus tells His children not to fear His closeness because, as he says, "*I have cleansed them with My blood and clothed them with My righteousness.*"

This, of course, is a true statement…if and when we repent of our sin. Although, nowhere within *Jesus Calling* is there biblical reference to exactly how one becomes "*cleansed*" or "*made righteous.*" To the reader not yet *born again* through a regenerated mind and sorrowful for their own sin, Jesus is right there "*hovering over*" us when we need Him. The subtleness of deception here is that we can become "*cleansed*" and "*righteous*" for only "*seeking His face*" in communion. The New Testament gives no indication that we are righteous before God without first repenting of sin. This is the simplicity of the Gospel of salvation—a concept completely absent in *Jesus Calling.*

The December 13 devotional is foreign to any Bible verse. Jesus begins by saying: "*Take time to be holy. The word 'holy' does not mean goody-goody; it means set apart for sacred use. That is what these quiet moments in My Presence are accomplishing within you.*"

These words may sound rational; however, the "holiness" of a believer is not accomplished through quiet moments spent with God. First Peter 1:16 says: **Be ye holy; for I am holy**. How does this happen? It is by becoming **the righteousness of God in Christ**, as stated in 2 Corinthians 5:21. It is through humble repentance and trusting in the Gospel of Jesus (Mark 1:15) whereby God imputes holiness and righteousness to us. Though spending quiet time with God keeps us close to Him, we are not made holy by doing so.

Is the real Jesus speaking through Sarah Young by way of mystic channeling? No. Mysticism focuses on the experience. But the Bible instructs us to exegete Scripture to hear from God. Again, Hebrews 1:1–2 (NIV) says: **In the past God spoke to our forefathers through the prophets at many times and in various ways, but in these last days he has spoken to us by his Son**. The words of Jesus and His life chronicled have "spoken" to us in the New Testament. However, the devotional *Jesus Calling* references only Bible passages which appear to agree with Sarah Young's personal channeled revelations. And because the author has published her messages from Jesus in the *first-person* format for all to read, this devotional might seem to have the same clout as anything written in the Bible. This is not conceivable because some of Sarah Young's statements from Jesus actually contradict the Bible. And the canon of Holy Scripture was closed within the first century of our Lord according to Revelation 22:18–19. The Holy Spirit then gives a doxology in verses 20–21, completely sealing the canon.

Though the content of *Jesus Calling* seems inspirational, the process by which it was written is not biblical: Jesus cannot be commandeered to give a daily word aside from Scripture. This modus operandi in *Jesus Calling* could easily propel many readers into anxious pursuit of their own personal daily message, thereby becoming highly susceptible to any spirit of deception. Regrettably, Sarah Young's devotional book has also been used as a study-tool guide in many Christian group gatherings.

The Shack

New Age Spirituality and *Universalism* theology was presented as doctrinal truth in the 2007 Christian fictional novel *The Shack*, written by William Paul Young. Many subtle messages of false doctrine appear in this wonderful story of God's love and forgiveness as it relates to human tragedy. The dramatic story of *The Shack*, also a box-office movie presentation in 2017, portrays a *Universal Christ* who forgives all humanity for their neglect of Him and His Word. Within the dialog of the story, traditional and biblical Christianity is presented as hypocritical and hurtful.

Halfway through *The Shack*, on page 122 of the book, God (portrayed as a woman named *Papa*) explains to the perplexed Mackenzie (the main character of the story): "*I don't need to punish people for sin. Sin is its own punishment, devouring from the inside. It is not my purpose to punish it. It's my joy to cure it.*"

How does the Bible respond to this statement?

> **And I will punish the world for their evil, and the wicked for their iniquity.** (Isaiah 13:11)
>
> **For, behold, the Lord cometh out of his place to punish the inhabitants of the earth for their iniquity.** (Isaiah 26:21)
>
> **But I will punish you according to the fruit of your doings.** (Jeremiah 21:14)

The New Testament reveals through the Gospel of Jesus Christ that man can escape God's wrath and punishment for iniquity. Yet the story of *The Shack* completely and decisively decimates this Gospel—declaring there is no punishment for sin!

On page 192 of *The Shack*, when explaining the vital connection of what Jesus did on the cross, Papa (God) tells Mackenzie: "*Through his death and resurrection, I am now fully reconciled to the world—the whole world.*"

This would be a biblically correct statement if just one word were changed: "*I am now [potentially] reconciled to the whole world.*"

The atonement of Jesus cannot possibly render a blanket pardon for the sins of all mankind—especially for those who don't believe that Jesus is the Reconciler between God and man. Biblical truth about God's forgiveness and man's reconciliation to Him is found in New Testament passages such as John 3:36 (NIV): **Whoever believes in the Son has eternal life, but whoever rejects the Son will not see life, for God's wrath remains on him**.

And Acts 17:30 (NIV) says: **In the past God overlooked such ignorance, but now he commands all people everywhere to repent**.

In chapter 16 of *The Shack*, on page 225, Papa explains that when Mackenzie forgave his father for abusing him as a child, his forgiveness did not create a relationship between them. This is true for humans, but human forgiveness and reconciliation is different from spiritual reconciliation with God the Father. Nonetheless, in the story of *The Shack*, Papa then correlates this idea of God's forgiveness to all mankind: she states, "*Forgiveness does not establish relationship. In Jesus, I have forgiven all humans for their sins against me, but only some choose relationship.*"

This statement is classic *Universalism* theology: *God forgives all people for their sin because of what Jesus did on the cross*. In the theology of *The Shack*, reconciliation with God is unavoidable. In contrast, Jesus said: **But he that doeth truth comes to the light** (John 3:21). Hence, we cannot come to Jesus "the light" without repenting of our sin.

Early in the story, Mackenzie's father, though a churchgoer, had not repented of his drunkenness and abusive ways and later dies with no evidence that he ever repented. Yet years later, when Papa shows Mackenzie a vision of souls on the other side, his father is observed enjoying a blissful existence. To the contrary, in Luke 13:5, Jesus said: **But, except ye repent, ye shall all likewise perish**. These simple words from Jesus totally destroy the *Universal Christ* theology of *The Shack*.

On page 112, Jesus explains the transcendence of God to Mackenzie, saying: "*God, who is the ground of all being, dwells in, around, and through all things.*"

Once again, this is occultic *New Age* terminology—that is, the Essence of God is everywhere and within all people—and after death, every soul naturally returns to God because it is part of God.

What does our Bible say about such a doctrine? Genesis 1:1: **In the beginning God created the heaven and the earth**...not "*In the beginning God distributed Himself.*"

Psalm 97:9 says: **For thou, Lord, art high above all the earth: thou art exalted far above all gods**...not "*For thou Lord are the Source in all things: your very Being is within me.*"

The heretical statements made within the story of *The Shack* cut to the doctrinal core of the Gospel of salvation—bypassing it and rendering it insignificant as the impetus for coming into right relationship with God the Father. With apologies to those who love this fictional story by Paul Young, the Holy Spirit did not inspire this novel. Though the narrative is intriguing, the god of *The Shack* is a god of Paul Young's imagination: it is not the God of the Bible. *The Shack* cannot be classified as *Christian fiction* but rather dangerous fiction because it is theological fiction in light of Bible truth.

The Shack is just one of many theological stepping-stones in society's trendy and marketable *New Age Spirituality*, now widely embraced within Christian circles and lining up with the end-time "falling away" stated in the New Testament.

What would the apostle Peter say about *The Shack*? **For we have not followed cunningly devised fables, when we made known unto you the power and coming of our Lord Jesus Christ** (2 Peter 1:16).

In exposing these examples of dangerous "Christian books," I am not judging the authors personally but judging what they write or teach compared with Scripture. God will judge them individually. The author of *The Shack* is actually a wonderful and compassionate man. I have nothing against Paul Young personally. However, because his novel is not based in sound Bible doctrine, it leads many undiscerning believers and unbelievers far from the Savior's plan of salvation and the understanding of God's holiness.

William Paul Young's life and how he came to write *The Shack* was highly publicized on Christian network TBN—which, because of their own position of ecumenism and apostate doctrine, supported Mr. Young's book with enthusiasm.

In 2004, a year before he began writing *The Shack*, Paul Young participated in a Christian think-tank forum of a dozen people to present and discuss ideas of how Christians could have better influence in society. When the day came for Mr. Young to share his views, the other participants were surprised and shocked when he presented a 103-page manuscript he'd prepared in support of *Universalism salvation*. In the manuscript, Young stated his total abandonment of the "*evangelical paradigm*" he grew up with. He verbally confessed his frustration with and rejection of biblical Christianity in favor of a *Universal* view of God.

In 2017, William Paul Young published another book titled *Lies We Believe About God*. In this book, he explains how Christians have been deceived through a misinterpretation of the Gospel and claimed to prove biblically that everyone is "*already saved,*" as he put it, that sin does not eternally separate us from God, and even that we will likely be given the chance to change our mind about the real love and forgiveness of God after we die. This idea goes totally against all Bible passages referring to the judgment—especially Hebrews 9:27: **And as it is appointed unto man once to die, but after this the judgment**.

In chapter 15 of *Lies We Believe About God*, Paul Young denies the doctrine of hell, referencing Bible passages containing the phrases **everlasting fire** (Matthew 25:41) and **a lake of fire burning with brimstone** (Revelation 19:20) as speaking of something other than eternal punishment for sin. Young asserts: "*This is a fire of love, that now and forever is for us, not against us.*" Amazingly, Mr. Young seems to have not noticed the words **cursed**, **everlasting punishment**, **prepared for the devil and his angels**, and **the fierceness and wrath of Almighty God** also stated within the context of these passages.

Since the theological blunders of *The Shack* and *Lies We Believe About God* stray far outside orthodox Christianity and the truthful Gospel of Jesus, we should know that God cannot have mercy on all mankind in the end. This kind of forgiving mercy renders a total rejection of God's holiness: it is greatly ignored and even mocked.

I've been accused by some of picking apart every incongruous detail or doctrinal error of these and other Christian books. Although, in Acts 17, the Bereans did the same thing! They scrutinized Paul's testimony against the ancient Hebrew text and the prophecy of the coming Messiah yet found no error in his words concerning Jesus. And it tells that the Bereans were "more noble" for their search of Holy Scripture. Through the same method of searching Scripture, I must declare the opposite for finding little biblical, theological, and doctrinal alignment with these "Christian books" I have critiqued. I am therefore not guilty of dividing the body of Christ but of strengthening it against the scheming forces of darkness.

Chapter 18

Irrefutable Discernment

We as Christians would love to see genuine revival in our time. Our hearts naturally yearn for it, and we should pray for the unsaved around us. Regrettably, however, a worldwide end-time revival of righteousness is not spoken of in the Bible. In the book of Revelation, Jesus rebukes and warns the apostate church to repent from her waywardness. Since a large portion of the church in America and around the world has lost its first love and has wandered from the Judeo-Christian principles it was founded upon, we are in line for the same harsh rebuke. This, in addition to the continued sin of the unregenerate, brought a great warning to America on September 11, 2001. But it was not heeded. Instead of turning to God in repentance, we erected an even taller building than the World Trade Center had been. God was again ignored in an attempt to prove our greatness and self-reliance. The warning from Isaiah 9:9–13 was not heeded by our government leaders: **And all the people…that say in the pride and stoutness of heart, the bricks are fallen down, but we will build with hewn stones… therefore, the Lord shall set up the adversaries…for the people turneth not unto him that smiteth them, neither do they seek the Lord of hosts.**

This sad scenario from Isaiah, chapter 9, has happened to us in America. Because of sin and neglect of God's Word of truth, our arrogant fist of defiance continues to shake at those who hate us rather than repenting and trembling in fear of Almighty God who was the One responsible for bringing this calamity on our nation. We will experience more of the same destructive judgment if we continue on the same path.

Unperceived rebellion

All Christians, whether they attend a Charismatic-type church, a mainstream Protestant denomination church, or a nondenominational church are not immune to false teachings. Liberal, apostate, or blasphemous concepts are not blatantly presented but rather are subtly introduced, sounding reasonable and rational—not ruffling too many feathers in the undiscerning minds of the faithful. Over time—perhaps decades—apostasy from the Gospel of Jesus is embraced unaware, aligning perfectly with New Testament prophecy that it would happen. Hebrews 2:1 warns of the potential Christians have to stray from sound doctrine: **Therefore we ought to give the more earnest heed to the things which we have heard, lest at any time we should let them slip**.

Psalm 118:8 also tells us to put trust in no man but only God and His Word. Yet in divisive ways of unrecognized apostasy and through vain philosophy, much of the church is now thoroughly penetrated with delusion. *Word of Faith*, NAR, *Universalism*, and *New Age Spiritually* books and material are available online and in every Christian and secular bookstore. Ignorantly enticed, Christians are easily seduced by these teachings: they are thrown off course from the simplicity of God's Word. Though the theological and doctrinal views of these movements may differ, they all have a similar theme of heresy and apostasy from the Gospel of salvation:

- *Word of Faith Christianity: "Incarnate Divinity"—equality with the Savior, embracing earthly prosperity as a component of the Gospel, unifying with Catholicism's heresy*

- *NAR (New Apostolic Reformation) Christianity: "Power Dominionism"—the prioritization of signs, miracles, and mystic/pagan practices to usher in the kingdom of God upon the earth*
- *Universalism Christianity: "Auto-Syncretization"—unavoidable unity with God: all humanity is exonerated through the cross of Christ with the axiom of eternal bliss for all*
- *New Age Christianity: "Quantum Spirituality"—the literal Essence of God within, compatibility with mystic/pagan practices, harmony with the cosmos*

These additions to and compromises of the Gospel of the Bible are Satan's strategy of deception. This gradual apostate shift easily takes root and progresses forward within the slumbering and distracted church, culminating in a *Universal Religion* which will one day be controlled by the anti-Christ man.

We must note that Jesus sternly warned the religious scribes and Pharisees: **You generation of vipers, how can you escape the damnation of hell?** (Matthew 23:33). Putting trust in vain philosophy or false religion will send us down the same path the scribes and Pharisees traveled. They couldn't see the truth for their religion and their vanity. Today, we hear varying forms of the same vain philosophy tugging at the hearts of millions of Christians:

- *All humanity has access to health and wealth through the cross of Christ.*
- *All humanity can benefit from direct divine revelation.*
- *All humanity is forgiven.*
- *All humanity is Christ.*

Since each of these doctrines bypass or overshadow any acknowledgment of sin, let's go back to Matthew 24:5 and read again what Jesus said: **For many shall come in my name, saying, I am Christ; and shall deceive many**.

We have now come full circle, and we can see the enemy's deceptive scheme against all of humanity—and especially professing Christians.

Amazingly, our Bible sums up its reply to all of these false doctrines in just one verse: **Put them in fear, O Lord: that the nations may know themselves to be but men** (Psalm 9:20).

This single verse totally annihilates the theory that man and God are involuntarily or unavoidably united—or even that a *born-again* believer has equal power with Jesus the Savior. We cannot mingle spiritual darkness with spiritual light to illuminate a brighter spiritual path. Again Jesus said we are separated from the Father: we are sinners until we reject all darkness and **come to the light** (John 3:21). He also said: **If therefore thine eye be single, thy whole body shall be full of light** (Matthew 6:22). When we turn from our sin and put faith in Jesus the Savior, we then walk in the Spirit and the Light of Righteousness—the Holy Spirit dwells within us. It is not a light of personal divine power, nor is it a magical shield against sin, nor does the indwelling of the Holy Spirit remove the guilt of committed sin—but convicts of sin (John 16:8). For this reason, believers who partake in mystical, experiential, or materialistic pursuits cannot see of their deception. Their spiritual eyes are not focused and single: they have not recognized the Holy Spirit and thereby have not fully surrendered to Him.

Make sure your election

The Old Testament refers to the elect as God's chosen people—the Jews. The New Testament refers to the elect mainly as those who are believers in and followers of Christ. They have repented from sin and place trust in the Lord Jesus Christ. In Matthew 24:24, Jesus said that even the elect of the last days will be preyed upon by false prophets who will show signs and miracles that divert attention away from the saving Gospel. The Greek Interlinear Bible interprets the last part of Matthew 24:24, **so as to deceive if possible the chosen ones**. To the reader of nearly any version of Matthew 24:24, it may appear that Satan will only attempt to deceive the elect, but he cannot...

because they are "the elect." This cannot be the correct interpretation of the verse. Why would Jesus warn His elect about deception if it were impossible for them to be deceived? It is up to the believer to discover and discern deceptive teaching. Jesus does not speak of any such immunity to deception. In fact, in Matthew 24:5, He clearly states many will be deceived by those claiming to be "as Christ." The teaching of a metaphoric duplication of deity and the inner-self transformation to become as Christ through a *born-again* conversion thus falls on Christians, not unbelievers. As such, when reading Matthew 24:24 in the midst of all surrounding verses and by making the connection with other warnings from the apostle Paul of **another gospel, which...ye might well bear with** (2 Corinthians 11:4) and **a falling away** (2 Thessalonians 2:3), we see it is very possible that some of the elect living at the end of the age will indeed be deceived by false Christs and false prophets. Therefore, as the elect, we are required to be diligent to sound doctrine and humbled enough to admit when we err in deception.

The church at Galatia was easily seduced by a perverted gospel (Galatians 1:6–7; Galatians 3:1–3), and Jesus warns that the church will encounter equally seductive dangerous doctrines in the final days as well. If it were impossible for the elect to be deceived, then Acts 20:30 refers to nothing of importance—**Also of your own selves shall men arise, speaking perverse things, to draw away disciples after them**. And in 1 Corinthians 10:12, Paul says: **Wherefore let him that thinks he stands take heed lest he fall**.

All of this leads to the reason the apostle Peter admonished: **Brethren, give diligence to make your calling and election sure: for if ye do these things, ye shall never fall** (2 Peter 1:10).

Titus 1:1 begins: **Paul, a servant of God, and an apostle of Jesus Christ, according to the faith of God's elect, and the acknowledging of the truth which is after godliness; in the hope of eternal life, which God, that cannot lie, promised before the world began**.

These verses and others indicate that we are not so fortunate to be chosen by God for salvation but rather that by responding to

God's "calling" in truth and by our "faith" and "diligence" to focus on "godliness," thereby have obtained "election."

We should therefore realize the ultimate seriousness of who Jesus spoke of as "his elect" in Matthew 24:31: **And he shall send his angels with a great sound of a trumpet, and they shall gather together his elect from the four winds, from one end of heaven to the other**.

Paul picks up on this future event in 1 Thessalonians 4:17: he says, **Then we which are alive and remain shall be caught up together with them in the clouds, to meet the Lord in the air: and so shall we ever be with the Lord**.

This is our hope for believing in and trusting in the Jesus of the Bible.

In Revelation 22:12, Jesus says: **Behold, I come quickly; and my reward is with me, to give every man according to his work shall be**.

And in John 6:29, Jesus said: **This is the work of God, that ye believe on him whom he hath sent**. The connection between Revelation 22:12 and John 6:29 is profound. The singular word "work" (*ergon*), meaning "act" or "deed," is the same in both verses. All good deeds we've done in our life are recorded in heaven and will be judged and rewarded by Christ Himself at His Second Coming. But in addition, since John 6:29 states that the act of believing in the Savior is **the work of God**, as such, we are also rewarded for our "act of belief" when Jesus returns as Revelation 22:12 states. These two verses reveal that the "act of belief" is the far weightier spiritual matter over the "act of good deeds" for gaining eternal life. We are rewarded not only for having faith in Jesus as Lord of our lives now but are also rewarded for believing that Jesus *was* Lord when He was first **sent** into the world (John 6:29). It is a past-tense reference: Jesus was "sent" from heaven to earth. When we believe this truth, we are rewarded for it. Though in a belief that Jesus was born only a man who merely functioned under the direction of the Holy Spirit, as is falsely taught today, our "deeds of belief" will be branded insufficient, and we receive a far lesser eternal reward. Read carefully the fullness of John, chapter 5: in verse 23, Jesus states, **He that honoureth not the Son honoureth not the Father which hath sent him**.

Literate mankind is responsible to read and study the instruction manual given to him for finding everlasting life. But when selfishly turning inward and only searching out passages that, when twisted just a little, seem to support the idea that God's greatest desire is for our earthly happiness and comfort, we then apostatize from the truth given for our salvation. Many false doctrines such as the spiritually *born-again Jesus* and the *Universal salvation* teaching have accomplished just that. This distraction and perversion occurring now within the worldwide church proves that there's an apostasy, not a revival, happening within the church. Even so, this is not a defeat for the Gospel of Jesus because His remnant church—the true and the faithful of God's Word will remain steadfast—even though they are fewer in number.

Jesus said: **Straight is the gate, and narrow is the way, which leadeth unto life, and few there be that find it. Beware of false prophets** (Matthew 7:14–15).

The last call

We must carefully listen to the heart of Jesus when He said: **And shall not God avenge his own elect...though he bear long with them? I tell you that he will avenge them speedily. Nevertheless, when the Son of man comes, shall he find faith on the earth?** (Luke 18:7–8).

Can you detect a tone of sadness in the Savior's call to the last generation of the Church Age? One day, God will quickly avenge His redeemed throughout all of human history. But on the day when the Lord Jesus returns, He is concerned that there may be very few living faithfully on the earth. Is this possible? Yes! Look at the very next verse: Luke 18:9 (NKJV) explains why Jesus said this: **And he spake this parable unto certain who trusted in themselves that they were righteous, and yet despised others**.

Similarly in our generation, though many churches continue to grow larger, there are Christians who inwardly detest the unbelievers who scoff at them—all while relying on their monetary works of obedience to be favored by God. But many of the unchurched around us are becoming increasingly interested in supernatural and mystical things. Have we shared with them the Gospel that saves sinners? Or have we only invited them to visit our dynamic *positive-confession*, miracle-teaching church so that they may also experience the same? If so, we have not proclaimed the Gospel of salvation to them! We are hypocritical, unfaithful believers in a Jesus of narcissistic perks, rather than a Jesus who saves from sin and hell.

Jeremiah 9:3 speaks of God's own people: **And they bend their tongues like their bow for lies: but they are not valiant for the truth upon the earth; for they proceed from evil to evil, and they know not me, saith the Lord**.

How can we apply this Old Testament passage to today's believers? Very easily: we need only to compare it with a few New Testament passages. If we **are not valiant for the truth** as Jeremiah says, we will be **tossed to and fro, and carried about with every wind of doctrine**, as Paul warns in Ephesians 4:14. We are easily deceived through Satan's **power and signs and lying wonders** (2 Thessalonians 2:9). We've become unfaithful to the Gospel of the Savior because we neglected the truth proclaimed from the heart of God.

The Bible tells us that God is loving and compassionate. But it also tells that we should fear Him. If we have no fear of God, our spiritual health is lopsided.

> **The fear of the Lord is the beginning of knowledge.** (Proverbs 1:7)

> **The fear of the Lord is the beginning of wisdom.** (Proverbs 9:10)

We find "knowledge" and "wisdom" through the "fear" of God by following His loving instruction. Though when favoring only certain passages or by altering or modernizing God's Word to fit our ever-changing hypothesis, we have no fear of Him but only a fabricated and superficial confidence in what we want Scripture to say. Will God have mercy on those who sincerely taught a misinterpretation of His Gospel? Will God have mercy on the listener who believed it? Scripture indicates the reverse.

Jesus cautioned the Jews, saying: **I honor my Father, and you dishonor me** (John 8:49). Jesus spoke the truth and was Himself the Truth of Righteousness. He warned the Sadducees, scribes, and Pharisees that they had not discerned the Scriptures and were stuck in religious form and pretentious self-exaltation. Jesus did not confront them with polite and congenial vocabulary but lambasted them with abrasive words—calling them "fools, vipers, and hypocrites" right in their presence! Certainly the book you've just read contains no harsher language or accusation than the Lord Jesus used.

According to the Bible, the Lord of heaven and earth will one day judge the lives of all people. All who rejected or ignored the salvation Gospel will not gain eternal life. Nor can anyone gain eternal life by only reading the Bible. Instead, the apostle Paul tells us to **work out your own salvation with fear and trembling** (Philippians 2:12). We must study God's Word, giving serious heed to its words: we must take it to heart and act upon it. Revelation 1:3 says: **Blessed is he that readeth, and they that hear the words of this prophecy, and keep those things which are written therein: for the time is at hand**.

Appendix

Defending the Bible

Our Christian beliefs are easily defendable when we know what the Bible declares. We can also be a better witness for Scripture and the Gospel of Jesus when we become familiar with other religious books and non-Christian teachings.

The Church of Jesus Christ of Latter-Day Saints (the Mormons) indirectly teach that the Bible is inadequate and unreliable. They claim that the Book of Mormon, first published in 1830 by founder Joseph Smith, compliments and helps to explain our flawed Bible. Within the introduction to the Book of Mormon, it states: "*The Book of Mormon is a volume of holy scripture comparable to the Bible. It is a record of God's dealings with the ancient inhabitants of the Americas and contains, as does the Bible, the fullness of the everlasting gospel.*"

This is a confusing statement and is even dangerously heretical seeing that Revelation 22:18 says: **If any man shall add unto these things, God shall add unto him the plagues that are written in this book.**

Hence, we can determine that the Book of Mormon has "added unto" the Bible because Joseph Smith claimed his revelation was "*holy scripture comparable to the Bible.*"

A century later, in 1938, a collection of sermons and writings of Smith's was published, titled *Teachings of the Prophet Joseph Smith.* In a commentary on page 327, Smith states that the writers of the Bible were "*ignorant translators, careless transcribers, or designing and corrupt priests who have committed many errors.*"

Smith's statement makes the Bible seem to have many incongruent and misleading passages needing to be explained by present-day more educated men who have additional revelation from God. This is blatant defiance of Revelation 22:18.

The Book of Mormon is in direct conflict with the Bible on several issues. Its primary error is discrediting what the Bible says about true salvation. The Bible states: **For by grace ye are saved through faith; and that not of yourselves: it is the gift of God, not of works, lest any man should boast** (Ephesians 2:8–9).

In contrast, the Book of Mormon states in 2 Nephi 25:23:

> *For we know that it is by grace that we are saved, after all we can do.*

Here, the Book of Mormon states that salvation comes by grace plus works—"*after all we can do.*" This robs the biblical Gospel of its true power—that salvation is from Jesus Christ only and what He has done.

In 1835, Joseph Smith obtained a partial scroll containing ancient records and writings purportedly written by Abraham. Smith personally translated this *Book of Abraham* into English, and it was later added to other writings by Joseph Smith and published in *The Pearl of Great Price*, which then became a part of the doctrinal foundation of the Latter-Day Saints Church. The *Book of Abraham* contains an unscriptural account of the origin of the universe, the plurality of gods, and the exaltation of humanity doctrines. The *Book of Abraham* (beginning at 3:27) tells how Jesus and Lucifer vied for the position of Savior of humanity before the world began. Jesus (named Jehovah and being the elder brother of Lucifer) was chosen by the Father and sent to earth to redeem souls and guide them to eternal life, and symmetry with God. This not only speaks against the Bible's declaration of a God who is far superior to humans, but also derives that Jesus and Lucifer were at one point created equal, completely nullifying the doctrine of the Trinity Godhead.

On other seemingly minor issues, the Book of Mormon also fails to agree with the Bible by stating, for instance, that Jesus was not born in Bethlehem but in Jerusalem (Alma 7:10). This falsifies the prophecy in Micah 5:2 that out of **Bethlehem**, a ruling king **shall come forth…from everlasting**.

Mormonism is an offshoot cult of Christianity; it is confusion. Joseph Smith, who lived some eighteen centuries after the New Testament was written, was a deceived false prophet according to God's final word in the book of Revelation.

The Muslim holy book, the Quran, is a book of disjointed statements with no continuity, no storyline, or timeline. However, because it flows with a poetic style in the Arabic language, it is a much beloved book in the Islamic world. The Quran is speculated to be written about five centuries after Christ—and mostly by the acclaimed prophet Muhammad. Its wording and arrangement have been changed from what was originally found.

The Quran mentions Jesus twenty-five times. But it speaks of him in confusing terms and not as the factual and decisive Savior of mankind.

In chapter 3, verse 45, it says: "*O Mary, indeed Allah gives you good tidings of a word from Him whose name will be Christ Jesus the son of Mary.*"

This verse states that Jesus was the "*Christ*" but that He was only "*the son of Mary,*" not the Son of God as the Christian New Testament states. A few verses later, in 3:59, it states that Allah created Jesus from the dust of the earth just as Adam was created. Which verse is truth? Was Jesus born of Mary, or was he formed from the dust?

Just prior, in 3:53, Jesus is called "*The Messenger.*" Then in 3:55, it claims that Jesus ascended to heaven before the Jews could kill him. Chapter 4, verse 157 specifically denies that the crucifixion of Jesus ever happened!

In chapter 19, verses 30–35, Jesus is stated to have risen from the dead and that He will one day come again. But wait…didn't Jesus ascend to heaven without dying in chapter 3, verse 55? Nonetheless, this verse in chapter 19 correctly tells of the return of Jesus…but then later clarifies that He will not rule as a triumphant King as the Christian Bible declares—but as a radical Muslim and an aid to a true Islam Messiah.

In chapter 43, verse 59, the Quran states that Jesus was only a mortal man whom Allah favored. Chapter 9, verse 30 warns that if anyone states that Jesus is the Son of God, they will be cursed! Yet in 57:27, it says: "*Jesus gave the gospel*"! But within the pages of the Quran, there is no statement telling that Jesus died for the sin of mankind. Instead, He was translated to heaven without being crucified. There is, therefore, no saving gospel message within the Quran. The Bible, however, clearly defines the Gospel as repentance from sin and the belief in the One who forgives that sin—Jesus, the Son of God, the Savior.

The supreme being of the Quran is *Allah*. The supreme being of the Christian Bible is *Yahuwah*. They cannot be interpreted as the same because Allah demands works to receive eternal life, and Yahuwah does not.

Judaism and Christianity are also in conflict with each other. Just as Muslims reject the teaching that Jesus was the literal Son of God, today, the majority of Jews still deny that the resurrection of Jesus ever happened. In the Judaism religion, their Messiah has not yet come. They believe Jesus was not a true prophet by Old Testament standards, and neither was he the Incarnation of God.

In Judaism's interpretation of their Bible, the Tanakh (the entire Old Testament), the coming Messiah will reinforce the neglected Mosaic ordinances of the Torah, the first five books of the Old Testament—known in Christian terminology as the Pentateuch. However, according to Jeremiah 31 (in the Old Testament), the "covenant" between God and His chosen people was to continue until the "new covenant" was made. The "new covenant" revealed in the New Testament is Jesus the Savior, and observance of the Mosaic ordinances are now justifiably removed. Yet Judaism does not recognize this as any such truth as per their rejection of the entire New Testament.

Another major disagreement unconverted Jews have against New Testament Christianity is that the King James translators changed the Hebrew word "damsel" to "virgin" in Isaiah 7:14, then repeated it in Matthew 1:23, saying: **Behold, a virgin shall be with child, and shall bring forth a son**. Judaism considers this a perversion of the Tanakh. However, from a convincing belief that the New Testament is truth and that Jesus was indeed the Messiah, the King James translators were actually correct. If only **a damsel shall conceive, and bear a son**, as was the original Hebrew wording of Isaiah 7:14, it therefore cannot be a genuine "sign" from the Lord, simply because any young girl has the potential to conceive a child. Therefore, a "virgin" birth is a "sign" from the Lord. It is not perversion of Isaiah 7:14 but is correct Old Testament hermeneutics in accordance with faith in Jesus of Nazareth as the Messiah—who was "born of a virgin."

No doubt, there are sincere people in these and other cult religions. But sincerity and trying to work our way to heaven won't get us there. The requirement for heaven's entrance is clearly defined in the Christian New Testament, which gives no conflict of who Jesus was, where He came from, or what happened to Him. In understanding the truth of the entire Old and New Testaments, we then realize that Jesus Christ, the only Righteous One, paid the ultimate price for our sin on the cross, and there is no other way to receive eternal life except by simple faith in this Savior. Other religious teachings of the Hindu Krishna or Gautama Buddha or the Islam prophet Muhammad do not agree with the Bible. Though similar in some humanitarian teachings with Jesus, none of these were the Incarnation of God upon the earth as is stated in Scripture. And no other person in history was prophesied to rise from the dead and did so as Jesus did. This single fact could be the justifiable reason that our Bible is called the Word of God.

About the Author

Born in Portland, Oregon, in 1953, Philip Smith is descended from a Christian heritage to the fourth generation. He was raised in the Nazarene denomination and attended Northwest Nazarene University in the early 1970s. He is very gifted to be an accomplished freelance artist, as seen on the cover of the book, and is now retired from the blue-collar job he also held.

At age twenty-three, Philip joined a large Charismatic church, where he was a member for twenty years. Afterward, he was part of a Baptist church and a Covenant church, then returned to his Nazarene roots.

Philip is married to his "Beverly-good-wife," and they enjoy being part of the extended family of God.